HOWELLS
AND THE AGE OF REALISM

HOWELLS
AND
THE AGE OF REALISM

BY

EVERETT CARTER

ARCHON BOOKS
Hamden, Connecticut
1966

FIRST PUBLISHED BY J. B. LIPPINCOTT COMPANY

REPRINTED 1966 WITH PERMISSION
IN AN UNALTERED AND UNABRIDGED EDITION

LIBRARY OF CONGRESS CATALOG CARD NUMBER: 66-15384
PRINTED IN THE UNITED STATES OF AMERICA

For Wife and Parents

ACKNOWLEDGMENTS

I am grateful to the John Simon Guggenheim Memorial Foundation for the grant which enabled me to finish this work. I wish to acknowledge the kind permission of Miss Mildred Howells to quote from her *Life in Letters of William Dean Howells* and from other copyrighted material of her father's; also my indebtedness to the Executors of the Mark Twain Estate for permission to quote briefly from materials covered by copyright, and to the following publishers for quotations from the following works: The Bobbs-Merrill Company, Inc., De Lancey Ferguson's *Mark Twain: Man and Legend;* Harvard University Press, C. M. Bowra's *The Romantic Imagination*, and Bernard DeVoto's *Mark Twain at Work;* Alfred A. Knopf, Inc., E. M. Forster's *A Room with a View;* Houghton Mifflin Company, Dixon Wecter's *Sam Clemens of Hannibal;* Liveright Publishing Company, Percy MacKaye's *Epoch;* Longmans, Green and Company, Inc., William James' *Pragmatism;* Oxford University Press, *The Notebooks of Henry James*, ed. F. O. Matthiessen and Kenneth Murdock; and Charles Scribner's Sons, *The Letters of Henry James*, ed. Percy Lubbock.

I also wish to thank the editors of *The Antioch Review*, *American Quarterly*, *College English*, *English Journal* and *English Literary History* for permission to use material which appeared originally in those publications.

CONTENTS

HOWELLS
AND THE AGE OF REALISM

PROLOGUE

This is the history of the growth of sensibility of a man and of an age, and part of the biography of ourselves.

It is the story of the growth of the mind of William Dean Howells; but this writer, even more than most writers, was made by and helped to make his age. And his age happens to be the age when much of the complexity of modern America was born.

That this is a study of a man's sensibility, rather than his biography, will be self-evident. Our first concern will not be with his life, with his small physical stature, his worldly rise, his social grace, his political conservatism which changed to radicalism, his devotion to his family. These are the materials for another story. Here we can tell briefly that he was born in 1837 at Martins Ferry, Belmont County, Ohio, one of eight children of a struggling printer and publisher, William Cooper Howells. William Cooper had been born in South Wales, had not been quite a year old when the family came to New York in 1808, had been four when it migrated by wagon and flatboat to Jefferson County, Ohio. As he grew to manhood, he had yearned to write and to paint, but had been able to take up pen or brush only after a day's labor at typesetting, or farming, or carpentering, or printing and editing a series of unsuccessful local journals. He was, William Dean wrote later and lovingly, "not a very good draughtsman, not a very good poet, not a very good farmer, not a very good printer, not a very good editor . . . ; but he was the very best *man* I have ever known." Of worldly goods William Cooper Howells gave his son little; but of the love of life and beauty and letters he gave him much. As the family followed the father about Ohio, from one ailing enterprise to another, William Dean received almost no formal education. "In school," he would say later, "there was as little literature as there is now, and I cannot say anything worse of our school reading; but I was not really very much in school, and so I got small harm from it." From his father, however, came the guidance he needed. When the boy began to show an interest in literature, the father could not only direct his choice, but could supply him with books out of the largest private collection in their Ohio town, a library which included names like Thomson, Cowper, Byron, Burns, Scott, Pope, and Dryden. From these beginnings, the son adventured on his own; he read voraciously; taught himself Spanish to read Cervantes, learned German to read Heine; he would take a volume of Shakespeare into the woods "at the ends of the long summer afternoons . . . and on the shining Sundays of the warm, late spring, the early, warm autumn." Thus did the young Ohioan prepare himself for the moment when he would meet the best minds of Boston and impress them so thoroughly that they would accept him as their equal and heir.

This self-education of a future arbiter of American letters went on during a series of moves: from Hamilton, where the father edited the *Intelligencer*, to Dayton where he tried unsuccessfully to revive the ailing *Transcript*, to Xenia and an experiment in primitive living in a log cabin beside a mill, to Columbus where, at the age of fourteen, William Dean became a compositor on the *Ohio State Journal*, back to the small towns of Ashtabula and then Jefferson, where the father became co-owner of the Ashtabula *Sentinel*. And finally, at twenty, William Dean was back in Columbus as reporter, editorial writer, and news editor for the *Journal*, poised for his flight into the larger world of eastern intellectual America.

These early years had their difficulties. There were the agonies of uprooting from beloved Hamilton to the "big" city of Dayton; there were the years of draining labor over the type-boxes, years which made him forever mindful of those who toil long and hard for little. There were strange fears which haunt the ignorance of childhood. He was convinced for some time that he was dying from a terrible, and wholly imaginary, disease. He was obsessed by a painful prudery which, on one occasion, made him shrink from the nudes in a panoramic painting, and on another caused him to think it shameful for the shopgirls of Columbus to show themselves in so "public a place as a restaurant."

But these were minor blemishes on a boyhood and youth which formed a sensibility whose main feature was a love of the normal, the open, the average of human existence. To be a boy in Ohio (or Missouri) in the 1840's and '50's might not have been the best fate in the world, but was surely close to it; and to be a boy there, at that time, in small towns, on a river; to be one of a large family with intelligent and loving parents, was certainly as good a life as one could wish. While the Howellses were not well off, in Hamilton everyone had enough and no one had too much, and all shared the river and its islands, on which the boys could enact the tales of "Simon Girty, the Renegade," or "Simon Kenton, the Pioneer," and the meadows and woods, and the friendly community, and could know for the rest of their lives that theirs was a place of "almost unrivalled fitness" to be the home of a boy, a place where the years seemed in retrospect, a succession of holidays, and "Saturdays spread over half the week." In this atmosphere, Howells could dream of being a "god of poetry and sunshine."

This was the cultured, if self-taught, young Midwesterner who, in 1860, began to contribute to the *Atlantic Monthly*, and to correspond with its editor, James Russell Lowell. And later in that year, he journeyed to Boston and was received with friendliness by his august correspondent who, in turn, introduced him to Oliver Wendell Holmes, James T. Fields, Hawthorne, and Emerson. "Nothing else so richly satisfactory . . . could have happened to a like youth at such a point in his career," Howells wrote afterwards. Having glimpsed the culture of Cambridge, he would never be content with any other life, although his entrance into that blessed society would be delayed for six years. Meanwhile he returned to Columbus for a few months and met a slight, fair girl with light brown hair, Elinor Mead from Brattleboro, Vermont, the daughter of a New England lawyer and banker, a girl interested in the arts, fond of sketching and painting, with one brother who would later become a successful sculptor, another who would be an able architect. She became his partner in a long and happy marriage. Like the union between Sam Clemens and Livy Langdon, it was the kind of a marriage which would do nothing to change Howells' feelings of "honor and worship for . . . girlhood and womanhood." Howells would occasionally chafe under the burdens of family, but he was almost always both contented, and grateful for the taste which his wife showed in helping him with his work.

As a reward for writing a campaign life of Lincoln, he was appointed United States Consul at Venice, where he spent four years from 1861 to 1865, and then returned to America with a girl baby, Winifred, the materials for two books of travel, and a longing to re-enter actively the world of American letters. He knew he would have to get some basis, some position in journalism, so he found employment with the New York *Times* and with the *Nation.* Then in 1866, he returned to his spiritual home, to Boston and Cambridge, and for fifty dollars a week happily agreed to read and edit manuscripts, read proof, and write the reviews for the *Atlantic.* In 1871, he was made editor-in-chief of this most powerful literary magazine of the day, and he continued in the position until 1881. During these years two more children were added to the family, Mildred and John Mead; during this decade too, he lived a life of contented awareness that he was part of the most gracious society of his times. In 1881, he left the *Atlantic* to devote himself to writing the fiction with which he had already begun to make himself known and which, by 1882, would call forth articles about him and Henry James "as thick as blackberries." Three years later he contracted with Harper and Brothers not only to provide them with a novel a year, but with a smaller book as well, and an essay on current literature for their monthly magazine.

The next years, 1886 to 1890, were crucial ones, and must necessarily be treated in some detail at a later point; but now we can say briefly that public and private crises changed both the man and his work. Sometime between the summer of 1886 and the fall of 1887 he was shaken by the unjust condemnation of eight anarchists to long prison terms or death by a partisan judge and jury in Chicago, and he risked his livelihood and his reputation in a vain attempt to save them. While the vision of the evil that men can do to men was sobering him, Howells was confronted with one of the tragedies that nature has in store for us: the chronic illness of his eldest daughter drew to its fatal end. It was a profoundly altered Howells that moved permanently from Boston to New York soon after, and made the larger city his home for the rest of his life. Nine years later, in 1900, he took up the department in *Harper's Monthly* known as "The Editor's Easy Chair," and conducted it for twenty years. By the turn of the century he had become a revered anachronism; he could, by 1906, tell of his grand-niece's complaint that his writing lacked virility; she defined "virile" as "very strong, don't you know; and masterful; and relentless; and makes you feel as if somebody had taken you by the throat; and shakes you up, awfully; and seems to throw you into the air, and trample you underfoot." Howells' reply showed his wry awareness that his age was past: "Good heavens, my dear! . . . I hope I'm a gentleman even when I'm writing a novel." His place in American culture seemed secure, however; he received honorary degrees from Yale, Columbia, Princeton, and Oxford; he became the first president of the American Academy of Arts and Letters in 1908, and held this office until his death in 1920 at the age of eighty-three.

This was clearly the life of a man devoted to writing. He passed no year and very few months from 1866 to 1920 without commenting about life and literature in either novel, short story, or essay. After his early self-indulgence in sentimental poetry and his biography of Lincoln, he began in Venice a long career of transmuting the stuff of his experience into fine and graceful literature. Observations of the life he knew began appearing in the Boston *Advertiser*, and were collected, with critical approval and profitable sales, in *Venetian Life* in 1866. This success was quickly followed by *Italian Journeys*. By then, Howells had returned to America to begin the steady production of what so shrewd a critic as Henry James could call the definitive picture of American life in American fiction. *Suburban Sketches* was the first, and then came the semi-autobiographical treatment of his own nuptial tour in *Their Wedding Journey*. From then on he created thirty more full-length novels, two long prose narratives which he preferred to call "romances," and five volumes of short stories. While this stream of fiction was coming from his pen, he was also turning out a quantity of critical material with which he helped to shape the taste and sensibility of his era. He did the prefaces for eighteen books by other authors, and through them and his reviews helped to introduce to America Tolstoy, Galdós, Valdés, Dostoevsky, Turgenev, and Zola. From 1867 to 1881 he wrote over four hundred and fifty book reviews for the *Atlantic*. From 1881 to 1886 he contributed criticism to *Harper's*, *Century*, and the *Atlantic*. From January, 1886, to March, 1892, he composed a monthly essay, the "Editor's Study," for *Harper's*. From 1892 to 1900 he wrote essays that went into three books of literary comment and criticism. From December, 1900, to his death on May 10, 1920, he wrote a monthly department, "The Editor's Easy Chair," for *Harper's*, and during the same years wrote over seventy critical papers for the *North American Review*. These are the rich materials from which the intellectual biography of a man can be constructed.

And when we discover what kind of mind this was, we begin to understand much about the age which made it and which it helped to make. The weight of Howells' work, appearing in the most influential magazines, exerted an immeasurable pressure upon the intellectual life of his day. He was read and appreciated by large numbers of the better minds in America for two generations. He was not only a novelist, but a critic, and an enormously influential one; as such he either attracted other writers to his field or repelled them with equally electrical violence. This mild, squat, gentle man was prophetically named. For thirty years he was dean of American letters. Other authors loved him or hated him. For Mark Twain he was guide and friend; the man with whom he could drink and smoke, and who taught him the way to handle his craft. But for Ambrose Bierce he was the monster of middle-class virtue, with a following of "fibrous virgins . . . and oleaginous clergymen." Some followed him slavishly, others agreed, disagreed, and then agreed again. For Hamlin Garland he was the great master, upon whom he waited, hat in hand, one day in 1885, and from whose lips he received the word about realism in literature. For Henry James he was the sympathetic and lifelong friend whose solid virtues as an artist he could admire, but of whose lack of the "really *grasping*" vision he could be early aware. To most of the significant younger men he was guide and helper; to others, he seemed an oppressive tyrant. Harold Frederic called him "the big man" on whose side of the literary wars he wanted to be; Stephen Crane acknowledged that Howells gave him his literary creed; Frank Norris was grateful for Howells' encouragement. But Theodore Dreiser interviewed him one day, and came away depressed by his bourgeois dullness, and seems to have regarded him, as did Sinclair Lewis, as the dead wood which had to be cleared away before American writers could move ahead.

As either a leader to be followed or a villain to be foiled, Howells was the kind of man whose presence obviously shaped his era, and his productive years deserve to be called the age of Howells. The dates of this age can be determined; it surely began after the Civil War when Howells published his travel books, when John De Forest wrote *Miss Ravenel's Conversion from Secession to Loyalty* (1867), when Mark Twain wrote *The Innocents Abroad* (1869). It reached its climax when Twain published its greatest expression: *Huckleberry Finn* (1884), and Howells its best work on a contemporary American theme: *A Hazard of New Fortunes* (1890). It can be said to have ended when in 1896 a disciple of Howells, Harold Frederic, wrote the story of America's fall from innocence, and called it *The Damnation of Theron Ware;* by then Howells and Twain had finished their best work, De Forest was almost forgotten, Hamlin Garland was turning to tepid Western romances, and Crane and Norris were beginning to experiment with new materials and new methods to express the bewilderment of a changed America.

The irony of Crane struck a new note, and one which sounded the end of the age of Howells. Irony sees man and his society and his struggles as mere delusive appearances, and is a concomitant of the tragic spirit. But Howells and the early Twain and De Forest were all satirists, not ironists, and their age was an age of comedy. For comedy is based upon a faith in the living, in the value of the world of appearances. The comic writer believes in the significance of the social organism of which he is a part, and since he believes in it, and is an artist, which is to say a highly organized and easily injured system of sensibilities with a vision of perfection, he tries to make this organism even healthier. Being an artist, he cannot help thinking how much better his world could be than it is, even though he deeply loves it as it is. He therefore judges his world, and shows how it falls short of perfection. De Forest and Twain and Howells were essentially comic writers whose satire was based firmly upon the fundamental proposition of their basic allegiance to the American culture in which they found themselves, because they believed that this culture promised most for most men. When they criticized aspects of this culture, as they were to spend most of their lives doing, they criticized it as only lovers can. Theirs was both a conscious, reasoned love, and an unconscious emotional involvement. De Forest could argue with his French friends that the republican system, best exemplified in America, was the safeguard of the liberty of the individual; Mark Twain could report his thrill at the sight of an American frigate in foreign waters as it "flung the Stars and Stripes to the breeze," and unashamedly worship it as "a vision of home itself and all its idols." Howells could write his sister: "No one knows how much better than the whole world America is until he tries some other part of the world."

In this, of course, they were presenting a thesis to which a minority in their own age could and did present the counter-thesis. Young Henry James, for example, travelling abroad, found other travelling Americans hopelessly "vulgar, vulgar, vulgar." And when viewing the scenery of England, he could not help seeing in it a mute commentary on the lack of inspiration in America for the artist. But Mark Twain, travelling across the countryside of France, yearned for the stagecoach of the western plains, and Howells would try "not to think of the Americans' faults"; for he found that "they are a people so much purer and nobler and truer than any other."

Then there is a third aspect of this study: it is a part of the biography of ourselves. One of the revolutions in thought in the past half century has been the willingness to accept the works of poets, dramatists, and novelists as evidence leading towards hypotheses about the condition of man. When statistical methods seem inadequate, when records of history appear only "the approximate vision" and "any attempt to say what is happening in the world . . . must be conscious of its own irony," when the mind of man cannot be laid on the dissecting table, social scientists are ready to turn to literature for a kind of knowledge about human beings. Freud's debt to Shakespeare and Dostoevsky, Toynbee's to the great mythologies are cases in point. The statement of one of our great poets, Robert Frost, has then a double force; his is the insight of a poet, and he is talking in turn about another writer when he says: "We are eight or ten men already, and one of them is Howells."

Frost, like every poet, spoke for himself and for us all. We *are* partly Howells. For his was the dominant and representative sensibility of the age which formed us—the era to which Allan Nevins, in writing its history, gives the name: "The Emergence of Modern America." It was the era when industrialization overtook us, when business became national, when the city rose, when our political ideas went through one of their major shifts and "liberalism" started to mean a belief in more government, and "conservatism" began to mean a belief in less. As modern America emerged socially and politically in this era, so did it begin to form itself in literature and philosophy. Those traits conventionally assumed to be American traits, concern for fact, pragmatism, optimism, were the basic attitudes of Howells and the movement in letters called American realism. A reverence for the material surface of things was the spirit behind its literary forms; a pragmatic rejection of the absolute and an acceptance of that which worked as right, gave the realistic writers their moral scheme; an optimistic belief in the possibilities of their contemporary world of middle-class, republican America gave their literature its comic texture.

These attitudes have been under attack for thirty years. Reverence for the fact has been named a gross materialism, pragmatism has been called no philosophy and amoral ethics, optimism has been labelled a myopic acquiescence in the evils of industrialism. The revival of Melville, the new appreciation of Hawthorne and James, the decline of Emerson and Whitman are part of a modern temper which has found the tragic vision of *Moby Dick* and *The Scarlet Letter* closer to what it feels to be the truth of the human condition. And in this temper, a large part of intellectual America has rejected that portion of itself which is Howells.

Nations are made up of individuals, and we know that an individual cannot safely hate himself without, at least, understanding himself. Howells' view of life, which he expressed through the form and content of his fiction and criticism, is, therefore, at least a view which we must understand before rejecting, and at best might be one which is still partly valid.

What this work is going to do is sympathetically to re-examine these attitudes as they appear in the works of Howells and those writers of his convictions: a giant like Mark Twain who was a part of this context and can be best understood in terms of it; a lesser figure like John De Forest; minor authors like Edward Eggleston and Albion Tourgée. And we will find that Howells' influence was not crass, or amoral, or blindly acquiescent. When we examine his literary forms, we will find them neither an attempt at unselective representation nor non-significant social history. When we understand his morality, we will find it neither a pious prudery nor an abandonment of a quest for the knowledge of good and evil, but rather a morality of relative and contingent values. Above all, when we investigate the nature of his optimism, we will find that it was neither smug, complacent, nor cowardly; that it called for an unceasing criticism of things as they are so that men might give thought to making them better. It is a not unworthy part of our cultural heritage.

CHAPTER I

BACKGROUND

In some sense, to understand the age of realism in America we have to go as far back as history. The quest of a man like Howells for a way to express in fiction what he felt to be the truth about the world is part of the total drama of the race. In that drama there have always been ages when men have given their commitments to physical things and social appearances, and they usually have followed, and in turn have been superseded, by ages whose search is for the meanings that lie behind, or above the world of things. At the beginning of the nineteenth century there had been a dominance in German and English thought of thinkers and writers whose vision was directed behind the world of physical appearances. Friedrich Schlegel gave the name "romantic" to these writers, and from Blake through Wordsworth and Coleridge to Keats and Shelley, the romantic imagination was concerned with a "search for an unseen world," with penetrating "to an abiding reality, to explore its mysteries, and by this to understand more clearly what life means and what it is worth."

In America, as so often happens, the romantic movement had come late, and it was in its flow, not its ebb, when William Dean Howells was born in Martins Ferry, Ohio, in 1837. To understand what Howells was (and what we are) one has to understand this: that he grew up intellectually in an America in which the romantics produced the greatest writing and thinking, but in which the neo-classicists were influential in a peculiarly fruitful way; he grew up in an America which produced Emerson and Thoreau and Whitman, and Hawthorne and Melville and Poe; but it was an America which also produced the staid humanistic culture of Brahmin Boston, under the leadership of James Russell Lowell and Oliver Wendell Holmes. He grew up at a time when the American romantics were trying to smash through the pasteboard mask of appearances into eternal truth, when Emerson, Thoreau, and Whitman were in quest of the meaning of this world as a symbol of the "real world"—the natural facts which were symbolic of the spiritual facts; when Hawthorne and Melville were trying to unravel the meaning of the eternal necessity of evil; when Poe was searching for the forms of unchanging, amoral beauty. But at the same time in America the Boston humanists were thinking and writing, men for whom the veil was not distortion or symbol, but reality to be treated for itself and on its own terms. It was a time, too, of the growing influence of those writers in America whose devotion was not to the true or the beautiful, but to the satisfaction of the prejudices and preconceptions of their audience. These were the sentimentalists.

The young Howells was produced by this intellectual environment. To understand how he grew, we have to understand the way in which he reacted to American romanticism, to neo-classicism, and to sentimentalism in the twenty years before the Civil War.

1. Strains of Idealism

The forces which produce a cultural climate made the major fiction of Howells' youth and adolescence darkly romantic. Hawthorne and Melville and Poe—all three wrote from a common temper. *The Fall of the House of Usher* and *Mardi* and *The Scarlet Letter* were truly all of one brood, all concerned with the truths which lay behind the world of appearances, all turning to the symbol as a means of fusing this truth with the physical, all immersed in a tragic vision of life. I love a man who can thunder

"No," said Melville, and he found that kind of man in Nathaniel Hawthorne. These writers of the pre-Civil War generation found the impulse to create and the materials for their creation in probing behind the façade of middle-class American life and society of their times. This is less true of Hawthorne than of Melville and Poe. The sensitive creator of *The Scarlet Letter* and *The Marble Faun* also wrote *The Blithedale Romance* and *The House of the Seven Gables*, both with the settings of contemporary America. But in his preface to *The Marble Faun* Hawthorne admitted that he could not find the materials for his art in the normal world of American social relationships. "No author, without a trial," he wrote, "can conceive of the difficulty of writing a romance about a country where there is no shadow, no antiquity, no mystery, no picturesque and gloomy wrong." He thought the day would be long in coming, when writers of romance would "find congenial and easily-handled themes . . . in any characteristic and probable events of our individual lives."

Perhaps it was Hawthorne's sad awareness of his inability to find the materials for fiction in the commonplace that led Howells to "come nearer" to the recluse of Salem, when he met him in 1860, than he "at first believed possible." But this nearness was only relative, and based upon the elder romancer's attempt to incorporate his own experience in fiction—*The Blithedale Romance*, which Howells mistakenly thought his best work. Howells never mentioned Melville, and treated Poe with the mixture of aloof admiration and lack of understanding which was his constant attitude to these romantics.

No, these great men of the American Renaissance had little to teach Howells, either in choice of material, or treatment of what is chosen. Theirs was another time spirit. Howells could admire it; he could even encourage others to follow their mode; but it was not for him. For they had not simply "the conception or intellectual perception of evil, but the grisly blood-freezing heart-palsying sensation of it close upon one." Although Howells could admit that this "morbid-mindedness" ranged over the wider scale of experience ("My way is still the byway, not the highway; the minor, not the major means"), with what Henry James called his incurable optimism, Howells naturally felt more with the men like Emerson, whose philosophical disciple, Walt Whitman, William James took as "the supreme contemporary example" of healthy-mindedness. These healthy-minded romantics expressed a basically optimistic American culture which was a major part of the intellectual soil from which Howells sprang, and from the very first, Howells strove for "grace" and for "light," for his soul detested obscurity.

Emerson, like Thoreau and Whitman after him, was essentially a philosophical idealist and a literary romantic, his eyes focussed on the spiritual world, of which the physical world was a symbol, on the "ideas" for which the objects of the "real" world were clothing, but his was a romanticism of light rather than of darkness. He saw the physical world not as shadowy and delusive; but as a total part of universal goodness, the way in which the Oversoul was made available to fleshly eyes. Although he was happiest when trying to capture the world beyond the world of the flesh and its eyes, he never scorned this world or sneered at it; rather, he insisted it be treated reverently, for it is the means through which men can know eternal goodness. Since the smallest and meanest thing is a symbol of the spiritual world, the smallest and meanest things should be examined carefully and lovingly, known intimately, and made the subject of poetry and fiction. The new American poet, when he comes, proclaimed Emerson, will be all that—he will be American; he will worship humble American things—"the meal in the firkin; the milk in the pan"; and he will write lovingly, too, of "tariffs, banks, commerce." And Emerson was talking not only of lyric verse forms, but of prose fiction as well. When Howells started writing, he could speak to an America which had heard Emerson proclaim the greatness of the commonplace. Put away the formal, transcendental structure of Emerson's philosophy, or, rather, hold it in the mind as a coloration rather than a creed, and you have left the moving power of the realist movement in America. Although not attracted to Emerson personally, Howells thought him "a presence of force and beauty and wisdom unaccompanied in our literature." Emerson's peculiar blend of idealism and realism lay under the thought of Howells and of the late nineteenth century.

And not only Emerson contributed to Howells' strong rooting

in idealism. For the entire Howells family was brought up on the doctrines of Emanuel Swedenborg, the Swedish mystic upon whose teachings Emerson himself had drawn so heavily. Swedenborg's metaphor in which he expressed the symbolic nature of reality was that of a macrocosmic man, a huge living figure which comprised the entire universe, of which actual man was a microcosmic duplication. Howells' father, "after many years of skepticism," embraced the doctrines of Swedenborg wholeheartedly. For him and for his children, the faith of Emanuel Swedenborg became "their life." In this creed, the boys were taught that "in every thought and in every deed they were choosing their portion with the devils or the angels . . ." Later, Howells maintained that his belief in the mystical system of Swedenborg was "a wholly outside" one, but we cannot feel that a faith in which a boy is reared during his formative years can ever be "outside"; the deeply imbedded belief that there is a supernatural order, together with a pragmatic willingness to let the unknowable and incommunicable stay unknown and uncommunicated—this is the kind of idealistic materialism which was the core of Howells, just as a kind of materialistic idealism was the center of Emerson.

2. The Classical Tradition

". . . most of the good things come from the mean of life . . ."
—Howells

When the circus came to Hamilton, Howells was one of the few boys who did not risk a ride on the elephant's back; and what was true of his taste in entertainment was true of his range of ideas as well. He did not wish to climb high or dive perilously deep. Although there were strands of Emersonian romanticism and idealism in the young Howells, very early in his adolescence other threads appeared, the threads of a concern with the material aspects of the physical world which can be perceived and analyzed by the common sense of the average man, and these threads finally made up the dominant color and texture of his mature life. In his formative years in Hamilton, Dayton, and Jefferson, Ohio, in the year he spent as a thirteen year old in a log cabin near

Xenia, Greene County, Ohio, in his earliest teens in Columbus, he took most pleasure in those writers who wrote with the conviction that sensibility, decency, decorum, and normalcy are the chief aims of civilized man's existence. The writers to whom he paid early allegiance, and his later discussions of the reasons why he liked them, show that the genesis of Howells' later thought was not in the line of Orpheus, but in the direct descent from the Ionian rationalists; Howells was not by temperament a Faust. And he seems to have turned the petals of his young attention towards the sun of the eighteenth century and its authors.

When, during the great Age of Reason, humanity became the primary concern of men, all of humanity's activities became fit subjects for literature. When Howells absorbed the eighteenth-century concept that man is the measure of all things, he had taken the first step in his education. When he was sixty, and relaxing in the "Easy Chair" of *Harper's*, he devoted part of one of his essays to a eulogy of the philosophy of the Age of Reason, which he summarized in three words: "humanity," "humaneness," and "sensibility." He quickly made it clear that he was not speaking of false and excessive emotionalizing when he talked of "sensibility"; rather, he meant the tasteful and sensitive sympathy for normal human experience. "If the eighteenth century could have lasted a few hundred years longer," he wrote, "it might have ended in the golden age."

The eighteenth century did not last, but its ideas stretched out to warm the youthful Howells. He had the love of good society and decent, decorous behavior which characterized the neo-classicists, and he was glad that he need not, as an artist, forgo the pleasures of good living among congenial people. "Instead of . . . sleeping in doorways or under the arches of bridges . . . we were good society from the beginning," he said later of his circle of literary acquaintances. Then he added: "I think this was none the worse for us, and it was vastly the better for good society." To the end of his life, he steadfastly believed, with the eighteenth century, that "most of the good things come from the mean of life which is rightly praised as the golden mean." He had the Augustans' traditional distrust of genius, of indulgence, of eccentricity, of extremes of any kind. He looked forward to a day when the "poor, honest herd of humankind" would no longer be imposed upon by the "'geniuses' who have forgotten their duty to the common weakness, and have abused it to their glory."

The writers from whom he derived these ideas were Alexander Pope and Oliver Goldsmith, and their spiritual American cousin, Washington Irving. He read all three before he was fourteen, and Goldsmith's *History of Greece* and *History of Rome* before he was ten. He knew Goldsmith's essays well enough by 1851 to be imitating them. From these and from *The Citizen of the World*, *The Vicar of Wakefield*, and *The Traveller*, he learned that "kindness and gentleness are never out of fashion," and that without them the best art cannot exist. Irving followed closely upon the heels of Goldsmith on the crowded schedule of the young Ohioan's reading. He read *The Conquest of Granada* in 1848 or 1849, and the *Knickerbocker History*, *Life of Goldsmith*, *Legend of Sleepy Hollow*, and *Bracebridge Hall* "later" but still in boyhood. And he found Irving, like Goldsmith, "not a master only, but a sweet and gentle friend, whose kindness could not fail to profit him." To Alexander Pope, the epitome of the Age of Reason, he paid the highest praise of slavish imitation. At the age of fourteen, he tried a long poem, patterned closely but unsuccessfully after the Pastorals. It began:

> When fair Aurora kissed the purple East
> And dusky night the struggling day released,
> Two swains whom Phoebus waked from sleep's embrace
> Led forth their flocks to crop the dewy grass.

Along with these three, Howells was schooled by Cervantes. Indeed, he explicitly rated the author of *Don Quixote* above Pope, and along with Irving and Goldsmith as one of his "first three loves in literature." He read the sadly hilarious stories of the Knight of Mancha in 1848, and reminisced that "the reading of *Don Quixote* went on through my boyhood." In his passion for Cervantes he taught himself Spanish, and by the age of fifteen planned to write a life of the great author. Later, but still in his teens, Howells found the hard little fragment by an unknown author that is the prototype of Spanish rogue fiction—*Lazarillo de Tormes*. While he thought it "gross in its facts" and "'unmeet for ladies,'" he deeply admired its "honest simplicity," its "pervading humor," and its "rich feeling for character." He still thought, in 1895, that "the intending author of American fiction would do well to study the Spanish picaresque novels."

At almost precisely the same time, in Hannibal, Missouri, a teen-age boy was falling in love with *Don Quixote*. What Sam Clemens, like Howells, found in the Spaniard was a deep reverence for reality. In the picaresque novel, the Spanish rogue wanders through a series of adventures; the unifying element is character, not plot; for there is literally no plot, in the sense of causal sequence of events from beginning to end. And through the episodic wanderings runs a strong feeling of sympathy for the common, the mean, the ugly, the low. In them, and especially in *Don Quixote*, the greatest of them all, Howells sensed a current of hatred and scorn for the warped, sentimentalizing, romanticizing of life by literature which could so twist the mind of the lovable tilter at windmills. Both Howells and the boy who later became Mark Twain believed that *Don Quixote*'s "free and simple design, where event follows event without the fettering control of intrigue, but where all grows naturally out of character and conditions, is the supreme form of fiction." Both Mark Twain and Howells were haters of the sentimental, as well as worshippers of the real.

Along with Cervantes, Shakespeare was an enormous passion of Howells' adolescence; he abandoned himself to a worship of his plays that "went to heights and lengths that it had reached with no earlier idol." He felt that Shakespeare created a complete world "as great as the creation of a planet." And for his own created world of fiction he often chose quotations from Shakespeare as the summaries and titles: *A Counterfeit Presentment, The Undiscovered Country, A Modern Instance, The Shadow of a Dream, The Quality of Mercy*.

But we note that he preferred the history plays because of his "instinctive liking for reality." In the histories, he "found a world appreciable to my experience," and even though that world was "inexpressibly vaster and grander" than his own "poor little affair," still there was "nothing abstract or typical in it."

As he did with Shakespeare, so did he with lesser figures: find in them one feature to admire, and this feature was their truthfulness to the average, probable course of human social existence. When he came across Dickens' work in 1854, he liked him and tried later to imitate him; Dickens, after all, was the idol of middle-class America as well as of England at the very time when a seventeen year old was most likely to be impressed by artistic success in others: "It was no more possible for a young novelist to escape writing Dickens than it was for a young poet to escape writing Tennyson." But his liking was tempered by a suspicion of the caricaturing which Dickens habitually used as his short-cut to characterization, and it was this "grotesqueness" which made Howells feel that he "admired other authors more." At the same time he read and admired Thackeray. But again, his admiration took a bent which strongly indicates the way the tree of his disposition was to grow. He selected *Barry Lyndon*, the life of an English picaro, as the best example of Thackeray's craft, and "the farthest reach of the author's great talent."

Just as his early literary passions indicate the direction of his development, so do his literary aversions. *Uncle Tom's Cabin*, whose sentiment moved him, never became a passion, and Harriet Beecher Stowe's famous work remained for Howells, after his first reading of it in 1852, an example of art submerged under moral. "Its chief virtue," he said later, "is in its address . . . to the ethical sense, not the aesthetical." After reading Scott's poetry in 1850, he did not turn to his novels until 1860, when he went through them all to pass the time while waiting for his passport as consul to Venice. He was lukewarm about him then, and later he became aggressive in his dislike. Sir Walter was the *bête noir* of the American realists. He became, for both Twain and Howells, the symbol of falsification in literature. Young people, the mature Howells said later, ought to be warned against him, and instructed "how false and how mistaken he often is."

Of the romantic poets, the young Howells read Byron and Wordsworth. He disliked Byron on first reading, and his dislike solidified and intensified. Ten years later, when an assistant editor of the *Atlantic*, he agreed to the publication of Harriet Beecher Stowe's defense of Lady Byron, a bitter attack upon the selfish immorality of the lame Lord, and in 1875, he wrote that "Byron is the essence of conscious romanticism, and modern in the worst sense."

The case of his attitude towards Wordsworth is more complex. Byron he could reject as escapist, poseur, profligate imposture of genius. But Wordsworth, after all, was the man who called for the romanticizing of the small, the humble. Yet, Howells said that he could "not make out that Wordsworth was ever a passion of mine." There should have been a measure of sympathy between the poet whose mission was to cast the aura of beauty about the commonplace, and the novelist who made the same mission his career. That there was this perhaps unconscious bond is suggested by Howells' borrowing of one of Wordsworth's lines and using it twice, at wide intervals, in his later career, to characterize his own work: "The moving accident is not my trade." But the way of the romantic mystic was not to be his.

His reading, then, carried up and through him the currents of the classical attitude in literature. Almost instinctively he accepted and loved those writers of the past, and those Europeans of the then-present, whose attention was directed towards the world of their social environment, and who found meaning and value, and therefore literary subjects, in the commonplace world of social experience.

3. The Brahmin Culture

"*. . . the open levels of their common humanity . . .*"
—Lowell

It was not only in his reading that Howells found these currents. They were vitally and colorfully embodied in some of the best-known intellectuals of the American scene in the twenty years before the Civil War. It is difficult, in the attempt to make valid generalizations, to convey an idea of the complexity of a cultural environment. Looking back upon the years between Jackson and Lincoln, we can agree that the American rebirth in the arts was associated with the names of Emerson, Thoreau, Hawthorne, Melville, and Whitman. These were the great creators of the age, and the motivating power of their creation came from the search, through intuition, for the meanings and values that lay behind the world of physical appearances; in short, this was a romantic age. But the American of 1850 would not have regarded it as such, especially if he had lived in Boston. For the ruling intellectuals of the day were not the seaman turned romancer, nor the recluse of Salem, but were, rather, men like James Russell Lowell and Oliver Wendell Holmes, those perfect epitomes of the neo-classical civilization which the descendants of the early unions of Puritan divines and merchant princes had so comfortably made for themselves in mid-nineteenth century Boston.

To this civilization Holmes gave in 1860 the famous label "Brahmin." But for thirty years, the substance of the culture which he named had been the pride of New England. Satisfied with the good society which their grandfathers and fathers had created for them to enjoy, the Brahmins provided the typical environment in which a literature dedicated to the sunny open spaces of social intercourse could flourish. This literature finally created its own medium—the *Atlantic Monthly*—the founding of which in 1857 gave Brahmin culture a national voice, and, ten years later, provided William Dean Howells with the instrument for forging a dominant school of American writers. It was fitting that the first editor of the *Atlantic* should have been James Russell Lowell, for here was the leader of the Brahmins; here, too, was the man most influential upon the development of the attitudes of the youthful Howells.

Lowell's general attitude towards literature defines the way in which a man's basic assumptions are almost always determined by his disposition. He was maturing at a time when the doctrines of Coleridge had become influential in the world of major English literature. As the professor of modern literature of Harvard, and leader among Boston intellectuals, Lowell could therefore not help being interested in the romantic doctrines of transcendentalism, and the impulse these doctrines had given to a kind of poetry which tried to soar into the world of noumena on the wings of emotional insight. Yet he could never shake off the uneasiness which he felt at such flights beyond the pleasant and comfortable confines of his well-ordered earthly existence. He even tried to rescue Coleridge's "imagination" from mysticism by defining it, in a telling blend of classical reasonableness and romantic metaphysics, as "the common sense of the invisible world, as the understanding is of the visible." But where Coleridge, and Emerson, had restricted the source of true poetic inspiration to the Imagination, Lowell insisted that both the poetry of the Understanding and the poetry of the Imagination were needed: "Great poetry," he wrote, "should meet men everywhere on the open levels of their common humanity." Then he added, and we cannot fail to note the depreciatory tone of the allusion to the Imagination: "and not merely on their occasional excursions to the heights of speculation or their exploring expeditions among the crypts of metaphysics." His most popular poem, *The Vision of Sir Launfal*, is a parable on this theme: Sir Launfal goes out on a romantic quest for the Grail, returns broken and unsuccessful, only to find Christ in the dusty beggar who had always been at his gate.

In the same year (1848) Lowell published his first series of *Biglow Papers*, homely verse diatribes against the Mexican War in the dialect and spirit of the New England farmer. Howells, a boy of ten, heard his father repeat passages of the poems, and they always were, for him, the first and best examples of what he later defined as literary "realism." When Lowell, a decade later, became the *Atlantic*'s first editor, he was in the profoundly influential position of the man whose favor Howells as a young potential contributor would be most eager to court. The editors of the *Atlantic* were his idols; publishing in its pages was his dream; he describes how each issue was eagerly received by his friends in Columbus; how he discussed its contents with them; how nearly sacred he felt its opinions to be. When his friend, J. J. Piatt, in collaboration with whom he wrote his first published book, *Poems of Two Friends*, sold a poem to the awesome journal in 1859, Howells wrote him that he was "glad and proud" that Piatt had made it, although "a mean little pang of envy was felt at first."

Then, a year later, Howells sent off a poem of his own, and felt the magnificent thrill when a check for twenty-five dollars came back, and with it, a letter of acceptance from James Russell

Lowell. He cashed the check, but kept the letter next to his heart, and felt for it "to make sure of its presence every night and morning and throughout the day." Naturally, when he made his pilgrimage a few months later, Lowell was the first man he called on in Boston. Lowell gave him his introductions to Boston literary society; Lowell was, for him, "the wisest and finest critic in our language"; Lowell would be for the young Howells "the largest part of that public of which I am conscious when I write."

Howells went off to Venice to spend four intensely growth-filled years there as United States Consul, and as surveyor and reporter of the Italian scene for the American people. His reading of the Italian dramatist Carlo Goldoni solidified many of his earlier convictions regarding the value of literature whose clear level gaze is focussed on materials of the social environment. He began to write a series of sketches of Venetian life which he sold to the Boston *Advertiser*. Lowell read them and wrote him to "keep on cultivating" himself. "They make the most careful and picturesque *study* I have ever seen on any part of Italy. *They are the thing itself*." Howells immediately replied that he was "particularly delighted" to learn that Lowell liked his work, because, while he wrote, he pleased himself with thinking that Lowell "and another dear friend" would see and read them.

The other "dear friend" was Oliver Wendell Holmes. Howells had met him during his memorable trip to Boston in 1860, when Lowell had been good enough to arrange a luncheon for Howells, Holmes, and James T. Fields, publisher of the *Atlantic*. At the conversation which followed, Holmes had laughed and said that this indeed was "the apostolic succession . . . the laying on of hands." What was being passed on was the quiet power of neoclassical Brahmin culture, flowing from its restricted core of Boston into the whole of American life, and somehow, Holmes sensed that this small young man from Ohio was going to be the medium through which that power was transmitted.

Holmes, like Lowell, was an epitome of the Brahmin culture. Born in Cambridge exactly a hundred years after Dr. Samuel Johnson, he was as much a living definition of the classical attitude as the arbiter of Boswell's England. "Boston State-House is the hub of the solar system," Holmes maintained, and he steadfastly held himself to a concern with civilized man organized decently into normal society, and the problems arising out of this kind of organization. He joined with Lowell in a distaste for the metaphysical questings of his more creative contemporaries, and talked of the "oriental side" of Emerson which reveled in "narcotic dreams, born in the land of the poppy and of hashish." The Calvinistic broodings about original sin which gave Hawthorne's dark allegories their haunting depths, the tragic conviction of the necessity of evil which gave Melville's romances their sombre power—these were not for Dr. Holmes, who had seen medicine make greater strides in twenty years than it had in two thousand. "If for the Fall of man, science comes to substitute the RISE of man, sir, it means the utter disintegration of . . . spiritual pessimisms," he said in one of his *Breakfast Table* dialogues. Howells saw in him a man, like himself, who did not want to transcend. "He liked horizons, the constancy of shores," Howells reminisced, and then added, "and I will own that I, for my part, should not have liked to sail with Columbus."

In the year Howells came east to enter the great world, Holmes had made a specific application of his neo-classical doctrines of humanism to fiction. In the series of letters which he prefaced to *The Professor's Story*, Holmes claimed that he was not writing "an 'imaginary' story or a . . . romance or anything of the kind." He insisted upon the truthfulness of his tale, and the value of its imitation of life. He was, he said, simply relating some interesting matters which had come to his attention and which he was reporting faithfully. He went on to jeer at a kind of fiction created with different motives: *that* kind of story, a made-up story, would have "a parcel of impossible events and absurd characters," while his story, he maintained, was simply the reporting of a series of events and the description of a number of persons in the world of his experience.

4. Sentimentalism in America

"I write of the anguish and suffering of an elderly widow with a drunken husband."

—Matilda Muffin

We notice that Holmes seems to have had a low opinion of "romances" and the "romantic." We can hardly imagine such complete shortsightedness on the part of such a truly capable man unless we recognize that "romantic," for a man like Holmes, meant a certain low form of literature which came inevitably to be associated with that word in America in 1860—the kind of literary lying for which we prefer to use the name "sentimentalism." For the sentimental novelists were corrupting America's taste and dulling its sensibilities when Howells was developing into his maturity. Was there concern about industrialism? Sylvester Judd could tell you that the factory girls worked in the Massachusetts mills like princesses in "an abode of enchantment," who tended their looms, during a troubled winter night, "as in the warmth, beauty, and quietness of a summer day." Did you want to find out how to conduct yourself in the increasingly predatory world of business? All you had to do was read of heroes like Horace Courtenay in *The Cabin and the Parlor*, who, in turn, "had read of so many who, like him, had started friendless boys, yet had finally won opulence and station"; or perhaps you would take the advice of the author of *The New England Village Choir*, who pointed out two roads to wealth open to every boy: one was "to become a clerk of some wholesale or retail merchant in Boston, and the other, to pass through a college." Were you concerned about slavery? You need not have been, for, as Caroline Lee Hentz told America in *Marcus Warland*, "It is a dark thread, but as it winds along, it gleams with bright and silvery lustre, and some of the most beautiful lights and shades . . . are owing to the blending of these sable filaments."

The widest range for the sentimentalizer, of course, was the relation between the sexes. In his last novel, *The Vacation of the Kelwyns*, the eighty-year-old Howells satirized this aspect of the stories of the 1860's and '70's. The "nascent fictionists of the *Atlantic Monthly* school" were the American tellers of tales in whom Parthenope, the heroine of his novel, revelled; and these romancers "inculcated a varying doctrine of eager conscience, romanticized actuality, painful devotion, and bullied adoration, with auroral gleams of religious sentimentality." From these writers, Parthenope derived her knowledge of life. Young ladies of marriageable age, she was given to believe, "ought to be won by heroes who sacrificed or ventured a great deal for them." This "great deal" might be as little as rescuing them "from some sort of peril" or as much as risking their lives for them "even when they were not in danger." If the heroes were not physically equipped for such deeds, they would at least have the good sense to "fall a prey themselves to some terrible accident" or to be taken with some sickness "in which the heroines could nurse them up from the brink of death to the loftier levels of life in happy marriage." This fictional world of Parthenope allowed for almost every sort of stubbornness on the part of the male character. If he were so mulish as to refuse to "fall sick, or imperil life or limb, or sublimely rest guiltless under the blame of some shame or crime that would otherwise be laid to the heroine's charge," he would at least have the sense to "believe some other man in love with her and give her up to him." These last tactics "would go far to win her, especially if the hero died of his renunciation or fell into a decline." Not that this was a one-sided fictional world in which the young mind of Parthenope was educated. The heroine, for her part, felt a kind of *noblesse oblige*—"a reciprocal duty to give him up to some girl whom she knew to be in love with him."

It would not be here a matter of serious concern if Howells had been describing the fiction of Ned Buntline or of the dozens of predecessors of Horatio Alger; this kind of popular literature we have always with us; but what he was describing was the literature of the intellectual elite. Sentimentalism had risen from the popular depths and spilled its mawkishness over the entire American literary scene by 1860. Remember that when Howells talked of sentimentalism in 1920, he talked of the "*Atlantic Monthly* school." American literature had reached the state, by the outbreak of the Civil War, where the arbiter of its tastes, the great *Atlantic*, spokesman for the culture of New England, and hence of the New World, had been invaded by sentimentalism, stereotype and falsehood.

An inadvertent acknowledgment of guilt was provided by Rose Terry who wrote her "memorial" in this magazine in 1860 under the pseudonym of "Matilda Muffin." Miss "Muffin's" purpose was to protest against the reading of her fiction as autobiography. Any resemblance between the characters and situations in her fiction and any real people either living or dead, or capable of any kind of life is purely coincidental—this might be the theme of her complaint. "Because I write of the anguish and suffering of an elderly widow with a drunken husband," Matilda asked, does that mean the reader should imagine that I am "therefore meek and of middle age, the slave of a rum jug?" She went on to dispute some of the other identifications her public had made: she had found herself "successively as figuring in the character of a strong-minded, self-denying Yankee girl,—a broken-hearted Georgia beauty,—a fairy princess,—a consumptive school mistress,—a young woman dying of the perfidy of her lover,—a mysterious widow." These were some of the stock characters which "peopled" the short stories and romances of the decade 1857-1867, as a reading of the pages of the *Atlantic* for its first ten years proves. For the *Atlantic* represented the highest cultural range in the spectrum, and as we descend lower we come to the more purple hues of synthetic passion and finally arrive at the ultra-violet ancestors of Deadwood Dick and his progeny, who were leering and posturing through the pages of the newly-born dime novel.

Deadwood had his spiritual counterpart in Loo Loo, who, in one of the first *Atlantic* serials of the same name, was a slave octoroon, white as a lily, and as pure and beautiful. The hero, Alfred Noble, owned her, but treated her like his own sister, and intended to bring her to a northern state, free her, and marry her. The villain, Grossman, swart and sensual, saw and coveted the beautiful slave; he forced an auction sale of the hero's possessions, and bought Loo Loo for his own base purposes. But the villain was foiled; Loo Loo was spared dishonor, and ended happily in the arms of her true love. "Three of Us," an early *Atlantic* short story, ended with the death of its heroine in an icy flood to save the life of an unworthy man she loves. "My Last Love" told of an old maid of twenty-seven who fell in love with a hunter who had accidentally wounded her. He was engaged to another whom he did not love, but the "old maid" said: "A promise is a promise, Mr. Ames. I have thought that a man of honor valued his word more than happiness or life." "Some Account of a Visionary" was the story of Everett Gray, who went through life being honest, tender, and righteous, and was paid in kind by the world with a life full of happiness. His father went bankrupt and honor bade Everett to free Rosa, his beloved, from their engagement, while he went away to Canada for ten years and made his fortune. Honor also forbade him to write to Rosa; but she remained constant, and he returned to her. Marian James, the authoress, exclaimed: "How they have loved, and do love one another . . . ! All the best and truest light of that which we call Romance shines steadily about them yet."

Stereotype and sentiment dominated the fictional scene when Howells took over the assistant editorship of the *Atlantic* in March, 1866. Running in *Harper's* at the time was *Armadale* by Wilkie Collins, England's gift to mid-century "effectism." Appearing in the current numbers of the *Atlantic* was *Griffith Gaunt*, by Charles Reade, and when Howells picked up the most recent copy of the magazine he was to edit, he must have seen Reade's acknowledgment of the baseness to which his art had sunk. What is the good of stories like his? "Now we all need a little excitement," he answered patronizingly. "The girl who satisfies that natural craving by what the canting dunces of the day call a 'sensational' novel, and the girl who does it by waltzing to daybreak, are sisters." A substitute for a waltz to daybreak—that was the way one of the most esteemed practitioners of the art of fiction thought of his craft. Characters in these novels and stories are subordinate to incident. Since the characters were types well known to any reader of fiction, there was little need for honest revelation of character through incident, and, therefore, the author could simply hold up the convenient signpost—the villain's black mustache, the heroine's blond beauty, and could expect the conventional response. Carolyne Ryder, the feminine "heavy" in *Griffith Gaunt*, is introduced as a "female rake. . . .

As dangerous a creature to herself and others as ever tied on a bonnet."

Such was the characteristic fiction that literate America was reading in this decade. Sentiment, stereotype, and striving for effect were the major literary techniques of the day. And Howells, who was to lead the rebellion against them, was enough a creature of his times to have taken his first faltering steps in both fiction and criticism in the direction of sentimentalism. We have noted that he sold some poems to Lowell and the *Atlantic* in 1860; one was called "The Pilot's Story." And what was the tale the pilot told in dactylic hexameters? Much like *Loo Loo*, which had appeared three years before, it was the somewhat stronger story of a "beautiful woman, you would have thought she was white," and her master and lover who wished to make her his wife. In order to manumit her, he took her north on a Mississippi river boat. Once aboard, he fell in with gamblers, the chief of whom cast lustful eyes upon the lovely quadroon. The hero lost his money to the gamblers, and finally, in desperation, staked the ownership of the slave girl upon the turn of a card. The gambler won the turn, and with it the girl; but she threw herself under the paddle wheels before he could take possession of his property.

Even after living in Venice for two years, and after having been exposed to the literary theories of Lowell and Holmes and, as we shall see, Thomas Wentworth Higginson, Howells continued to think of fiction in terms of sentiment. True, it was poetic fiction which he thus considered, but nevertheless a story he was working over during the first part of his stay in Italy might almost be a caricature of the already-caricatured sentimental. It was his only attempt to deal with the Civil War in fiction, and dealt with it, as he later wryly acknowledged, in "a fashion so remote that no editor would print it." He called it, tentatively, "Disillusion: A Little Venetian Story." It would deal, he wrote a friend and prospective publisher, with a pair of lovers; indeed, with two pairs of lovers. And traditional sentimental arrangement was the motivation of the plot: the young enthusiastic girl, Howells wrote in a short prospectus, would promise herself to a man she did not love, as he started with the first volunteers of the war. In her immediate regret at having so bound herself, she hoped that he would not live to fulfill the engagement. His death is reported, and, stricken with remorse and half-crazed, the girl comes to Europe, and promptly falls in love with another. Meanwhile, her betrothed turns up alive and well, and true to their sentimental code, the hero and heroine are willing to place their false ideas of honor above their true feelings. But, as Howells added, the whole thing ended like a comic opera. He had prefaced the synopsis of his plot with the hope that the work, sold at twenty-five cents, might pay, but, fortunately, no one believed him.

He also had been guilty of writing a great many poems in imitation of Heinrich Heine, all the expressions of whose mind, he later acknowledged, were "tinged . . . with . . . passionate sentimentalism." But Lowell, in 1864, wrote him that he must "sweat the Heine" out of him "as men do mercury," and Howells heard him, and wrote a young poet and fellow townsman in 1865 that "the German poetry" was the best of the subjective sort; but that he valued it less than he once did, and indeed, liked objective poetry better. In 1866, he looked upon his poetic sentimentalizing as a closed chapter in his life. He had already written of his pilot's story that it was "a misfortune," and then in 1866, back from Venice and Europe to plunge deeply into American life and letters, he told Thomas Wentworth Higginson that his poetry had been written more than six years before, that he had almost entirely changed since then, that he counted the author of it dead, and himself his literary executor, who had no right to meddle with his work, but had merely to raise money on the verses and apply the proceeds to the relief of his family.

CHAPTER II

THE ATTACK ON THE SENTIMENTAL

1. Beginning the Attack: Higginson

By 1866, then, back from his European withdrawal, and hired, at the suggestion of James Russell Lowell, as assistant editor of the *Atlantic*, William Dean Howells, creature of his times, worshipper of the actual, but with a strain of idealism and mysticism which could never be erased, one-time dabbler in sentimental poetry and fiction, had resolutely set himself against his previous tendencies and the prevailing current of his times. His initial impulse to begin to form a credo of criticism and then of creation—a yard stick by which to judge the works of others and then his own work—was a negative impulse; he simply was against the kind of prettified falsehoods which were passing as current in American literature during the 1860's and '70's. And in this revolt, as in everything else, he was not an innovator, but a representative. For at the same time, other sincere writers in America were finding the impulse for their own criticism and creation in a revolt against sentimentalism.

One of these writers was Thomas Wentworth Higginson, who ought to be remembered not only as the man who first recognized and encouraged Emily Dickinson, but as something more—as the man who first, in influential circles, spoke up clearly and roundly against the currency of sentimentality in fiction, and who foretold, indeed, who publicly demanded the coming of a literature which was to be given the name "realistic." His advice was couched in a form which probably came to Howells' attention in 1862. Higginson called it "A Letter to the Young Contributor" and in the "letter," he told the hopeful author that he must remember to give the present, the familiar, the commonplace, its rightful position in American literature. In his reviewing for the *Atlantic*, both before and immediately after Howells became its assistant editor, Higginson continued to wage his fight for an indigenous American literature, whose allegiance was to the commonplace facts of daily experience, by vigorously attacking the sentimentalism of his day. In 1866 he flattened a novel called *Esperance*, the most recent contribution of the sentimentalists, with a devastating summary of its faults. "Espy," as she was styled, was a "young girl who seeks her destiny" and encounters, in the course of that search, "innumerable crises" during which "father and mother desert her, several lovers jilt her." She would, as Higginson bitingly reported, "be much obliged to you to point out any specific sorrow of which at least one good specimen has not occurred within her experience." Higginson then admitted that it seemed "rather hard, perhaps, to devote serious censure to a thing so frail." But, he said, unless the critic takes it upon himself to do so "how are we ever to get beyond this bread-and-butter epoch of American fiction?" A little later, after Howells had joined the staff of the *Atlantic*, Higginson published another essay that anticipated much of what Howells had to say. Pointing to writers like Balzac, Higginson declared the French novels superior to the English "in keeping close to the level of real human life." He deplored the consistent use, in both English and American fiction, of "the sensational and the exaggerated. . . ."

The next thirty years witnessed the growth of a group of American writers bound together by their disdain for the meretricious and their allegiance to the real, as they saw it. Some of them wrote well, many of them wrote poorly; the value of what they finally did had no necessary relation to their motives. Often Twain and occasionally Howells were able to achieve the justness of internal relations which makes for artistic distinction. Eggleston, Tourgée, Bret Harte almost invariably failed, almost always slipped into one kind of sentimentalism while they were attacking another. But they all partook of a common impulse—a desire to satirize false views of life, and the literature which encouraged them. By finding in anti-sentiment a motive for creation, these writers were underscoring the parallel between their age and other ages of reason in Western culture. When Cervantes wrote *Don Quixote*, his original purpose was to lampoon those romances of chivalry which told of impossible deeds by impossible people, spurred by impossible motives. Fielding, a century later but separated in spirit from Cervantes by no more than an outstretched hand, could not stomach Pamela's pious hypocrisy, and wrote *Joseph Andrews*, in part, to ridicule Richardson's sentimentalizing of the subject of virtue assailed. Jane Austen's *Northanger Abbey* was her satiric commentary on the spectres of the Gothic romance which were occupying much of the attention of the English reading public at the beginning of the nineteenth century. The point of view of a Cervantes, a Fielding, an Austen was like that of Howells, and it was not unnatural that the impulse that motivated these writers should have also motivated Howells and writers in America who were akin to him.

2. Howells' Defense of Romance

An attack on the sentimental was, then, the initial force in the development of American realism. In understanding it, we must keep in mind the meaning of the term for the age, and its distinction from the quite different mode of fiction which we call the "romance." Howells and his followers were against sentimentalism; they respected, even when they did not wholly understand, the romance.

In opposing sentimentalism, they defined it simply as literary lying: giving the reader what he wants, even if what he wants is falsehood. There was no conception of the possibility of an honest sentimentalism which organizes an excessive emotion into the pattern of an integrated work of art; there was no sympathy for the possibility of using stock, stereotypical characters as useful symbols, as Emily Brontë had done with Heathcliff, or Hawthorne with Chillingworth. The reason is clear: by 1870, sentimentalism in America was simply pandering to the emotions of its readers, and had earned the right to be classified by the historian of the type as a "disease." It took a sly peek at the various aspects of American life, and over them threw the veil of rosy-hued sentimental distortions. About social relations, about the rising tides of industrialism and urbanization, about slavery, the sentimental writer had his saccharine say. Against this kind of falsification the satire of the realists was directed.

But "romance" for Howells was another word; Twain would generally lump the two together, but Howells felt that the romance was a different, and possibly a higher window in the tower of fiction. It represented, for him, a different type, governed by different rules. He tried to distinguish between the "novel" as the realistic mode of fiction, and the romance as a type more elevated, more self-contained, less dependent upon direct relations with the world of observed, contemporary appearances. In this he was following Hawthorne who had pointed out that the "novel" is the classical mode expressing itself through prose fiction. In his Preface to *The House of the Seven Gables*, he declared that the "Novel" must be judged on the basis of its fidelity to the normal and commonplace facts of the physical world as perceived by human vision—"fidelity, not merely to the possible, but to the probable and ordinary course of man's experience" was the way he put it. On the other hand, Hawthorne went on, the writer of a "Romance" may "claim a certain latitude." He may present "the truth of the human heart . . . under circumstances, to a great extent, of the writer's own choosing or creation." The author of a romance, then, may create a world in which his characters may move; the writer of a novel must accept the ordinary world, allow his characters to move within that world, and report their doings.

Howells, it is certain, had read *The House of the Seven Gables* and, therefore, indubitably its Preface too, before he had visited Hawthorne in 1860. But had his memory needed jogging, James Russell Lowell had made the same distinction between the two types in a review of Harriet Prescott's *Sir Rohan's Ghost* in the *Atlantic* of that same year. He commended the author for calling her work "Romance" and thus "absolving it from any cumbrous allegiance to fact." Minute and accurate delineation of character, the review went on, "is unessential in a romance, belonging as it does properly to the novel of actual life."

This distinction, this "crucial definition," may have impressed itself on Howells in 1860; it certainly did after he had seriously begun evolving his critical standards in 1872. For in this year, he clearly stated this difference in his own words, and from that time on, he almost invariably makes the distinction. Even the characters who appear as authors in his novels are made aware of it. In *The World of Chance*, Percy Ray, an aspiring young writer, sent his book, "A Modern Romeo" to a publisher; the work apparently dealt with a created world of the artist's own choosing—the world of a re-enactment of the Shakespearean tragedy in which a modern young girl, placed in a mesmeric trance by her father, is taken for dead by her lover, who then kills himself. "It's not, properly speaking, a novel, you see," Ray told the publisher. "It's more in the region of romance." Howells had first spoken clearly of these two types in connection with Charles Dickens, and thereby displayed a critical shrewdness about that great author unmatched in his day. Dickens, Howells felt, was not always a novelist, but often a writer of romances. His grotesques, his symbolizations of good and evil moving about their fog-shrouded world, Howells believed, had the validity of their author's own choosing; they existed in a "created world," and hence were creatures of a romance; Dickens was not, Howells thought, "a novelist in the sense of a writer of realistic fiction."

The following year, he reviewed a work called *Joseph Noirel's Revenge*, and felt that there was exaggeration and excess which should be called to the reader's attention. But these were not in themselves, he thought, the qualities which would determine the success or lack of success of the fiction. For, he said, "The book is a romance, not a novel, and it would not be right to judge it by the strict rules of probability applicable to the novel." He was more specific about the dual standards of criteria a few months later when he defended Thomas Bailey Aldrich against the charge of being fanciful. "Certain premises must be granted the story-teller," Howells said with regard to Aldrich's *Prudence Palfrey*. And the only consistency that "can be fairly expected of a romancer" is the "internal harmony and proportion of his own invention." In 1879, his old friend W. H. Bishop sent him a manuscript and Howells liked it and recommended it to Osgood for publication; when it came out, Howells reviewed it, and praised Bishop for calling his work a "romance." And then he added an insight which explains a good deal about the two types of prose fiction: a romance, he said, is "like the poem, at once more elevated and a little more mechanical than the novel." What he sensed, but did not express, was that the poetry of the romance was aimed at the "truth of the human heart," to put it in Hawthorne's words, or, as we would prefer to say, at the truth of the human subconscious.

Not until the turn of the twentieth century did Howells realize that psychology would force a revision of this critical definition, and when he realized it, he realized the coming of a new age in American literary sensibility. The master of this new age was his lifelong friend, Henry James, Jr. Howells knew there was something different about James from the moment he met him—something that would force him out of the main current of the thought of his half century, to become a prophet of a new generation of writers. The two young men first met and talked together in the fall of 1866, when Howells was beginning his career on the *Atlantic*, and when James was starting on his dedicated career as a story-teller. "Talking of talks," Howells wrote a friend, "young Henry James and I had a famous one last evening . . . in which we settled the true principles of literary art."

What they talked about can be inferred: the ways of looking at life through literature; the techniques that one might use to portray the truth. And it is equally certain that Howells quickly appreciated that James' forte was to lie in a version of the romantic quest—in the attempt to use the prose story as a means of piercing the veil of appearances. His early encouragement of James was all in the direction of "romance." And in 1882, when he wrote his essay on "Henry James Jr.," he singled out his romantic qualities for special praise. He ranked "A Passionate Pilgrim" above all his other short stories, and "for certain rich poetical qualities, above everything else that he has done." And then he went on to lament James' loss of this poetic quality (a loss which James was to make up with a vengeance in his later work, beginning with "The Turn of the Screw," and going on through his three late and great psychological romances). "Looking back to those early stories," Howells wrote, "where James stood at the dividing of the ways of the novel and the romance, I am sometimes sorry that he declared even superficially for the former." And then Howells went on to underscore this observation: "His best efforts seem to me those of romance, his best types have an ideal development."

The fight of Howells, it can be clearly seen, was not a struggle against romance. He understood that there were several roads to literary truth, that one of the best, perhaps, he would occasionally admit, even *the* best, might be the road that led to the stars—the road of romance; he simply felt that it was his call, and the call of his age, to be earthbound, limited, humble. His was the perceptive stroll down main street, not the vault into the unknown. His opposition was to sentimentalism—to the telling of the currently popular lies about life in order to satisfy the prejudices and preconceptions of the audience.

3. The Rejection of Europe: Howells and De Forest

"America is beginning . . . to judge the old world. . . ."
—The Nation

Howells was able to start his career of anti-sentimentalism in a way that met the approval of enough thinking people so that his challenging of popular prejudice did not doom him to unpopularity. This was fortunate and typical. He was a man of his times, a priest and not a prophet, not the prescient dreamer whose originality society either rejects or cruelly punishes, but the leader who can lead because he is so much what his followers are.

His hitting upon a popular mode of anti-sentimentalism was fortunate, too, because Howells was a truly professional writer—

one of the first America had. For him, writing was principally the creation of beauty and truth which could be understood and enjoyed, and bring financial rewards to the creator. He was one of the first American authors to make his living by his pen, and a pretty good living it was. Before the Civil War, Howells wrote once, there were many good authors, but none of them lived from their writings. The Brahmins were men of independent means. Hawthorne and Melville depended somewhat precariously upon political appointments for their bread and butter. Poe lived, barely, by loans. Thoreau subsisted on pencil-making, school-teaching, the bounty of friends, and, for a very brief period (he claimed), from the produce of Walden; Emerson only achieved partial independence after insisting upon his share of his dead wife's inheritance. But Howells was a professional almost from the year of his return from Europe, and by 1885 was the highest paid American novelist, reportedly able to demand five thousand dollars for a serial, besides a royalty on the published book. After 1885, Howells was under contract for ten thousand dollars a year. He continued some arrangement with *Harper's* until 1920. At his death in 1920, his estate was valued at $199,923. Writing is a trade, a craft, the Reverend David Sewell tells his protégé in Howells' *The Minister's Charge*, and Howells always regarded it as such. He took a dim view of the Carnegie public libraries because they might diminish the size of the book-buying public; and when, in 1898, a firm wanted to put out an edition of Mark Twain's works and asked Howells, one of Twain's best friends, to write an introduction for it, Howells said he would be glad to—for fifteen hundred dollars. When they would not meet his price, he politely declined. Yes, Howells was a professional, and as such he was not one to write where there was no audience. So it was fortunate that his first moves towards literary realism and anti-sentimentalism were in a direction which happened to coincide with the reading tastes of an appreciable section of the American public. His attack upon an idealized conception of the Old World, his realistic treatment of persons and places hitherto held in romantic awe was the kind of iconoclasm a growing American sense of cultural independence could welcome.

Howells' first considerable works were two travel sketches of Italy, the first entitled *Venetian Life*, the second *Italian Journeys*. Howells showed a close observation of, and sympathetic interest in, the small, homely details of Italian existence. His cook, her family, the gondoliers, a policeman, a cripple trying on a suit of clothes in a local store—these are the things of which his two travel books were made. And he showed that there was a certain self-consciousness in his rigid avoidance of the unusual; in the realm of the beautiful, he wrote in *Venetian Life*, "there is a perfect democracy . . . and whatsoever pleases is equal to any other thing there, no matter how low its origin or humble its composition." And in *Italian Journeys* he adopted as his motto the line from Wordsworth which we have already noted: "The moving accident is not my trade."

The same tone had been evident in the travel books of another pioneer in American realism: John De Forest's *European Acquaintance* and *Oriental Acquaintance*. De Forest, whose part in the growing realist movement was to be crucial, had, in 1858, published a travel book which poked sly fun at the scenes and people of the Old World. De Forest built the book around his search for the various kinds of cures which were popular at the time: hydropathy, where the sufferer was wrapped in sheets, left to soak in water, and then compelled to walk about dripping and shivering, like a damply apologetic ghost; or the "straw cure," where the invalid was buried in straw, and left to chafe himself into a supposedly salutary discomfort. And during this search, De Forest consciously avoided conventional, worshipful reactions to the Continent. "I have no intention of describing Venice at length," he said in *European Acquaintance*, "inasmuch as it has been visited by other travelers equally well provided with Murrays." This, or a more outright debunking, was the general tone. He told of a young Scotsman pointing his clay pipe towards one of the grandeurs of the Old World and saying: "You don't mean to say that those are the real Alps?" When assured that they were, he expressed his disappointment. His brother chided him: "For shame, you barbarian!" The "barbarian" rejoined that he expected to "grow up to the sentiment, by-and-by," but for the present "they look confoundedly small." The people of Europe, as well as the landscapes, were levelled by the view of the observer. "The plebians of Rome, the blouses of Paris, the b'hoys of New York, the filibusters of New Orleans were the same race," De Forest said, and all could act "like heroes and ignoramuses." The "nymphs" of Graefenberg, with their sunburnt legs scratched by brambles, were, "Alas for the romance of these sylvan scenes . . . more frail than fair, the morals of the peasantry for miles around Graefenberg having been lamentably corrupted by its unscrupulous bachelor patients." The mysteries of Europe became not mysteries at all; a house in Berlin, "haunted" by rumblings, and rollings, and strange bursts of laughter, was discovered to be situated over a beer-room and billiard hall.

Through this voyage of the discovery of the oneness of all men and all countries moved De Forest, the American proud of his homeland, proud that it was the country where the idea of the free individual was carried fullest into action, and challenging his continental friends "to produce a land in which society is more stable or prosperity more equally divided." He was able to laugh good-humoredly at himself when he discovered that he had used his *Dictionnaire de poche* for some months before discovering that *Poche* was not the author of it. He unashamedly danced the Negro *Juba* at a party, and found himself a crazy success. Europeans begged to be taught it. His most faithful pupil was a "severe Swiss minister . . . with stern black eyes, and a long beard of apostolic dignity," and day after day he used to "hear him double-shuffle, or hoe corn and dig potatoes around the billiard room."

This was the tone that Howells struck successfully in his travel books *Venetian Life* and *Italian Journeys* eight and nine years later. Howells saw Pompeii, enjoyed it, but could not help expressing his disappointment, for an "exuberant carelessness of phrase in most writers and talkers who describe it" had led him to expect more than was there. Before appreciating it for what it is, he declares, the visitor must "cast out of his knowledge all the rubbish that has fallen into it from novels and travels." Like De Forest, earlier, he saw the underlying sameness of poor men everywhere. In *Italian Journeys,* he viewed a colorful Italian crowd in winter with pleasure, but it was a pleasure tinged with melancholy at the knowledge of what was concealed beneath the display. He knew that it had "nothing but a cup of coffee in its stomach"; that it had "emerged from a house as cold and dim as a cellar"; that it would presently "go home to dine on rice and boiled beef." At the station of Castellamare he saw "a curious cripple on the stones,—a man with little, short, withered legs, and a pleasant face," and watched as he was measured for a suit of clothes, "twirling and twisting himself about in every way for the tailor's convenience." And as well as the little sadnesses, he saw the humor in the commonplace. Not only were the Italian legions a "thirsty host" as evidenced by the number of wineshops; he found them a bloodthirsty people as well, to judge from the number and colorfulness of the signs of the barber-surgeons. He saw that, as he went south from Venice, "science grew more and more sanguinary." The barbers' signs showed bleeding at the elbow, then from both elbow and wrist, and finally, at Naples, he observed "the exhaustive treatment of the subject . . . , the favorite study of the artist being to represent a nude figure reclining in a genteel attitude on a bank of pleasant greensward, and bleeding from the elbows, wrists, hands, ankles, and feet."

Involved in this discovery of De Forest and Howells that people, even in the heretofore culturally idolized and feared Old World, were essentially one in their common humanity, was an intellectual patriotism, an assertion of the equality of America, and hence the dignity and value of American civilization. This kind of cultural patriotism endowed the early anti-sentimentalism of Howells, as it did the attacks upon falsity by De Forest and Twain, with a basic appeal to his American audience. *Venetian Life* sold well and was well reviewed. In all three major periodical reviews, the word "delightful" appeared; readers remarked upon its "pleasant flavor of individuality" and its "beauty of finish"; there was surprised admiration for the native gentility of someone born in Ohio, and for the implicit attack upon sentimentality in the work. "Most tourists," one reviewer emphasized, "go to Venice with *Childe Harold* and Rogers' *Italy* in their minds and hands." But to Howells, "Lord Byron is neither a hero nor a historian . . . and he quietly tells the truth about the Bridge of Sighs."

Most important of all, the *Nation*, which Howells regarded as the supreme arbiter of American letters (he wrote Henry James that it was the "one critic for 40,000,000 of people") perceived what Howells was doing, and proclaimed the superiority of his achievement. The reviewer saw that his age was becoming an age of skepticism replacing an age of sentimentalism. "The author of *Italian Journeys*," this reviewer declared, was "certainly a sentimentalist" at one time. But he had seen his error, and now was satirizing his own sentimentalism, and thus became a humorist. "As a humorist," the reviewer then said, "he is the superior of all other American writers." With this kind of acceptance, Howells could feel encouraged to proceed in the direction of deepening his realism.

And then a year after his own success, a volume came across Howells' reviewing desk which climaxed this series of travel books written by pioneer realists to tell the truth about the parent culture of Europe. It was called *The Innocents Abroad* and reminded Howells that there was a writer appearing on the American scene who, like himself, was dedicating his life to the truthful reporting of that which he saw, and to the blasting of sentimental falsehoods.

4. The Rejection of the Old World: Twain

Samuel Clemens was two years older than Howells, and like him the son of a provincial family of small means. His parents had migrated from Columbia, Kentucky, to Jamestown, Tennessee, where they bought 70,000 acres of rich land between the Cumberland and the Tennessee rivers—bought them for less than a cent an acre and lived out the rest of their lives in the false hope of immense riches. From Jamestown they had come to Florida, Missouri, where Sam was born in 1835, and from there to Hannibal, where he grew up to adolescence on the bank of the trafficked Mississippi. Like Howells, he had set type for his family's newspaper, but, unlike Howells, had wandered to Cincinnati, New York, and Philadelphia, had become a river-boat pilot on the Mississippi, had gone West to the lure of the silver mines of Nevada, had reported for the Virginia City *Territorial Enterprise*, had left

Virginia City, a jump ahead of the sheriff, for San Francisco, and San Francisco two jumps ahead of the chief of police for the Mother Lode country. He had adopted the pseudonym "Mark Twain" from the call of the leadsmen on the river, whose shout that the safe two-fathom point had been reached was the sweetest sound a pilot could hear, and had written some highly successful accounts of his trip to the Hawaiian islands for the Sacramento *Union*. On the strength of these letters he had been commissioned to write a similar series during a cruise to Europe and the Holy Land on the *Quaker City*. The series appeared as *The Innocents Abroad* in 1869.

His purpose, Twain declared at the very outset of his book of travels, was the purpose of De Forest and Howells: to "suggest to the reader how *he* would be likely to see Europe and the East if he looked at them with his own eyes instead of the eyes of those who traveled . . . before him." At once, then, he identified himself with the American reader; he would make "small pretense of showing anyone how he *ought* to look at objects." He would let them look through his eyes. He was an innocent, with other innocents, and he reported what he saw, with the directness of the child. When he found something he could genuinely admire, he told about it; but when he found pretense and humbug, when he saw something distorted by sentimentalism, he stripped the veil from it by comparing romantic exterior with inner truth: for example, his description of the Portuguese boatmen "with brass rings in their ears, and fraud in their hearts." He could appreciate the Europeans' ability to forget the work of the day when it was done; he was pleased to find his party of tourists relax their pace; he noticed "the absence of hog wallows, broken fences, cow-lots, unpainted houses" and the presence of "cleanliness, grace, taste in adorning and beautifying." But the ignorance, the superstition, the fraud which masquerades as quaintness, the squalor that pretends to beauty—these he demolished with mining-camp humor. Of the Azores he saw that there was "not a modern plow in the islands, or a threshing-machine," for at any attempt to introduce them the good Portuguese "crossed himself and prayed God to shield him from all blasphemous desire to know more than his father did before him." In Italy he found "the home of priestcraft—the land of poverty, indolence, and everlasting unaspiring worthlessness." In Venice, he felt it "a sort of sacrilege to disturb the glamour of old romance" that pictured her as a thing of beauty, but he was compelled to report that in place of the "fairy boat" and the "gay gondolier in silken doublet" there was actually "an inky, rusty old canoe" and a "mangy, barefooted guttersnipe."

Where other travellers had come to worship at the shrine of European culture, Twain was an unabashed practical Yankee, who liked to revel in the dryest details. The great cathedral at Milan, he reported with a straight face, was "five hundred feet long by one hundred and eighty wide"; it had "7,148 marble statues . . . one thousand five hundred bas reliefs . . . one hundred and thirty-six spires." The bill so far, he calculated, footed up to "six hundred and eighty-four millions of francs." In front of the Last Supper, he looked hard, looked again, and could only report that the colors were "dimmed with age"; the countenances "scaled and marred," and nearly all expression "gone from them." Then he saw others about him, standing entranced before it and ejaculating over the "matchless coloring" where there was no color, the delicacy and feeling where there was only a dead blur, and he could only turn away with wryly good-natured sadness at the ability of some to see that which was not there.

He never gave up pricking the bubble of pretentious untruths about the glories of our parent culture, and about the supposed superiority of its storied, aristocratic past to the democratic bourgeois American present. His two best works of historical fiction, *The Prince and the Pauper* and *A Connecticut Yankee in King Arthur's Court*, are excursions into the past not for nostalgia or escape, but for demonstration of the superiority of republicanism to aristocracy, industrialism to agrarianism, and reason to superstition.

In the first of these fictions, Tom Canty, the pauper, became a prince by the change of costume; the prince became mad Tom by shedding his jewels for rags. Tom managed his new job, after training and practice, but the prince never learned the complexities of existence as a pauper. Tom, as the poor boy turned monarch, heard of the enormous indebtedness of the crown and faced it in practical fashion: "'Tis meet and necessary," he told the courtiers, "that we take a smaller house and set the servants at large." He remembered just the right kind of place, one that "standeth over against the fish-market," when a pressure on his arm from Lord Hertford reminded him that he was in a fantastic world of nonsensical traditions, a world in which his direct and intelligent approach was "foolish" and his practical speech was "strange."

While Tom learned how an aristocratic system could enslave the minds of the aristocracy, the little Prince learned how it could warp men's feelings and crush their bodies. Two gentlewomen befriended him in prison, and he begged them for assurance that they, at least, would not receive the lash. They tenderly told him that they would not; he found, instead, that they were burned at the stake, while their daughters struggled to die with them. And in this insane world, the little Prince's sanity seemed mad. Overcome with horror at the women's "heart-piercing shrieks of mortal agony," he could say nothing, and Miles Hendon took this silence as growing sanity. "His disorder mendeth," thought that young nobleman. "If he had followed his wont, he would have stormed at these varlets, and said he was king, and commanded that the women be turned loose unscathed. Soon his delusion will pass away and be forgotten, and his poor mind will be whole again." Then Hendon added, "God speed the day!" and his exclamation underscores the controlling purpose of the book —a hymn in praise of the progress of the race which can finally achieve the sanity of the little Prince and thereby understand the irony of Hendon's musings.

With this development of historical fiction as an allegory of human progress, and as an indirect glorification of democracy, science, and reason, Howells was in thorough accord. He had received *The Innocents Abroad* joyously, relishing it as "an amount of pure human nature . . . that rarely gets into literature." He liked *The Prince and the Pauper* "immensely." Although he wanted it to be even more satirical than it was, he found "the whole intention, the allegory, splendid, and powerfully enforced." And then, eight years later, Howells hailed Twain's climactic defense of America against the old world as "all good," with "passages in it" that did his "whole soul good." For *A Connecticut Yankee in King Arthur's Court* was the definitive statement of this phase of the anti-sentimentalism of the American realists.

The theme of this picaresque fantasy of the Yankee "Boss" in the land of the Round Table was the same as that of *The Prince and the Pauper*. The tone of triumph of the first book, however, was muted in the later, and greater, work. Much had happened in America between 1880 and 1888 to make it doubtful that the healthful forces of social, economic, and religious enlightenment had triumphed as completely as had been expected. *The Prince and the Pauper* could end with the real king happy on his throne, and promising a new order of justice and tolerance after his education in democracy. But after Hank, the Connecticut Yankee, had almost succeeded in making over the depraved sixth century in the image of the American nineteenth century, the force of superstition proved too powerful; Merlin and the Church demolished his works and put him into a sleep which was not broken for thirteen hundred years.

Before Merlin worked his final wiles, however, the Yankee, singlehanded, had given him a run for his money. For he was imbued with the democratic faith in man: "A man *is* a man, at bottom. Whole ages of abuse and oppression cannot crush the manhood out of him." And so he dreamed of transforming the country into one where "the whole government" would be placed "in the hands of the men and women of the nation, there to remain." And he actively engaged in the necessary reforms towards this end. For this apostle of progress, everything about the nineteenth century was better—even the cuss-words; when the king and a knight swore at each other, Hank flung out "a hair-lifting soul-scorching thirteen-jointed insult which made the king's effort poor and cheap by comparison." Hank got his "out of the nineteenth century where they know how."

Twain, then, made a lifelong career out of the assertion of the superiority of attitudes dominantly American. And although the works of Howells and De Forest never reached the same heights of satiric invective against European civilization, they did more quietly assert the same acceptance of their American environment which we find in Twain. The anti-sentimentalism of all three, as well as of the host of lesser writers who followed them, quickly turned to native subjects, and found their deepest meaning in their exploration of the vices and follies of their own people. But underlying their uneasiness with the life of their America—an uneasiness that often became irritation—was the conviction that their America was the best society the world had yet known. Theirs was a lovers' quarrel with their world. And theirs was truly a comic age.

5. The Attack on the Sentimental in Literature: Howells

As Howells did in his trans-Atlantic sketches, so he did in his writings on the American scene. When, after taking up the assistant editorship of the *Atlantic* in 1866, he turned his eyes upon the humanity of his own country, he began the same comic attack upon the lie that gave his books of foreign travel their secure place in the history of the anti-sentimental. In both his criticism and his first hesitant steps in fiction he showed that his underlying motive was to oppose the flood of literature which was not teaching men the truth, but was telling them the kinds of sugar-coated lies which would satisfy their preconceptions.

The longest notice Howells wrote in his first year at his new job was of Charles Reade's *Griffith Gaunt.* It must have taken some courage for the new young editor to review a work which had run in the magazine which had just hired him; but Howells was eager and wrote Fields that he hoped no one else would be engaged to do the review. It took little reading between the lines to see the essentially uncomplimentary tone of the notice Howells gave the novel. Although he approved of those aspects of the work which were natural and realistic, he was guarded in his highly qualified praise and pointed out the essentially contrived nature of a tale which began with the words: "Then I say, once for all, that priest shall never darken my door again," and continued through twelve installments of historical romance.

He took off the gloves when dealing with the work of another sentimentalizer the following year. His review of Dr. Holland's long narrative poem *Kathrina* showed American writers what they could expect from the new assistant chief of the *Atlantic*. The review had double force, for it followed on the heels of a piece by Higginson on "Literature as Art" which had repeated again that writers were true to their calling if they kept close to the levels of actuality. Then Howells stripped off the hopeless tangle of pathetic fallacies which clothed *Kathrina*, and showed it for what it was—a wallow of sentimental clichés in which lambkins and tearful heroines and impossibly upright young men rolled in saccharine abandon.

He never again was as harsh in his attacks upon the writings of his sentimental compatriots during his tenure on the *Atlantic*, and generally was more positive in his attitude, contenting himself to review those works about which he could comment constructively in his effort to build up a school of realism in America. But he was consistent nevertheless in his opposition to art which imitated art instead of life, and to the tendency of authors to look at experience "through somebody else's literary telescope." He used another figure of speech to express the same kind of literary sentimentality in 1874 when he complained of Thomas Bailey Aldrich that he "is apt, if anything, to be over-literary, to see life through a well-selected library window." He tried to encourage Aldrich to break the sashes of the window and to "step quite out of doors." But by 1880, Howells was forced to admit that Aldrich continued to prefer looking at life through literature and "giving not so much the likeness of what he might see . . . as the likeness of something that has pleased him in books."

From 1881 to 1885, Howells devoted himself to the writing of fiction, with only the occasional break of an article like that on Henry James, Jr., which set the English critics on their ears by declaring that James' art of fiction was a finer one than that of Dickens and Thackeray. But in 1885, he returned to regular reviewing for *Harper's Monthly* and for six years he wrote a monthly feature, "The Editor's Study," in which he fought the battle for realism and against sentimentalism. During these years sentimental fiction had assumed a new guise—the historical romance; and it was with the sentimental version of the historical romance that Howells crossed swords in what became one of the bitterest literary battles in American critical history.

We must repeat our words of caution here about the nature of these difficult terms "romance" and "romantic." "Romance" as a way of looking at life through literature which, like a poem, is at once "more elevated and more mechanical than a novel"; romance in which "you concede the premises as in a poem, and after that you hold the author only to a poetical consistency"—to this way of seeking truth through literature Howells was, we have already seen, friendly and understanding. He had some reservations about the ability of a writer of less than superior talents to handle the recreation of the past: "it is hard to get nature to take part in one's little effects when it is an affair of contemporary life; if it is an affair of life in the past her co-operation is still more reluctant." But the great writer, he felt, could understand the oneness of all people at all times, and make his work as true when it concerned remote times and places as when it concerned the now and the here. "Do I, then, wholly dislike historical fiction as impossible and deplorable?" he asked after describing the fatuities which were spawned at the end of the nineteenth century. And he answered: "On the contrary, I like it very much." He then gave a list of historical romances which he admired, a list headed by *War and Peace*, which "presents an image of the past that appeals to my knowledge of myself and of other men as unimpeachably true."

But when lesser talents tried the historical romance, the result was simply another example of lying about life which Howells knew was bad art and worse morality. He tried several times to find another term for "bad" historical fiction. Fiction, he once said, can be used to portray either the ideal or the real; "that which it is loath to serve is the unreal"; for the "unreal," he suggested, "we have no name for but romanticistic."

Since others, however, called sentimental historical fiction "romance," Howells usually went along with them; and it is true, of course, that the writers of historical tales usually deal with painted dolls going through stereotyped patterns of action in front of papier-mâché settings. And towards this kind of fiction, Howells' attitude varied between scornful condescension and positive distaste. Sometimes he would say that this kind of writing might serve a harmless, although useless service for readers who cannot face life but must see it through the mists of distance "in which all the disagreeable details shall be lost." He struck the same note in talking about the absurdities from Rider Haggard. They are intended, he said, to take the reader's mind, "or what that reader would probably call his mind, off himself." The Rider Haggards have their place, he sometimes felt; the world likes to forget itself and escape into the "horrid tumult of the swashbuckler swashing on his buckler." But more often he was bitter about this use of his craft to enable people to escape from the realities of the life about them, for he saw that only through facing these realities could they cure some of the diseases that were corrupting the American life he loved. Our well-to-do classes, he wrote, use the historical romance as a means of escape from the "facts of the life of toil" just as those who do the toiling use sentimental fiction to escape from the severities of their existence. After the war with Spain, he saw the resurgent interest in the form as evidence of another kind of escapism. Ashamed of ourselves because of our "lust of gold and blood," he wrote, we welcome "the taradiddles of the historical romancers as a relief from the facts of the odious present."

The false and mistaken sentimentalist view of life was the major target not only of Howells' criticism, but of his fiction. Beginning with his first sketches in 1870 and 1871, and continuing through his last novel which appeared in 1920, he consistently made his opposition to the sentimental view of life an important motive of his work. Sometimes he would bring up the subject almost incidentally: in *The Rise of Silas Lapham*, for example, when conversation at the dinner party where Lapham showed himself in all his touching vulgarity turned to the latest novels, and a clergyman vigorously indicts those which falsify life. But often Howells' anti-sentimentalism was much more than just a passing comment. It was the motive and meaning of his work, and it was symptomatic of the significance of the anti-sentimental impulse to the spirit of the age of realism that Howells' first prose story to achieve national publication was a comic treatment of the gap between the real and the sentimental view of the real.

The story was called "A Romance of Real Life." It told of a writer who had been musing how real life could supply "all the people of romance, who had but to be hospitably treated in order to develop the deepest interests of fiction, and to become the characters of plots so ingenious that the most cunning invention were poor beside them." The writer's reveries were interrupted by a grizzled old mariner, whose touching air of unaffectedness immediately won the author's heart. The mariner was looking for his children—those who remained to him after his wife and baby had been carried away by smallpox while he was on his voyage. Deeply moved, the writer spent the next days helping the sailor find his daughter. He finally succeeded, and with a light heart went up the steps of the daughter's house to break to her the news of the impending happy reunion. But the girl greeted him with a loud, hoarse laugh, and while she caught a fly on the door-post and deftly picked it to pieces, the writer learned that the "sailor" had just come out of State Prison, where he had been put for bigamy, and that kindly friends were trying to see that he was kept away from his children.

There were several kinds of satire on sentimentalism in this little story. There was the portrait of the fraudulent sailor who deluded not only the author, but himself as well. The fraud had read *Two Years Before the Mast* and "why should he not place implicit faith on all the fictions reared from it?" He convinced himself of the "reality" of his own falseness. And the writer himself provided the reinforcement of this little satire on seeing life through literature. For Howells finally absolved the "sailor" of all moral obliquity and, in an act of author-intervention which he would rarely commit again in his fiction, stepped in to say: "I can understand how one accustomed to value realities only as they resembled fables should be won to such pensive sophistry."

"A Romance of Real Life" was included in the volume entitled *Suburban Sketches* which appeared in 1871, and with it appeared another fragment of Howells' opposition to sentimentalism. It was entitled "Scene" and it described how the same writer moved through an Irish neighborhood and noticed an unusual activity. He was told that a girl had just drowned herself. "Upon this answer that literary soul fell at once to patching himself up a romantic story for the suicide, after the pitiful fashion of this fiction-ridden age, when we must relate everything we see to something we read." The author, however, forwent his romantic musings and simply told what he saw. And what his eyes showed him was a sight deeply significant: the corpse lay in the bottom of a cart, and over it were piled the baskets in which the grocers had delivered their sugar and flour, and coffee and tea. And as the cart jolted along, the street urchins danced about it with wild yells of mirth.

For the rest of his life, Howells' concern with sentimentalism that falsifies our perception of life, that slides in between the eye and the thing and blurs the outlines of reality, continued to be a major theme in his fiction. Indeed, it was the central meaning of two of his best works written before 1885, *A Foregone Conclusion* and *Indian Summer*.

A Foregone Conclusion was an international novel to which Howells turned his hand after making initial ventures in the field of long fiction on American subjects–*Their Wedding Journey* and *A Chance Acquaintance*. The idea had obviously been in his mind for at least eight years, for in 1866 he wrote a piece for the New York *Times* on the subject of the celibacy of the Italian priesthood. Marriage for priests, he asserted then, should be approved as a means towards improving the tone of both religion and morality in Italy. And perhaps he had seen in the treatment of a priest in *Griffith Gaunt* both the proof that the subject had possibilities for fiction and the example of how this subject should not be treated by the sincere writer. Instead of the overstated heroics of Reade's substitute for waltzing till midnight, Howells wrote the understated story of Don Ippolito, an Italian priest who succumbed to a fleshly love for a handsome American girl, Florida Vervain. The story was seen from the point of view of Ferris, an artist, who, like Howells, had temporarily taken a consulship in Venice. Ferris was deeply involved in the tale, for he too had fallen in love with the vital Florida, but he forced himself passively to watch the development of this strange attachment. Don Ippolito was led on because of the lack of restraint with which Florida conducted herself towards what she imagined an asexual tutor. When she finally realized his tragic situation, she reacted with an impulsive gesture of the maternalism which Howells knew so clearly is a true motivation of women. Caught up in a surge of compassion and sorrow, she "flung her arms about his neck, and pulled his head down upon her heart, and held it tight there, weeping and moaning over him as over some hapless, harmless thing she had unpurposely bruised or killed." She then thrust him away, and with her rejection, the priest was completely lost.

Don Ippolito's story was a minor tragedy, a tragedy in the conventional and classical sense of the word—a tragedy because it was the tale of an essentially noble man betrayed by what was false within, a minor tragedy because Don Ippolito's was a weakness which totally precluded greatness. His fault was what Howells feared might become the fault of his age, the fault of a sentimental withdrawal from reality. Don Ippolito could not visualize the vastness of America, and Florida told him that he never would if he did not think about it more practically. "Practically, practically," lightly retorted the priest. "What a word with you Americans!" But in this story it was the practical which was the truthful, and the escapist dream world of the priest which was the lie. "It's amazing," Ferris tells Florida, "it's perfectly amazing that you should have been willing to undertake the job of importing into America that poor fellow with his whole stock of helplessness, dreamery, and unpracticality."

Florida and her mother had thought seriously of enabling the priest to make his escape from the Church and from Italy. When Ferris had tried to reason with him and them, Mrs. Vervain had defended their actions by appealing to intuition over reason, and Ferris could only silently bow his head. But intuition, of course, the intuition of a sentimental woman, was proved wrong, and reason was proved right. And when it was, and Don Ippolito had brought death to himself, and almost brought unhappiness to Ferris and Florida, Ferris looked back upon the priest's history and saw it as the life of a victim of sentiment; Don Ippolito, although in many things "the soul of truth and honor," Ferris told Florida, "was such a dreamer that once having fancied himself afflicted at being what he was, he could go on and suffer as keenly as if he really were troubled by it." The priest, Ferris continued, took the traditional sentimental refuge of blaming his circumstances in place of his own insufficiency. Even his love for Florida seemed to Ferris to have "a great share of imagined sentiment in it"; rather than passion, "it was the gentle nature's dream of a passion." As a victim of sentiment, Ippolito never succeeded in becoming real; he "at last ceased to be even the memory of a man with a passionate love and a mortal sorrow."

Howells again took up this theme of the dangers of sentimentalism in *Indian Summer*. This story of a middle-aged bachelor and two lovely women, one his own age, one much younger, good-humoredly explored the effects of "a bad thing" which developed itself into "manifold and astounding evils." Colville, a newspaper publisher in the autumn of life, could perhaps be excused for so exaggerating the "bad thing," for he had been trapped by it into risking the loss of the woman who could make his life meaningful. The evil was the mistaken and childish view of love and matrimony which Imogene Graham, the beautiful young girl, had derived from poems and novels, and had tried to apply to the realities of human relationships. She sentimentally imagined that she had a mission with regard to Colville; he had had a shattered love affair, and Imogene put herself into the role of the self-sacrificing heroine who would make up to this attractive older man the wrong that another member of her sex had done him long ago. Flattered by her illusions, Colville, lonely and at loose ends in Florence, allowed himself to be pleasantly deceived into thinking she loved him. Mrs. Bowen, constrained by convention, could only watch hopelessly and passively, as the visions of the young girl threatened to turn into the painful reality of an unsuitable marriage.

Had Colville been a foolish unrealist, the triangle would have had the makings of a farce. But on the contrary Colville was a hard-headed, commonsensical man, almost the ideal of classical virtues. He believed in ghosts, he told Imogene, but he was in no hurry to mingle with them, and he would not believe a ghost were a ghost until the specific example of the genus proved its existence to him. He agreed, with the old minister, that "Nature is a savage"; after having been driven on by her, Colville said, "some fine morning we wake up" and find that she "has got tired of us and left us to taste and conscience." How much more dangerous the disease of sentiment could be, then, when it could soften the hard head of a Colville. And soften it sentimentalism did. He even found himself mouthing the phrases out of books, like, "if they loved each other they need not regard any one else," and it was with a kind of "dull surprise" that he saw that the platitude sufficed for Imogene. Although he came to realize that the child was "full of fancies" about him, and that her love for him was a mistake of her romantic imagination, when she insisted upon trying to live an impossible dream of self-sacrifice, Colville "could not endure to fall short of her ideal of him . . . no matter what error or calamity the fulfilment involved." Mrs. Bowen, in love with Colville, could help neither of them.

Only a lucky accident saved them. Colville was trampled by a horse as he melodramatically tried to save Imogene, and the shock of the incident shook the sentimental chaos into reasonable order. Colville came to consciousness in the comfort and quiet and orderliness of Mrs. Bowen's home, and knew that he would like to remain there forever. But sentimentalism almost had the final say. After the two middle-aged lovers confessed their affection for each other, Mrs. Bowen was constrained to act the part she thought was meant for her; she would renounce Colville because she had unworthily loved him while he had been engaged to another. But her daughter Effie came in upon the situation, and the child's wail of pain immediately revealed the false inhumanity of her mother's pose. " 'Oh you must stay!' " Mrs. Bowen told Colville, "in the self-contemptuous voice of a woman who falls below her ideal of herself." And *Indian Summer* left no doubt that Howells, like the other serious writers of his time, was trying to teach his generation that this was the most beneficent fall of all—the fall from false ideals and sentimental visions of human behavior to the good of an empirical solution. Mr. Waters, the old New England divine who acts as the chorus in the comedy, summarized the meaning of the story: "We are a long time learning to act with common-sense or even common sanity in what are called matters of the affections."

6. The Attack on the Sentimental in Literature: Eggleston, Harte, Twain

"*. . . as through a glass eye, darkly . . .*"
—Mark Twain

The writers of his age who partook of Howells' acquiescence, who rooted their satirical realism in the soil of their basic devotion to American republicanism, science, and the doctrine of progress, invariably found their initial impulse to write truthfully as a reaction against the sentimentalizing of life in literature. A man like Edward Eggleston, the circuit-riding Methodist minister from Indiana who wrote two of the early novels of local color and brought the life and dialect of the Midwest into American literature, felt strongly that fiction must serve humanity by writing its truthful personal history; he also felt that good fiction must first undo the harm wrought by the sentimental lie. So he frequently interrupted his narratives to explain the difference between the popular falsehoods about human beings and the sober and unexciting truth. Ralph Hartsook, the young teacher who played the principal role in *The Hoosier Schoolmaster* (1871), noticed the pretty and friendly Hannah at a spelling bee, and felt that the wilderness of ungracious coarseness into which he had come might be made less desolate by her presence. He walked her home, and Eggleston observed that the reader would undoubtedly expect him to describe the two lovers strolling over the shadow-flecked path under the "silvery moonbeams" as they came "down in a shower—to use Whittier's favorite metaphor," with the evening star "shedding its benediction on them." But Eggleston would do no such thing, for the plain truth of the matter was that "the moon was not shining, neither did the stars give their light." Instead, it happened to be inclement weather indeed, and the black boughs of the maples swayed in a very unsentimental wind.

As he would provide no bland sop for the palates tenderized by the unreal stories of contemporary love, neither would Eggleston provide spice for those readers whose tastes had been dulled by the "Cayenne pepper of the penny-dreadfuls." When the schoolmaster awakened in the middle of one of his first nights in his new surroundings, it was not to the stirrings of a trap door or, even better, to the rustling of nameless beings in subterranean passages, but to the very ordinary unrest of a troubled mind. "It's so pleasant to have one's hair stand on end," Eggleston said. "But if you want each individual hair to bristle with such a 'Struggle in the Dark,' you can buy trap-doors and subterranean passages dirt cheap at the next news-stand."

Had Eggleston been a humorist, he might not have been forced into so explicit a statement of his anti-sentimentalism. Like Bret Harte, and like Mark Twain, he might have used the most effective weapon in the arsenal of the commonsensical—the sharp edge of satire. Bret Harte was making his splash in literary America with his stories about the Far West at the same time that Eggleston was publishing his Indiana tales, and he was consciously, though not always successfully, basing his fiction upon his experience; he claimed that all of his characters had "a real human being as a suggesting and a starting-point." When Howells reviewed Harte's *The Luck of Roaring Camp and Other Stories* he saw that they were a contribution to America's growing knowledge of the actualities of her multi-faceted life, that they brought the society of the Far Western frontiers into the nation's literary consciousness. Howells saw, too, that Harte had often slipped into sentimentalism. (Characters like Cherokee Sal and Kentuck in the story which gave its title to the volume were typical toughs, female and male, the prototypes of the ruffians with the hearts of gold who people so many of our motion pictures.) But Harte, nevertheless, erred unwittingly, for he had, through the pages of San Francisco's *Golden Era* and *The Californian,* carried on a brilliant satirical campaign against the falsifications of life purveyed by the sentimental novelists. His blows in the war on the lie took the form of a series of *Condensed Novels* which imitated the impossible content and the inflated style of sentimentalists, and the subjects of his satire ranged from the dime novelists (one of the "novels" is called *The Hoodlum Band; or, The Boy Chief, The Infant Politician, and The Pirate Prodigy*) up through the Indian stories of James Fenimore Cooper.

The condensation called *Muck-a-Muck* was a summary of the

sentimental faults of Cooper's fiction—the falsity of his characters, the absurd inaccuracy of his settings, the contrivance of his plots. The characters were Judge Tompkins, his beautiful daughter Genevra Octavia, Muck-a-Muck, and Natty "Bumpo." Their impossible dialogue ranged from the literary cadences of Cooper's well-born simulacra to the close-lipped understated homeliness of the Deerslayer. When the judge addressed his daughter about a common household matter, he spoke thus: "Genevra, the logs which compose yonder fire seem to have been incautiously chosen. The sibilation produced by the sap, which exudes copiously therefrom, is not conducive to composition." Upon which Genevra answered, "True, Father, but I thought it would be preferable to the constant crepitation which is apt to attend the combustion of the more seasoned ligneous fragments." Or she confided in Natty Bumpo: "Methinks 'twere pleasant to glide ever thus down the stream of life, hand in hand with the one being whom the soul claims as its affinity." Whereupon Natty: "Ef you mean you're on the marry... I ain't in no wise partikler."

Natty Bumpo was one aspect of the sentimental love of the unspoiled children of nature—the noble savage ("Noble being!" Genevra thinks to herself. "Reared in this wild seclusion, yet he has become penetrated with the visible consciousness of a Great First Cause"). Another side of noble savagery was exhibited in Muck-a-Muck "the haughty aborigine,—the untaught and untrammelled son of the forest." Over the "bare and powerful breast" of the graceful savage was pasted "a quantity of three-cent postage-stamps which he had despoiled from an Overland Mail stage." The Noble Savage spoke in low, sweet, mellifluous tones, full of the primitive poetic imagery which Cooper would have had his readers believe the normal conversation of the red man: "Why does the Pale Face still follow the track of the Red Man? Why does he pursue him even as *O-keechow* the wild-cat chases *Ka-Ka* the skunk?" And while he spoke he quietly abstracted a silver spoon from the table or slipped a silver cake-basket beneath his blanket "to conceal his emotion."

Harte satirized Cooper's ignorance of the settings of his stories as well. In a sylvan atmosphere, Judge Tompkins' log cabin was "embowered in buckeyes." Outside it was humble; inside was "an aquarium, containing gold-fishes . . . a magnificent grand piano . . . paintings from the pencils of Van Dyke, Rubens, Tintoretto, Michael Angelo, and the productions of the more modern Turner, Kensett, Church, and Bierstadt."

The plot matched characters and setting. At a point in the story (any point), Genevra for no apparent reason put on a white bonnet and lemon-colored gloves and plunged into the depths of the pine forest. She had not, naturally enough, "proceeded many miles" before she tired; or rather "before a weariness seized upon her fragile limbs." She was startled by a low growl, and by a sight which might well freeze her blood with terror. Down the path, "in Indian file, came a monstrous grizzly, closely followed by a California lion, a wild cat, and a buffalo, the rear being brought up by a wild Spanish bull." But Natty, of course, appeared on the scene, and with one well-aimed bullet felled all five of the beasts.

The well-aimed bullet of ridicule was easily the most effective weapon used against sentimentalism. The other, and greater, humorist who shared honors with Harte as the interpreter of the colorful society of the Far West did not always get along well with the author of the *Condensed Novels.* But with Harte's attack on Cooper, Mark Twain was in wholehearted agreement. Twain's most detailed work of literary criticism, as a matter of fact, came from his compulsion to detail "Fenimore Cooper's Literary Offenses" after two professors and an English novelist had combined to declare Cooper a great artist in fiction. Mark demurred. And the tribute to Cooper which irked him most was the tribute to Cooper's supposed gift of observation; Mark began his essay by quoting Professor Brander Matthews as saying that " 'the craft of the woodsman, the tricks of the trapper, all the delicate art of the forest, were familiar to Cooper from his youth up.' " This, added to Professor Lounsbury's declaration that *The Pathfinder* and *The Deerslayer* " 'were pure works of art,' " and Wilkie Collins' assertion that " 'Cooper is the greatest artist in the domain of romantic fiction yet produced by America,' " was more than Twain could bear. "Cooper's art has some defects," he asserted with the air of calculated seriousness which often prefaced his wild flings of satiric exaggeration. And then he began his attack: "In one place in the *Deerslayer*, and in the restricted space of two-thirds of a page, Cooper has scored 114 offenses against literary art out of a possible 115. It breaks the record." The rules governing literary art, Twain made it clear, should be the rules of the realist: that literary art should have a "life-likeness" and "seeming reality"; that it should deal with the life the author knows, and deal with it accurately; not that the author must try to reproduce life, or confine himself purely to the level of objective experience; far from it; after all, this was the author of the *Connecticut Yankee* talking. But literary artists should "confine themselves to possibilities and let miracles alone; or, if they venture a miracle, the author must so plausibly set it forth as to make it look possible and reasonable."

Cooper fell hopelessly short of these standards, Mark insisted. Against the measure of the rule that "the personages in a tale shall be alive, except in the case of corpses, and that the reader shall be able to tell the corpses from the others," Cooper's all-pure heroines and all-heroic heroes, his noble savages and intrepid frontiersmen, dwindled into false nothingness. Against the laws which demand at least a kind of internal consistency, Cooper also sinned. It is expected, said Mark, that "when a personage talks like an illustrated, gilt-edged, tree-calf, hand-tooled, seven-dollar Friendship's Offering in the beginning of a paragraph, he shall not talk like a negro minstrel in the end of it. But this rule is flung down and danced upon in the *Deerslayer* tale."

Above all, Cooper had no real knowledge of what he was writing about: "one of his acute Indian experts, Chingachgook," pronounced "Chicago," turned a running stream out of its course and found the tracks of the last person in the slush of its bed. "No," said Twain sadly, "even the eternal laws of Nature have to vacate when Cooper wants to put up a delicate job of woodcraft on the reader." And he summarized his diatribe by declaring that Cooper "saw nearly all things as through a glass eye, darkly."

7. The Attack on the Sentimental in Society: Twain and Warner's *The Gilded Age*

This ridicule of Cooper came at the end of the nineteenth century, but Twain's scorn for the glass eye of the literary falsifier had been evident as early as *The Innocents Abroad* and had been a consistent theme in his work. We may recall his reaction to the story spun by the Swiss guide about an iron hook in the castle wall: "wonderful story, wonderful lie." As he wrote to Mrs. Mary Mason Fairbanks, one of the "innocents" with whom he was abroad in 1867, he had but one desire: to be "authentic." With this as his standard, he could never pass up an occasion to attack those who were telling falsehoods about the life he knew and loved. When he and Charles Dudley Warner wrote the most elaborate work of satiric realism written by Americans in the nineteenth century—the joint effort they called *The Gilded Age*, thereby giving a name to an entire era—they wrote an attack in fiction upon sentimentalism in literature as it operated in the social and economic and political life of America.

Two stories were written by the collaborators, and it has been conventional to say that the book falls apart because the two appear to have only a remote connection. But viewed as an attack on a false view of reality, the two stories are seen immediately to have an organic connection. One story they told was an imaginative account of Mark's own history and the history of his family, and a projection into the future of what could have happened to them, given the kind of people they were. For the fictional Hawkins family, like the real Clemens clan, had been victimized by the great sentimental myth of financial success, the myth which assured Americans that fabulous wealth was always available for those energetic enough to get it. As a counterpoint to the story of the downfall of the Hawkins family, Twain and Warner wrote of the Bolton family and Philip Sterling; the Boltons found that speculation could bring only misery, but they were rescued by the hard work of Philip, who turned from will-o'-the-wisp adventuring after gold mines to prospecting for good, black, productive, unromantic coal. The interplay of the two stories made the moral clear: dreams of glory bring disaster; only hard work brings happiness. The Hawkins family was a family cursed by a sentimental dream, a dream without reasonable foundation in the world of reality, a dream of great wealth to come from the 75,000 acres of Tennessee land in which Silas Hawkins had speculated. The dream, Washington Hawkins realized at the end, was an illusion which he chased "as children chase butterflies." He lifted the curse of the dream by tearing up the tax bill for the land, and letting it go, and with it, the false hopes of speedy and painless riches.

Twain and Warner embodied the spirit of speculation in a great comic creation: Colonel Beriah Sellers. Sellers was a confidence man, the drummer of eternal progress, the kind of character who had writhed in symbolic evil when seen through Herman Melville's eyes; but Melville's was a tragic vision, and Twain's a comic, and so Twain's creation was satire at its best; a ridiculing of vice for the purpose of reform, a ridicule that carried with it the basic love of the life to be reformed. Sellers was at once a ridiculous and a beloved figure, the only character in American literature worthy to be mentioned in the same breath with Sir John Falstaff. Around his knees clustered his adoring children and their worshipful mother, though Sellers gave them turnips for food ("examine them—examine them," he bellowed jovially to Washington, "see how firm and juicy they are") and a candle behind the isinglass door for warmth ("A little idea of my own, Washington—one of the greatest things in the world!"). He first projected a monumental world-wide promotion in eyewash: the "Infallible Imperial Oriental Optic Linament and Salvation for Sore Eyes." Then he attempted a diversion of one of the tributaries of the Mississippi to make a killing on improved real estate; then he promoted a plan to sell the Tennessee land to the government as a site for a Negro university. And finally, when Washington tore up the tax bill to the 75,000 acres, and with it the curse of speculation which had ruined his family, Sellers shook his hand and announced that he, too, would make a fresh start; he would go into the law: "There's worlds of money in it! —whole worlds of money! Practice first in Hawkeye, then in Jefferson, then in Saint Louis, then in New York! . . . Climb, and climb, and climb . . . it's as clear as day—clear as the rosy morn!" So Sellers careens out of the story as he entered, the spirit of speculation, the ruinous, beloved corrupter of his age.

The Gilded Age, then, was a criticism of a society which had been "sold" by the mythology of the barker and his literary counterparts, the sentimental novelists; and in its parts it often made the general satire specific, dwelling in detail upon the contrast between literary realism and literary sentimentalism. At a crucial point in the story, Laura Hawkins, about to use herself as a lure for the vote of Senator Dilworthy, stepped aside into a bookstore, and there enacted a little comedy of the conflict between the false and the good in literature. Laura asked the clerk for "Taine's *Notes on England*." (Taine, as we shall later discover, became about this time the prophet of the literature which tries objectively and truthfully to observe its society.) The clerk smiled vaguely, and admitted his ignorance of it. Laura then asked him for the *Autocrat of the Breakfast Table*. But the purveyor of sentimental trash could not be expected to know the work of the Dr. Holmes whose intelligent observations of society were a forerunner of realism. He assured her "with cold dignity, that cook books were somewhat out of their line." Laura found a copy of *Venetian Life* and leafed through it with pleasure, but the insufferable clerk thrust under her nose a work he thought "one of the best things that's come out this season—'The Pirate's Doom, or, The Last of the Buccaneers.' " Laura pushed it gently aside and attempted to continue with *Venetian Life*, but the clerk continued to try to force on her one he's sure she'll like: "It's full of love troubles and mysteries and all sorts of such things. The heroine strangles her own mother. Just glance at the title, please, —'Gonderil the Vampire, or the Dance of Death.' And here is 'The Jokist's Own Treasury, or, The Phunny Phellow's Bosom Phriend.' "

A society composed of people like the bookstore clerk, Twain and Warner felt, would become a society living in a nightmare world of sentiment where justice would become injustice, where healthful, rational social procedures would be supplanted by illogical mass insanities. "Would be"? Indeed, when writing *The Gilded Age*, the authors already had proof of popular sentimentality all about them. In San Francisco, for example, a woman had cold-bloodedly tracked down her unfaithful lover, had shot him, had been freed by a court which had decided that she had killed in a flash of insane jealousy, and then had been lionized by the public. So Twain and Warner wrote *The Gilded Age* towards a climax at which Laura Hawkins was declared "not guilty" of murdering her lover by virtue of insanity. (At almost that very moment the nation's political health was restored by the exploding of the scheme for the Negro university.) When Laura was freed, the judge was described as sentencing the woman who "was of an unsound mind, with a kind of insanity dangerous to the safety of the community . . . to the care of the Superintendent of the State Hospital for Insane Criminals, to be held in confinement until the State Commissioners on Insanity shall order her discharge." Laura was led away by the officer and conveyed to the hospital and there—but then the authors broke in upon their narrative and begged the reader's pardon. This, they explained, is what would have happened had they been writing a novel, the form of prose fiction which is an expression of a civilized society. But this was the history of their times, instead of a novel—the history not of a civilized society, but of a society which threatened to become uncivilized by the usurpation of reason by passion. And so they were compelled to go back and tell the reader what actually did happen to Laura: she left the courtroom to the cheers of the multitude, who had just swarmed over her attorney "in a transport of gratitude," and she went free to accept an offer of twelve thousand dollars for a lecture tour on "The Revelations of a Woman's Life."

8. The Attack on the "Fungus Crop of Sentiment"

The social madness engendered by sentimentalism that most seriously concerned Mark Twain, and many of his contemporaries, however, was not the strange regard for lovelorn lady murderers. It was rather the warped reverence for the slaveholding South. Howells, in his semi-autobiographical *Their Wedding Journey*, caused Basil March to summarize the fears of the realists:

"I suppose that almost any evil commends itself by its ruin; the wrecks of slavery are fast growing a fungus crop of sentiment, and they may yet outflourish the remains of the feudal system in the kind of poetry they produce."

Howells himself was not in the vanguard of this phase of anti-sentimentalism. The reason is simple; he had been away from America during the Civil War; he had no direct experience with either the conflict or with the social system which engendered it; and his theory of literary realism demanded that he write about that which he knew. He sympathized deeply with the Union, and knew that "every loyal American who went abroad during the first years of our great war felt bound to make himself some excuse for turning his back on his country in the hour of her trouble." He portrayed Kitty Ellison, the gallant and charming heroine of *A Chance Acquaintance*, as the daughter of a Kansas Abolitionist and follower of John Brown. He channelled some of his own guilt at leaving his country during the war into a dislike of the English for siding with the Confederacy. But the problem of the South was not a major concern of his fiction.

Not so with the other realists. John De Forest and Albion Tourgée made the telling of the truth, as they saw it, about the Civil War and its aftermath a central motive for their fiction. And while Mark Twain had been physically and emotionally detached from the conflict, he, and George Washington Cable, were both concerned with the "fungus crop of sentiment" that was developing about the old South.

De Forest was the first of these writers who found their impulse to create in a revulsion against the sentimentalizing of the South. A native of New Haven who had, as we have seen, instinctively defended American values on foreign shores, he enlisted early in the First Company of the 12th Connecticut Volunteers and became a major by the time of the war's end. He wrote long letters home about his experiences in the campaigns around Port Hudson and in the occupation of New Orleans, and after the war's end began to shape them into the novel which he called *Miss Ravenel's Conversion from Secession to Loyalty* (1867). His heroine, Lillie Ravenel, the daughter of a Northern doctor, had been brought up in the South, and was completely seduced by its dream of magnolias and moonlight. Colburne, a lank Yankee lawyer, had nothing to attract her. Colonel Carter, a dashing Virginian who represented all the glamorous decadence of the South, won her completely. The two men become, in their treatment, symbols of the two civilizations. Carter, like the South, and like many corrupt people, was "generally very agreeable"; Colburne comparatively drab and, to Lillie, unattractive. "But pleasant as our corrupt friends are apt to be," De Forest commented, "you must not trust your affections and your happiness to them, or you may find that you have cast your pearls before the unclean." Lillie found that her pearls of devotion had been cast before uncleanliness; for Carter turned out to be a philanderer, and the cause of the South, the cause of oppression. With both this private and this public revelation, Miss Ravenel was converted to loyalty.

As Howells said a few years later, the dangers of sentimentalizing the South were overwhelming. Even Dr. Ravenel was represented as still somewhat under the influence of the "aristocratic glamour" of the system of slavery. But he shook it off, and proceeded to become the spokesman for the realistic North. When Lillie praised the beautiful relationship she thought existed between chivalric and benevolent Southern planter and grateful serf, Dr. Ravenel countered with the facts about the seamy sides of slavery—the loosening of morality, the invitation to cruelty. When Lillie complained about the coolness of the Northern ladies to her, he defended the reasonable behavior of the North against the primitive impulses of the South; the Northern ladies only glared at their enemies; the Southern would have scarcely let them off "with plain tar and feathering." And Dr. Ravenel was aware of the more subtle danger in the sentimentality inevitably attendant upon the problem of white and black; either the Southerner stereotyped the Negro as a sub-human, or the Northerner sentimentalized him into the noble savage; both of these approaches were fatal, Dr. Ravenel knew. So he started a freedman's community based upon the hard realities of the fact that the Negro is a human being with special problems of cultural as well as economic poverty. There are very few Uncle Toms, he told the man associated with him in this enterprise, and the reconstruction of the Negro can only succeed if realism breaks away from both Northern and Southern sentimentalizing of the black.

This basic theme was supported and illustrated by the most detailed picture we have of the Civil War in fiction. And the combination of anti-sentimental theme and honest treatment of the life the author knew well immediately struck Howells as marks of greatness. *Miss Ravenel's Conversion,* Howells wrote when it came out, is our first American novel to find its way with sureness. He praised its honesty, its fidelity, and above all, its comparative abstention from the greatest crime of sentimentalists—sentimental intervention of the author. This was an opinion which Howells never relinquished. Although *Miss Ravenel's Conversion* sold poorly, although it had never been serialized because of the frankness of its treatment of the liaison between Carter and Mrs. Larue (in order to have it printed at all, De Forest had to put some of Mrs. Larue's conversation into French), Howells, in 1887, still persisted in calling De Forest an American realist worthy to be named with Tolstoy.

De Forest carried this theme into the post-Civil War decade with his novel *Kate Beaumont,* in which the sentimental tradition of honor, resulting in the code of the feud, was shown in all its pernicious evil. The eye of a young Northern scientist was the realistic point of view from which this aspect of Southern falsification of the values of life was seen, and it saw that living according to sentimental codes of behavior can only bring unhappiness. After *Kate Beaumont,* this vein ran out, and De Forest never matched his first impressive work. But another Northerner who had seen the Civil War and its aftermath at first hand took over where De Forest had left off.

The soldier, carpetbagger, and judge with the improbable name of Albion Winegar Tourgée was driven to fiction in order to tell the truth about something he felt had been the subject for sentimental lies. De Forest had been concerned largely with the war itself; Tourgée, who had gone into the South on the "fool's errand" of reconstruction, was largely concerned with post-war materials. There he saw not only the conscious evils of slavery, but the "unconscious evils . . . the very ones which had left their marks upon character." He described some of these conscious and unconscious evils in *A Royal Gentleman (Toinette)*, in which Geoffrey Hunter, a wounded and blinded soldier, instinctively debased the girl who tenderly helped him, when he discovered her to be "a very likely yaller girl I used to own." And Toinette, the beautiful mulatto who had been, up to that point, the "free, white, intelligent, interesting, beautiful Mrs. Hunter" could only start "like a guilty loiterer" and answer "instantly, with the inimitable and indescribable intonation of the slave: 'Sir?' "

His two succeeding works, *A Fool's Errand* and *Bricks without Straw*, dealt more specifically with the period of the Reconstruction; the first of these, *A Fool's Errand*, was an attempt to set the record of Reconstruction right. Comfort Servosse was the "fool" in question, and his name was but thinly concealed allegory for the spirit with which Tourgée insisted many of the maligned Reconstructionists went South. The book described how every effort at rebuilding the conquered country and at elevating the freedman to a position of human dignity was crushed by the ravages of the Ku Klux Klan. Tourgée documented a succeeding edition of the story from records of Congressional committees and government bureaus. "Not only is the truthful intent and spirit of the tale manifest on every page," he asserted, "but it is a fact that the greater portion of the incidents of the narrative were actual occurrences, of which the author had either personal cognizance or authentic information." *Bricks without Straw* narrowed down to a more dramatic treatment of the evils of the Klan, showing it as it destroyed a promising co-operative community of freedmen led by a stalwart ex-slave, Nimbus. And Tourgée stepped out of his narrative to condemn the "fungus crop of sentiment" which prevented the North from giving Nimbus the bricks and the straw. " 'Curse me this people!' said the Southern Balak—of the Abolitionist first, of the Bureau-Officer next, and then of the Carpet-Bagger," Tourgée wrote in his summary of the paradox. "The Northern Balaam hemmed and paltered, and then—*cursed the children of his loins!*"

Tourgée, making an attack upon the lie about the Negro and the white the basis of his work, was unfortunately not artist enough to understand that there are other lies an author may tell about human relationships; and his works often slipped into sentimentality of another and subtler kind. His white people spoke as the reader of fiction would like to think they speak; his incidents, when they left the realm of the conflict between struggling black and domineering white, were what Tourgée's feminine readers thought life should be, rather than what Tourgée knew it was: Lily Servosse made the traditional wild and heroic night ride to forestall a Klan raid in the nick of time, for example. But despite these weaknesses, the Reconstruction novels of Tourgée were symptomatic of the development of anti-sentimentalism.

Less serious than Tourgée's work, more deft in their artistry, but concerned with the same attempted revelation through fiction of the truths about racial relationships were the stories of George Washington Cable. This man who first and definitively caught the color of the French-American culture around New Orleans was a strange creature, a Puritanical Southerner watching the drama of blood lines hopelessly entangled by the excesses of ancestors; there was something of Hawthorne in his conviction that the sins of the French settlers, who spread their seed without discrimination, were visited relentlessly upon their descendants. The short story "Belles Demoiselles Plantation" was a summary of the theme that ran through most of his tales, and his only successful novel, *The Grandissimes.* It concerned "the proud Creole family of De Charleu" which had risen "up, up, up, generation after generation, tall, branchless, slender, palm-like; and had finally flowered" in the seven beautiful daughters of old Colonel De Charleu, the owner of the plantation which he named for his daughters. Another line of this family was represented by Injun Charlie, the descendant of the original Comte De Charleu and his Choctaw wife whom he had discarded and left to starve. Injun Charlie was wealthy; Colonel De Charleu deeply in his debt; yet the Colonel was driven by pride to attempt to purchase the last remaining Charleu property that still remained in the hands of the half-breed. Injun Charlie refused; his blood said to him: " 'Charlie! If you sell dat old house, Charlie, you low-down old dog, Charlie, what de Compte De Charleu make for you grace-granmuzzer . . . !' " Instead, he offered to buy Belles Demoiselles, and was scornfully rejected. But the Colonel then found out that the plantation was doomed, that it was being undercut by the Mississippi and would be carried away by the river; he hastened into New Orleans to sell the worthless property to the half-breed, concluded the last of the many swindles by which the whites had denied the colored their birthrights, and returned to the plantation just in time to see it disappear beneath the waters of the river —with his seven beautiful daughters carried to their destruction with it.

Southerners were quick to see the basic criticism of their morality which runs through Cable's works, and his name became an ugly word in the lexicon of the people of New Orleans. Their reaction was summarized in the words of Abbé Adrien Rouquette, who asked: "What would you . . . say, were you to see a buzzard, glutted with carrion, lightning heavily upon a consecrated shrine?" The buzzard, of course, was Cable, and the consecrated shrine, the sepulchre of white racial integrity. "What would you . . . say," Rouquette went on, "were you to behold a jackal disinter a cherished corpse, drag it away, tear it to pieces, and devour its lacerated flesh?" These are the only fit comparison, he said, for the writings of "this heartless and grim-humored dwarf."

Although Cable's small stature and his Presbyterianism were often the object of Mark Twain's less caustic criticism, Twain was essentially one with Cable in his attack upon false and immoral attitudes towards the non-Caucasian races, and regarded him as one of the few post-war Southern writers of value. They barnstormed together, and Twain would often lead him by the hand to the edge of the lecture platform and introduce him as "my little brother," which, in a sense, he was. What Cable did on his small canvas, Twain did in his sweeping pictures of the Southern scene in *Huckleberry Finn* and *Life on The Mississippi*. *Huckleberry Finn* was partly an attack upon the Southern view of the Negro. "Goodness gracious! Anybody hurt?" asked Aunt Sally when she heard of an explosion on the river. "No'm. Killed a nigger," was Huck's answer. And much of the book was concerned with Huck's inner struggle between this attitude and his profound conviction that Nigger Jim was a human being—one of the best he had ever known.

There was in *Huckleberry Finn*, too, a criticism of the sentimentalism of Southern behavior. The Shepherdson-Grangerford feud was shown in all its senseless, sickening perversion of a code of "honor." The perversion, Twain thought, was part of a culture molded by sentimental literature. Huck and Jim encountered an old wreck of a steamboat that had killed itself on a rock in the river. Nigger Jim didn't want to go "fool'n long er no wrack," but Huck wished the adventure of boarding it, and found there corruption and decay, thievery and murder. The name of the wreck was the *Walter Scott.* Sir Walter, Twain suggested later, had a large hand in "making Southern character, as it existed before the Civil War." After the French Revolution, he said, had left the world in its debt for the advancement of "liberty, humanity, and progress," along came "Sir Walter Scott with his enchantments, and by his single might checks this wave of progress, and even turns it back; sets the world in love with dreams and phantoms; with decayed and swinish forms of religion, with decayed and degraded systems of government; with the silliness and emptiness, sham grandeurs, sham gauds, and sham chivalries of a brainless and worthless long-vanished society." While most of the world had shaken off his harms, Twain added, "in our South they flourish pretty forcefully still."

Howells, too, recognized the dangers of the "fungus" of sentiment about the lost cause of slavery, and encouraged those who tried to root out this growth; he successively cheered on De Forest, Cable, and Mark Twain, and was editor of the *Atlantic* when its reviewers were praising Tourgée for his honesty in meeting the problem head-on. But he had no experience with the problem of slavery, or with the South. Since he was convinced that he should write about that which he knew, he was compelled for twenty years to treat these problems only indirectly. When he did finally turn to them, it was in a work which explored a much subtler and more lasting aspect of America's dilemma than any of the works of his contemporaries; he picked up the theme which De Forest had first sounded: the two edges of the evil of sentimentalism about races in America. For there were not only the lies about the problem told by the unreconstructed Southerner; there were also the unrealistic views of the Northerner who would make the Negro something more than man is; there was also the whole range of subtle variations in sentimental response to the question, and it is this range which Howells was the only writer of his time to explore.

The exploration was conducted in a novelette which appeared in 1891, entitled *An Imperative Duty;* it concerned a problem which has since captivated the imagination of many other writers. We remember it, for example, in *Kingsblood Royal,* the late novel of Sinclair Lewis, in which Kingsblood, the red-headed member of a Midwestern country-club set, suddenly discovered that an infinitesimal part of his heredity was Negro, and thereupon martyred himself and his family by proclaiming his "taint" to the world. The essential unrealism of this fiction is exposed by a reading of the healthful reasonableness of a story like *An Imperative Duty*. For in it, Howells tried to face the question of what a woman under similar conditions would actually do, given the circumstances of her world; and, in honestly tracing out the probabilities of the action, he also succeeded, without overt preachment, in exposing the essential evils of the American treatment of its black minority.

The "white" who discovered her taint of blackness was Rhoda Aldgate; Dr. Edward Olney, from whose point of view the story was seen, remembered her as a dark beauty "with a rich complexion of olive . . . and . . . hair crinkling away to either temple." He recalled her face with a sense of its being a lovely mask, even a tragic mask, worn "over a personality that was at once gentle and gay." Olney had been subtly prepared for the drama of racial tensions in which he was to take part by observing the contrast between the Negroes and the whites of the lower class in Boston. He thought of how the Negroes wished to imitate the manners of the best among the white race, while the young white girls and their fellows tried to mimic the worst. When he attended Mrs. Meredith, the aunt of Rhoda Aldgate, the brash ignorance of an Irish bellboy compelled him to raise the problem of the contrasts between minority races, and Mrs. Meredith eagerly seized upon the theme. He then learned that Rhoda's birth was clouded and her aunt felt she must tell her, although the girl had no inkling of her "taint."

Olney's reaction was sensitively handled; there was some stain upon the poor child's birth, he thought, some "ancestral infamy," perhaps some criminality among her forebears, and he was "not shocked; he was interested by the fact." Then he heard Mrs. Meredith gasp out, "My niece is of negro descent," and he instinctively recoiled from the words "in a turmoil of emotion for which there is no other term but disgust." It was an emotion which was "profound and pervasive." His deepest being "expressed itself in a merciless rejection of her beauty, her innocence, her helplessness because of her race." Howells saw into the nature of man, for he insisted that "the impulse had to have its course"; before he felt pity, he felt repulsion. And once again he gave his healthful, sane answer to the worship of the primitive impulse and its unreasoned manifestations: this impulse must be controlled by reason. Olney mastered it immediately "with an abiding compassion, and a sort of tender indignation."

But he had other unreasons to combat. One of them had set the drama into motion: the sentimentality of a Mrs. Meredith who had tried to meet the questions of life with answers supplied to her not by experience but by convention, and whose unrealism was compounded by a false sense of the nature of moral obligations. Olney had already theorized Mrs. Meredith "as one of those women . . . to whom life . . . remains a sealed book, and who are always trying to unlock its mysteries with the keys furnished them by fiction." And so she made the initial mistake of thinking it somehow her duty to tell the truth, despite the anguish it might cause, and only too late realized the evil of her position, and took the final escape from reality through an overdose of sleeping pills. Then the problem descended to Rhoda herself; what is the "right" course to follow after learning her ancestry? The books had told her, too, what she should do. And the dictates of a Puritan civilization, which had carried the cult of personal conscience into an obsession with duty, impelled her to reenter the Negro race, to try to educate them, and elevate them. Is it not cowardice to desert them, she cried to Olney, and "live happily apart from them, when—" "When you might live so miserably with them?" Olney finished for her. And so Olney brought reason to bear on their incipiently tragic situation, and turned it into a comedy. For he was one who knew that "the tame man, the civilized man, is stronger than the wild man . . ."

and that "vice is savage and virtue is civilized" and that problems such as theirs must be met as civilized beings would meet them. Rhoda at first was unconvinced, and persisted in the desire to martyr herself; but finally her love "performed the effect of common-sense for them, and in its purple light they saw the every-day duties of life plain before them." They kept Rhoda's secret, they married, and they lived out their days in Italy. He still had to struggle with the Puritanism in her "which so often seems to satisfy its crazy claim upon conscience by enforcing some aimless act of self-sacrifice." But he was able to reason her out of these moods by representing to her "that it would not be the ancestral color . . . but the ancestral condition which their American friends would despise if they knew of it." And presumably this answer satisfied her.

While he told this urbane and civilized tale, Howells skilfully handled the most subtle aspects of the problem. One of these was the difference between someone who has a stake in the question, and someone who has not. Olney, an impersonal observer, saw the Boston Negroes and was filled with a sense of their essential grace, good humor, and dignity. Rhoda, who had shared these feelings, was suddenly changed from an impersonal bystander into one deeply involved in the racial problem; and when, after learning her ancestry, she walked dazedly into the midst of Negroes, "a new agony of interest in them possessed her." They became hideous to her, "with their flat wide-nostriled noses, their out-rolled thick lips . . . they seemed burlesques of humanity, worse than apes, because they were more like." The ways of the unconscious reactions to problems of race were well known to this novelist, too, although he showed only their conscious manifestations. The deepest antipathies of our being are for that which we fancy we have wronged. Rhoda began to hate the race of which she was so minutely a part because she felt she had rejected them. But Olney refused to hate either them or her. Perhaps he should, he said shrewdly, if he had come of a race of slaveholders. "But my people," he tells her tenderly, "never injured those poor creatures, and so I don't hate them, or their infinitesimal part in you."

An Imperative Duty, then, was a treatment of the theme which so often occupied the writers of Howells' age who were one with him in their attack upon sentimentalism. Less direct, less dramatic, but in its small, fine way as true and as telling as *Miss Ravenel's Conversion* or *Huckleberry Finn*, it was Howells' contribution to the disabusing of America's mind of the false and deadly stereotypes and stock reactions to the problem of the Negro in America. It was part of the attack on sentimentalism which gave the realistic movement in American letters its initial impulse.

CHAPTER III

TOWARDS A PHILOSOPHY OF LITERARY REALISM

1. The Reason for Realism

"He . . . can write solely of what his fleshly eyes have seen."
—Henry James

But "no" is not the kind of word upon which men can build; the impulse to destroy the lie in literature was a negative impulse; and writers must not only be against something; they also have to be for something. It is not enough to be just against untruth; an artist must feel that "this world means intensely, and means good" in order to justify his absorption in its appearances. Why is it that writers over the Western world returned to the physical world for the materials of their fiction, and to an objective selection from the events of that world for their method? Part of the reason why realism came in America, of course, as it had been coming in France, and in Russia, and was to come in Spain, is that there were intellectual attitudes floating in the solution of our culture which could be precipitated by the currents of post-war developments. Some of these attitudes we have already noticed. Emersonian transcendentalism revered the smallest and most humble bits of the world of experience; it took only a change in emphasis to make over transcendental concern for the commonplace into realistic concern for the immediate, the familiar, the humble, and the low. The Scottish philosophy of common sense "dominating the intellectual atmosphere of most American colleges and universities in the decades immediately following Appomattox" filtered down into the periodicals and the newspapers to color the attitudes of the generation. The answer this philosophical school would give to the difficult problem of "how do we know things?" would be: "We know them through perceiving them"; and in reply to the skeptical doubtings of a Berkeley and a Hume about the trustworthiness of sense perceptions, they would give the "common-sense" answer: Dr. Johnson kicking the stone to prove the existence of the material. In pre-war America, too, the Brahmin civilization of Lowell and Holmes had kept very much alive the neo-classical tradition of humanism with its concern for the world of the senses, and with its fundamental distrust of the "crypts of metaphysics."

These were the native sources from which De Forest and Twain and Howells—all three of them, as well as a host of their followers later in the century—could draw when they turned naturally to a reporting of the world of their experience. In "common-sense" terms they never doubted that they need do anything else than observe carefully and honestly and report truthfully in order to arrive at truthfulness, and hence beauty, in fiction. Twain wanted above all to be authentic. No other literature is worth writing, Howells wrote to a young poet in 1867, except that which expresses the life one has lived. The only secret of art, said Howells to another friend in 1871, is to observe with the naked eye.

It is fruitless to hope to find out "why" this should be; as Howells wrote later to T. S. Perry, realism cannot be said to have been caused by anything; it just "came," and seemed "to have come everywhere at once." The generation of Howells was swinging away from the otherworldliness of Hawthorne and Poe. Almost instinctively, as we have seen, Howells read and loved those authors whose concern had been with man's social circumstance; instinctively, he turned away from Wordsworth and Coleridge, from Poe and Sir Walter Scott. He quickly abandoned his adolescent imitations of Heine, and his immature apings of the sentimentalists, and agreed with Lowell that he must write of that which he observed and knew himself. In one of his early letters to Mrs. James T. Fields after he assumed the assistant editorship of the *Atlantic*, he complained of the impossibility of finding people who could write short, lively sketches, and made it clear that he was searching for contributors who would base their work on observed material. While no discernible critical standards operated in his reviews in the first years for the *Atlantic* (he wrote in 1867 that "there is hardly any law established for criticism which has not been overthrown as often as the French government"), hints of his allegiance to fiction based upon personal experience had already begun to appear. He liked Bayard Taylor's "faithful spirit" in which he "adhered to all the facts of life he portrayed." He wrote to Don Lloyd Wyman, who wished advice, and asked if his poems expressed the life he had lived or had known, and added that only such poems are worth reading. He admired Henry Ward Beecher's "felicity in expressing the flavor and color of New England life." Mark Twain, he told readers of the *Atlantic*, had an honest and observant eye, "honest enough to let himself see the realities of human life everywhere." He cheered for T. B. Aldrich's *The Story of a Bad Boy*, which was obviously the story of the author's own life, and it was this element of autobiography which Howells seized upon as the reason for its success. Aldrich did a new thing, Howells wrote; he told "what . . . life is" instead of trying to teach "what it should be." And in this direction, Howells said, lay "the work which has long hovered in the mental atmosphere . . . pleading to be born into the world,—the American novel, namely." Soon after reading *The Story of a Bad Boy*, he started on the writing of his first novel; and it was a novel in which he simply took his experiences on his own delayed honeymoon and gave them "the form of fiction so far as the characters are concerned." He wrote his father that this was the path in literature which he believed he could make "most distinctly" his own. Henry James testified that Howells was beginning to dedicate himself to a reporting of that which his "fleshly eyes" could see.

But why should such observation be "art"? Why should people be interested in reading works based upon observation by "the naked eye"? What is the beauty and morality of a work of fiction whose base is a fidelity to actuality? Howells and Twain never considered such matters systematically. They and De Forest, and Bret Harte in the Far West, were creatures of their time. And yet their concern with the physical world had, in France, produced a social philosopher and a literary critic who gave system and justification to man's concern with the observable. And when Howells, and men who thought and wrote like him in his own age, turned their attention to a careful examination of the probable and the commonplace as the materials for their fiction, they were sometimes unconsciously, but more often consciously, basing their attitude towards fiction upon a theory of aesthetics which had been fashioned to meet the needs of a world which was being transformed by the application of the scientific method to the material and the moral universe.

2. The Scientist as the New Hero

Howells' was an age which saw about it everywhere the success of the empirical method. In the thirteen years from 1865 to 1878, applied science doubled America's capital investments; in 1864 the Bessemer process for converting iron to steel was first used commercially in America at Wyandotte, Michigan; three years later 2,600 tons of ingots were produced, a volume which increased four hundred-fold by 1879. In 1859, the first successful oil well in the United States was sunk near Titusville, Pennsylvania; by 1864 the area was producing more than 2,100,000 barrels. Railway mileage doubled in the seven years between 1865 and 1872. In this atmosphere of material expansion, the inventor became the new hero. James Parton's *Famous Americans of Recent Times* (1868) devoted a third of its space to men of science, and Howells thought that Parton wrote of them "with the most heart," that he interested the reader deeply in their lives. For the inventors, said Howells, "are the discoverers of our time, and it is they who carry forward, in their true spirit, the magnificent enterprises of other days. . . ."

While the applied sciences were transforming the face of

America, the theoretical scientists were busy overhauling its mind. Darwin published his findings in 1859, two years after the first issue of the *Atlantic*, and during the next twenty years, the periodicals of the day were still busy explaining the implications of his theory to their audience. While Darwin was casting doubt on the biblical account of mankind's development, geologists like Louis Agassiz at Harvard were forcing Americans to question the literal truth of the story of the world's creation in the book of Genesis. If they were to go out to Plymouth Rock once a year, Agassiz told his listeners, and brush silk just once, and lightly, over the monolith, and keep this up until the rock was worn down to a pebble, they would have a concept of the length of time our earth was a-borning. While geologists like Agassiz were upsetting Fundamentalist religious concepts, physicians like Oliver Wendell Holmes were challenging old beliefs about the mystical origins of personality, and would have no truck with either the pessimism of the Calvinists or the optimism of Platonic concepts to which Wordsworth had given new prestige. Don't talk to me about children coming into the world trailing clouds of glory, the doctor told the minister in *Elsie Venner;* and then the man of science went on to say that children are more likely to trail clouds of hereditary mental disorders.

And with men like Agassiz and Holmes, Howells felt himself instinctively at home. We have already seen how large a part Holmes played in the early encouragement of the young poet from the West, and Howells continued to avow his indebtedness to the little doctor and his hardheaded empiricism. Like Holmes he felt "the inquiry was inquiry, to the last," and he had the "scientific conscience that refuses either to deny the substance of things unseen, or to affirm it." The "Goethean face and figure of Louis Agassiz" were also dear to Howells; he later portrayed David Sewell, the sympathetic pastor in *The Minister's Charge*, as an admirer of the geologist who could "make every inch of the earth vocal, every rock historic, and the waste places social."

The admiration for the scientist became a commonplace of realistic fiction. As the clear-eyed observer, he was portrayed as seeing through sentimentality to the truth: De Forest's Dr. Ravenel, or his young scientist in *Kate Beaumont;* Mark Twain's empiricists: the Connecticut Yankee, Tom Canty, Pudd'nhead Wilson, even Huck Finn himself. Huck was really an empiricist; his belief in magic was not unscientific; far from it; as Frazer has pointed out, the basic beliefs of magic and science are the same —each accepts as empirically true any result which consistently follows the same activities (an experiment in one case, a ritual in the other). Huck putting the legend of the genie to the test of actual performance, and rejecting the story as untrue when the stipulated action did not have the stipulated result, is a symbol of the age's trust in the scientific method: Tom Sawyer, we may remember, had insisted upon the truth of the Aladdin legend. Huck's reaction was that of the empiricist: "I got an old tin lamp and an iron ring, and went out in the woods and rubbed and rubbed till I sweat like an Injun, calculating to build a palace and sell it; but it warn't no use, none of the genies came. So I judged all that stuff was only just one of Tom Sawyer's lies." Colville in *Indian Summer* and Olney in *An Imperative Duty* are less vivid, but equally symbolic characters in their representation of the empirical attitude towards truth and morality. It is no coincidence that Olney should be portrayed as a doctor; it is equally significant that Warner and Twain made Ruth Bolton, the heroine of *The Gilded Age*, a medical scientist.

Howells' generation was one in which science, both theoretical and applied, was either capturing or oppressing the imagination of creative artists. Men of letters at this time either absorbed its truths and went on to create literature which accepted what they understood was its message about the place of observation in art, or they rejected it, and wrote sentimentally, or not at all. Thomas Bailey Aldrich mourned that

> Romance beside his unstrung lute
> Lies stricken mute.
> The old-time fire, the antique grace,
> You will not find them anywhere.
> Today we breathe a commonplace,
> Polemic, scientific air. . . .

And Aldrich wrote novels like *Prudence Palfrey* which Howells saw were simply the sentimental stereotypes of a poet longing for what he thought was Romance. On the other hand, the Southern poet, Sidney Lanier, tried hard to make the poet at home in the new world of science; and while he failed in his own poetry, he made some remarkably acute observations about the nature of prose fiction and its relation to science, while in poetry he tried to reconcile art and empiricism:

> And Science be known as the sense making love to the All,
> And Art be known as the soul making love to the All,
> And Love be known as the marriage of man with the All—
> Till Science to knowing the Highest shall lovingly turn,
> Till Art to loving the Highest shall consciously burn,
> Till Science to Art as a man to a woman shall yearn.

The blend of the two, we see, was not signally successful. But his lectures on the novel were shrewd evaluations of the place of the scientific attitude in fiction. Like Howells and Hawthorne, he suggested that the term "Romantic" defined the literary attitude which was fundamentally poetic. The "realistic" attitude, he said, was a combination of the poetic and the scientific, while "those who entirely reject the imagination" could be termed "the Naturalistic school. We are prepared," he continued, "to study the novel as a work in which science is carried over into the region of art."

3. Taine in America

"Try to understand yourself. . . ."

In France, a generation earlier, a philosopher had come forth who had made the techniques and attitudes of the new science the basis of a system of thought. August Comte had proclaimed that the scientific attitude towards society and its problems was the right one. Just as it had alone proven of use in unlocking the mysteries of the physical universe, so it would alone be of use in solving the questions of the moral universe. Comte aimed at taking human social thought out of the two childlike and adolescent stages of development—the theological, in which all phenomena are ascribed to supernatural causes, and the metaphysical, in which preformulated, *a priori* principles are considered the causes of events. The new stage, said Comte, the positive stage, is one in which the supernatural is ignored and the metaphysical is discarded, and observation, analysis, and classification take their place.

Hippolyte Taine took positivism and made it into a literary credo, and it was Taine's positivistic theory of the source and function of literary expression that became the basis of conscious American realism.

Taine was almost unknown in America before 1870. There had been a review of his work in 1861 when M. H. Harisse had summarized the latest developments in French criticism for the *North American Review.* But the attitude of this early notice was that here is a young and brilliant Frenchman with a rather difficult philosophy of aesthetics and criticism in which we are interested but with which we cannot wholly agree. Then Edward Eggleston read Taine's *Philosophy of Art in the Netherlands,* and wrote a brief review of it for the *Independent* in 1870. A few months later, he was encouraged to write a story for *Hearth and Home.* The story extended through three issues; and while he was writing it, Eggleston remembered the philosophy of art formulated by Taine—that to be a great artist, one must express one's own times, and the attitudes of one's own people; that the greatness of the art of the Netherlands was its willingness to use common materials and familiar subjects. Eggleston came to his brother, George Cary Eggleston, and announced that he was going to "write a three-number story, founded upon your experiences at Riker's Ridge." Then, George recorded, the incipient novelist went on to "set forth his theory of art—that the artist, whether with pen or brush, who would do his best work, must choose his subjects from the life that he knows." And to justify his choice of theme, Eggleston "cited the Dutch painters" as well as referring to "Lowell's success with the Biglow papers."

Out of this fortuitous combination, out of Taine, Lowell, and the desire of the *Hearth and Home* for a story from Eggleston, came *The Hoosier Schoolmaster,* an early landmark in the development of realism in America. Despite its open mawkish sentimentalism, the novel was rich with regional dialect, and remorseless in its truthful portrayal of the hard-shelled farmers of Indiana. And in 1874, Eggleston added to his picture of the Midwest in *The Circuit Rider*. In the preface to this book, he expressed with clarity and precision the aim of realism in literature, and it was an expression which clearly shows the influence of the Frenchman who pointed out that an artist must deal with his contemporaries. Eggleston asked the reader who might be offended by his treatment of the rougher side of religion to remember "the solemn obligations of a novelist to tell the truth." He insisted that the title of "novelist" could only be given to him who tries with whole soul "to produce the higher form of history, by writing truly of men as they are, and dispassionately of those forms of life that come within his scope."

Howells had hailed *The Hoosier Schoolmaster* as a contribution to the development of a native school of realism. But this review had been one of a group which Howells wrote from 1867 to 1872 which had shown a catholicity of taste confounding to any attempt to draw consistent attitudes from them. They had praised historical romances and imaginative fantasies by Edward Everett Hale, and Dion Boucicault, as well as the realism of De Forest and Eggleston. But in 1872 Howells, too, read and reviewed a work of Taine's—his *History of English Literature*.

Taine's transformation of Comte's philosophy of social positivism into the conception of literature as a product of the "*race, milieu, et moment*" of each author is well known. What has not been so well remembered was Taine's penetrating formulation of the justification for, even the necessity of, a literature which plays its part in the positivist program. Literature, Taine said in essence, must be the principal method by which society and men are observed, analyzed, and classified. Fiction should be the scientific laboratory of society—the laboratory in which the complex components of our social system are mixed with each other, so that the race may watch the experiment, see the result, and be better able to make decisions affecting its life.

The romantics, said Taine, had been afflicted by the malady of the age—the bewilderment that came from the "reign of democracy which excited our ambitions without satisfying them" and the "philosophy which kindled our curiosity without satisfying it." The romantics had agreed that "there is a monstrous disproportion between the different parts of our social structure," and had seen that "human destiny is vitiated by this disagreement." But the answers of these "unfortunates" had been to "let deep and strong sensations reign upon you . . . cultivate your garden, re-enter the flock . . . take holy water, abandon your mind to dogmas."

These answers, said Taine, proved ineffectual, and his generation saw the true reply, the "deeper answer . . . in which issue all the labor and experience of the age, and which may perhaps be the subject matter of future literature: 'Try to understand yourself, and things in general.'" Yes, said this observer from France, his generation, too, was afflicted with the malady of the age, and all it could hope to do, in hopes of an eventual cure, was to strive to arrive at the truth; it must study man; he is not "an abortion or a monster, but he is in his place and completes a chain. . . . He is like everything else, a product, and as such it is right he should be what he is." The task of literature is to seek the truth about him, in all his relations. In this employment of science, and in its counterpart in letters—realistic fiction—"there is a new art, a new morality, a new polity, a new religion."

Howells reviewed Taine's *History of English Literature*, in the February, 1872, issue of the *Atlantic*. His notice was concerned with the one-sidedness of Taine's approach to literature. He called his method of showing the influence of environment upon art "admirably brilliant and effective," but he warned the reader against a too inflexible application of this theory. Howells pointed out that the personality of each great writer must be considered along with the general circumstances of his time and people.

Then, a year later, Howells became thoroughly saturated with Taine's theory of realistic literature as the laboratory of mankind. For in April, 1873, A. G. Sedgwick, normally the political reporter for the *Atlantic*, stepped out of his conventional role and wrote a review of George Eliot's *Middlemarch* which applied the philosophy of Taine to contemporary literature in English. Sedgwick was trying to discover why Eliot's detailed analysis of human action made her so great a figure in contemporary literature. He found the answer in Taine. He started his review with a long quotation from the *History of English Literature*, and these are the words which Howells, if he had not already read them, must have read and reread in manuscript, proof, and final form in the office of the magazine he was editing. For he was an uncommonly scrupulous reader of the material that went into the *Atlantic*. Besides his reading of manuscripts before their acceptance, he went over the proofs of each article "making what changes" he chose to make, and "verifying every quotation, every date, every geographical and biographical name, every foreign word to the last accent, every technical and scientific term." The article was then sent back to the author, and after author's changes, was read by Howells again.

What he read and reread in Sedgwick's article was a summary of Taine's justification for literature in an age of science. Sedgwick quoted the French critic on the failure of the romantic writers from 1800 to 1830 to give any answers to the great problems facing the nineteenth century, and then continued the long quotation, which is worth reproducing in full, for it seems to have struck exactly the note which writers in America, seeking the reasons for their instinctive yearning towards the actualities of their provincial environments, found so sympathetic. Of the great romantic writers, of Byron and Shelley and Keats, and their sensitivity to the monstrous disproportions which they felt to be the fact of their society, Taine asked the following questions, and Sedgwick reproduced these questions, and Taine's answers to them, in their entirety:

> "What advice have they given us for its remedy? They were great: were they wise? 'Let deep and strong sensations reign upon you; if your machine breaks, so much the worse. . . . Cultivate your garden, busy yourself in a little circle; re-enter the flock, be a beast of burden. . . . Turn believer again, take holy water . . . aspire to power, honor, wealth.' Such are the various replies of artists and citizens, Christians and men of the world. . . . There is another and deeper answer, which Goethe was the first to give, which we begin to conceive, in which issue all the labor and experience of the age, and which may perhaps

> be the subject matter of future literature. 'Try to understand yourself and things in general.' A strange reply, seeming barely new, whose scope we shall only hereafter discover. For a long time yet, men will feel their sympathies thrill at the . . . sobs of their great poets. For a long time they will rage against a destiny which opens to their aspirations the career of limitless space, to shatter them, within two steps of their goal, against a wretched post which they had not seen. For a long time they will bear, like fetters, the necessities which they must embrace as laws. Our generation, like the preceding, has been tainted by the malady of the age, and will never more than half be quit of it. We shall arrive at the truth, not at calm. All we can heal at present is our intellect; we have no hold upon our sentiments. But we have a right to conceive for others the hopes which we no longer entertain for ourselves, and to prepare for our descendants the happiness which we shall never enjoy."

But, Sedgwick wrote, we are not anywhere near those fortunate times which Taine foresaw in the future. "For the present, we," like the romantics, "live in a period of intellectual and moral tumult." Modern life is "too complicated, too revoluntionary, too full of sudden surprises and absurdities, too sad, too merry, too horribly real, too shamefully false. . . . Our business *is not creation, but criticism.*" Eliot's maxim, and our motto is, only slightly to alter Taine's words: "Know thyself and things in general."

Before Sedgwick's article appeared, Howells had seemed in doubt about the purpose which he felt literature should have. In his February, 1873, review of Turgenev, he had declared: "It is hard to reconcile the sense of . . . artistic impartiality with one's sense of the deep moral earnestness of the author's books." But in 1874, nine months after Sedgwick's forceful recapitulation of Taine, Howells seemed able to reconcile art and morality, and the reconciliation was based upon the positivistic philosophy of the French critic. In that year, Howells wrote that autobiography is "the most precious contribution to men's knowledge of each other," and that inventive writing reaches its greatest ethical heights when it enables men to know each other better by giving the reader the "facts in man's consciousness or experience."

In the same year, Howells ran a searching article on *The Growth of the Novel* by G. P. Lathrop, in which Lathrop took up the question of fictional morality in an age of science, and gave it Taine's answer. Lathrop scoffed at the attempts of Richardson and the sentimentalists to "impose a mechanical morality upon us," and then went on to underscore the positivist's contention that morality in the novel can only consist in telling us the truth about our actions, so that we may have clear understanding of what we are like. "It is only through clear perceptions into the true quality of our common nature," wrote Lathrop, "that the *foundations* of morality are deepened and secured." And in 1885, Howells, through one of his most sympathetically portrayed characters, pointed out the immorality of sentimental literature, when viewed from the standpoint of positivist ethics. The Reverend Mr. Sewell turns to the Coreys' dinner guests in *The Rise of Silas Lapham* and tells them flatly that "those novels with the old-fashioned heroes and heroines in them . . . are ruinous." He goes on to explain his startling statement by saying: "The novelists might be the greatest possible help to us if they painted life as it is, and human feelings in their true proportion and relation, but for the most part they have been and are altogether noxious."

The following year Howells began writing the series of monthly essays in *Harper's* called "The Editor's Study," and for six years he made these articles the medium through which he tried to convince the public of the merits of positivism as a basis for morality in literature. To enable humanity to know itself better—this is the burden of literature, he repeated again and again through the pages of the magazine. It was in one of these essays that he echoed Sedgwick's paraphrase of Taine, and said that he could not thank the writer of false fiction who "teaches us not to know, but to unknow our kind." This direct echo of Taine's justification for fiction in a scientific age Howells repeated in many ways. Fiction, he said, in commenting upon Mary Chase Wyman's "powerful sketches" is a place where "men and women . . . wish to meet other men and women in literature . . . to hear them speak out the heart of human passion in the language of life." Someone wrote to him and complained about false and injurious notions that could be traced back to the reading of novels. Howells agreed with his correspondent, but claimed that the term "novel" could not be rightly given to works which falsify life. Before we can call it a novel, especially before we can call it a good novel, he said, "We must ask ourselves . . . is it true?—true to the motives, the impulses, the principles that shape the life of actual men and women?" And then he specifically gave the positivist's justification for this kind of truthfulness: "If the book is true to what men and women know of one another's souls it will be true enough, and it will be great and beautiful."

The reason for this equivalence of truth and beauty, Howells believed, lay in the function of literature as the laboratory of man's behavior, where a reader may watch an experiment in social relationships, and can find out what will happen, given certain personalities reacting to each other under certain conditions. Just as an experiment would be false and injurious if it were "rigged," so a novel would be misleading and harmful if the people, or the circumstances, were contrived and arranged without regard to the truth of men's motives and passions, and the facts of their physical surroundings. Like the scientist, the novelist, Howells felt, "contributes his share to a thorough knowledge of groups of the human race under conditions which are full of inspiring novelty and interest."

In this feeling, of course, he was elaborating and adapting to American conditions the basic ideas of Hippolyte Taine. And he continued to the end to feel that any philosophy of art must be based upon what men know of the laws of natural science. At the beginning of the twentieth century, as we shall see, Howells realized that his own view of truth as that which might be perceived by the senses and objectively analyzed and classified was being replaced by more subtle and complex considerations. He was not able to grasp the new conceptions, but was entirely willing to admit their truth. In an "Easy Chair" essay in 1903, he conducted an imaginary conversation in which he brought out the parallel between the inductive method of science and the realistic method of fiction. The inductive method, he showed, was the objective assembling of facts from which the scientist could draw generalizations; the technique of the realistic novelist was the objective assembling of facts of human nature under conditions of "novelty and interest" which would enable the reader to make valid and usable generalizations about human nature. But a philosopher who is present points out that induction is being gradually replaced by a newer method—that of "boldly supposing a case . . . and then looking for occurrences to verify it." The new scientific way is "first the inference and then the fact." The favorite literature of the new reading public, it is then suggested, is "quite in the spirit of the new science. . . . Its bold events, its prodigious characters, its incredible motives, were they not quite of the nature of the fearless conjecture which imagined long and short electric waves, and then spread a mesh of wire to intercept them and seize their message?" All this is said, of course, in a tone of almost disbelieving good humor, the product of a state of mind which can intellectually grasp the possibilities of truth in the statement, but cannot constitutionally be convinced of it. But nevertheless, the possibility is stated, and stated convincingly, and shows the essential liberality of the man who is perfectly willing to change his basic creed of fiction to meet changed conditions of man's perception of truth. His own life and his own art were dominated by the positivistic concern with the objective observation, analysis, and classification of human life.

4. The Autobiographical Method: Howells

In a world where the scientific method was raising the hopes and stirring the imaginations of men, a school of letters created a literature for that world and tried to find the answers to such questions as: What is the function of literature? How do we know literature is good or bad? What kind should we write and encourage others to write? The answer Howells gave to these questions, and by giving it helped to encourage the talents of De Forest and Eggleston, Garland and Frederic, as well as the greatest of them all, Mark Twain, was simply "be true." This was to be the test of a "good" work: "Is it true?—true to the motives, the impulses, the principles that shape the life of actual men and women?" With this kind of truth, he told young writers, your books cannot be bad, morally or artistically. Without it, "all graces of style and feats of invention and cunning of construction are so many superfluities. . . ."

But then the question: How to be true in fiction?—how to say what is actual through something which is made up, invented; in short, which is a fiction? Howells knew well the depths and subtleties of the problem, knew that there were other roads to literary "truth"—the road Hawthorne took, the road Henry James was to take—roads which led through the brilliant strangeness of physical romance or the arc-lit phantasms of psychological romance. But Howells and his age felt that before writers could go *above* or *beneath*, they had to go *in*. Before they could attempt to tell the truth about the extraordinary, they had to tell the truth about the ordinary. How could they plumb the depths or reach the heights when there was so much to be learned about the levels, so much falsehood and sentiment to be dispelled before writers and readers could know the verities of their own social existence?

So this was the task the age of Howells set itself—to tell the truth, through fiction, about the ordinary world of physical experience. And the first way to do this, they felt, was to narrow the gap between fiction and nonfiction, to write fiction that was largely autobiographical, that was one's own experiences clarified by the perspective of the fictional technique. The novel, Howells felt, becomes the only true autobiography, for only by putting on the "mask" of the teller of tales can a man show his real face beneath it.

Strangely enough, as we have seen, it was Thomas Bailey Aldrich, the purveyor of sentimentalities, who brought home to Howells the lessons which the Brahmins had been trying to teach him. For with the reading of Aldrich's *The Story of a Bad Boy*, Howells became convinced that the future of his generation lay in fictionalizing its personal experience, in immersing itself in the contemporary American atmosphere and telling what it knew about life from what it had seen, heard, smelt, sensed about it.

This was the way to fulfill the mission of literature in the positivist's scheme, then: take your materials directly from your personal perceptions of the life about you. When Howells created authors to people his novels, he had them go through his own experience of searching for and then finding this literary creed. Both Brice Maxwell, in *The Story of a Play*, and P. B. S. Ray, in *The World of Chance*, found that they only wrote good literature when they turned away from invention and back to life for their models. Maxwell, a dramatist, found his most recent work falling to pieces until he wrote into it the circumstances of his own courtship and marriage. With his wife's help, he reproduced the exact situation, the exact words, and the play became honest and strong. So well did he do his job that the rest of the novel could be concerned with his wife's unreasoned jealousy of the actress who plays her part.

Like the authors in his novels, Howells drew his fiction from his life. Shortly after reading Aldrich's little tale, Howells wrote his father that he was working the stuff of his last summer's travels into the "form of fiction so far as the characters are concerned." The result was *Their Wedding Journey*, the first of a series of thirty novels which, with one exception, are of people, places, even actions which had come under Howells' direct or indirect observation.

Their Wedding Journey was almost pure autobiography—the description of the travels of Howells and his wife, who were given the names of Basil and Isabel March. He used these two representatives again and again, in *A Hazard of New Fortunes* and *Their Silver Wedding Journey* as major characters, and as onlookers and Greek chorus in *A Chance Acquaintance*, *The Shadow of a Dream*, *A Pair of Patient Lovers*, and *The Circle in the Water*. They were disguised enough to provide the necessary mask; but the mask was transparent. Behind the Marches were the Howellses, and the fictional characters matured and grew old, along with their prototypes, a couple who "had been happy together. That is to say, they had made up their quarrels or ignored them." And they found their favorite activity still the divining of "the poetry of the commonplace."

In recasting his personal experience, Howells found his method;

but where was he to find his materials? What he knew about, he wrote about, and in so doing he postponed his artistic maturation; for to practice the method he had chosen, a man must have lived and experienced deeply, and must have profoundly thought upon his life and experiences; there could be, and always have been, young poets; there could be young writers of romance; but there are rarely young novelists; invention is a gift of youth, but re-creation the reward of age or, at least, of maturity. Only part of the reason for Howells' insubstantiality for the first dozen years was his avowed dedication to the commonplace; the other and more important reason for his initial slightness was that he simply did not know enough. As a reporter on the *Ohio Journal* he had refused an assignment which would take him into the police courts, and it was with a sense of self-accusation that he was to show Basil March, his literary counterpart, turning his wife away from a case of poverty with the suggestion that they go to the theatre. Quite naturally, then, the course of his development was an elongated spiral, starting from the small circle of courtship and marriage in middle-class American society, widening slightly to include the same problems amid the additional complexities of the international scene, then gradually taking more and more of American life into its widening sweep: the helplessness of woman in a masculine society *(A Woman's Reason)*, the effects of Puritanism on American character *(Dr. Breen's Practice)*, the ethical behavior of man in a capitalist society *(The Rise of Silas Lapham)*, and finally the terrible problem of the relation between laborer and capital in *Annie Kilburn* and *A Hazard of New Fortunes*. (That the spiral then contracted is one of the reasons why we can assign a terminal date to the age of Howells.) And at each stage the widening figure, for all its limitations, swept into American literature more of middle-class life than had ever been there before, and each expansion represented a corresponding extension of the horizons of Howells' perceptions, for he clung tenaciously to the simple empirical test of truthfulness: to write of what he knew.

Delayed maturity was the major price he had to pay for adopting the autobiographical method. Another, lesser risk is run when one takes characters from the life one has known: the prototypes sometimes recognize themselves. Howells learned this early, for in one of his novels, originally entitled *Private Theatricals*, he told the story of a stage-struck woman he had observed at a New England resort, and no less an authority on feminine histrionics, real and fancied, than Fanny Kemble told him that his "Mrs. Farrell" was "terrific," and implored him to give her the "Small Pox." But the prototype set up a cry of threatening rage, causing the suppression of its appearance in book form until 1921, after the death of the original of Mrs. Farrell and her protesting friends. The reaction to *Private Theatricals* probably made Mrs. Howells feel more keenly than her husband the social risks of transforming personal life into fiction, for she tried to divert her husband from the subject matter of his next novel, *The Undiscovered Country*, which had for its background and its people the remembered experiences of Howells and his family in 1875. They had taken a house for six weeks at Shirley, Massachusetts, close to the settlement of Shakers, that austere religious sect whose sincerity and simplicity moved Howells deeply, appealing to latent religious feelings which later were to flower into a kind of Christian socialism. On friendly terms with many of them, he studied their community and wrote an article about them for the *Atlantic*. But he felt, too, that they presented "temptations to the fictionist," and in 1880, *The Undiscovered Country* began appearing in the *Atlantic*. Experiences from two worlds were unsuccessfully fused in the work—the world of the Shakers and the world of a Boston intellectual society which was once again becoming interested in mesmerism, hypnotism, and spiritualism. In evolving his story, Howells could remember the earnest sincerity of the believer, the scorn of the skeptic, the unctuousness of the fake; he had known them all, the first two at Henry Wadsworth Longfellow's home, when Longfellow's brother-in-law, Appleton, would defend the possibility of calling upon spirits from another world and recount the "facts" of a séance where the souls of the departed "outdid themselves in the athletics and acrobatics they seem so fond of over there." And he had heard the great Louis Agassiz say slowly and firmly: "*I say that it did not happen.*"

By far the greater bulk of his novels, which he produced at

the rate of one every two years, showed the same relation between his experience and his fiction. The characters in his second, *A Chance Acquaintance*, were patterned after some young people he had met aboard a steamer on the Saint Lawrence during the travels which he had reworked into *Their Wedding Journey;* and the problems of this boy and girl leapt to his imagination as the subjects for his next work. In telling their story, he was too much concerned with using them to illustrate a thesis, in this case that, in America, East is East and West is West, and the twain can meet but only rarely marry happily. The imposition of the thesis impaired Howells' allegiance to the truth of his subjects; when writing of a Boston aristocrat it was almost impossible to prevent the stereotype from slipping between pen and paper. Ruefully Howells admitted to Henry James that he had allowed Arbuthnot, the Boston hero, to become a "simulacrum"; but he promised not to repeat the error.

During these early years, when his American experience seemed to be yielding not even the slight tissue he needed for his creation, he would turn to another scene and another society which he knew well: Italy and Americans living abroad. *A Foregone Conclusion* was set in Venice, its protagonists members of the American colony there, and an Italian priest who was drawn briefly into their circle. Howells patterned its comical-tragical hero, Don Ippolito, after an Italian cleric, either a Padre Libera or a brother of the Convent of San Lazarro, Father Giacome Issaverdanz, even to his mechanical inventiveness, and to the handkerchief in his sleeve, daintily ready to conceal the effects of a pinch of snuff. Howells' Venetian experiences again served the purposes of his fiction for *A Fearful Responsibility*, admittedly a much slighter affair than *A Foregone Conclusion*, lacking the "strong motive" of his earlier story. But it came just as certainly from life; in this instance, out of the life of Howells' immediate family. His wife's sister, Mary Mead, a lovely girl of eighteen, had come to stay with the Howellses in Venice, and had proceeded to conquer all the available men, native and foreign. One of them came one day and stood on the balcony with Mary while Mrs. Howells, unobserved, sketched what she thought the picture of a tender moment in youthful courtship. To their horror, she and her husband learned that it was the picture of a rejected proposal. Howells elaborated his wife's sketch into a short novel which had experience just as surely for its model. To shoulder the "fearful responsibility," he created a professor with his own Midwestern background, his own unfulfilled yearnings to write a history of Venice (he had written Charles Eliot Norton that his acquisition of wife and children made this dream impossible of fulfillment), and his own American middle-class suspicion, which he could laugh at but never overcome, of continental morality. He even gave the professor his own dislike for the English because of their "brutal exaltation" of the Union's misfortunes during the Civil War.

In 1882 he published *A Modern Instance*, the deepest study of American society he had yet written and the first major American novel to deal primarily with an unhappy marriage. The initial impulse to write the story had come when Howells saw a production of *Elektra*, and was set to musing on the oneness of human nature at all times, in all ages; within himself he felt the stirrings of man ill-accustomed to his new state of monogamy. And so he gave life, in fiction, to that part of himself which he knew he must suppress in order to live the good life of reason, and created Bartley Hubbard. (Mark Twain, that other exemplary husband, insisted that *he* was Bartley Hubbard, the low-principled errant of the novel.) Howells did not have to go so indirectly to personal experience for many of the other aspects of his book. When he had begun his own career in letters, some "softening cynic" had told him: "Get a salaried place, something regular on some paper." And he had his protagonist receive, and follow, this same advice, and contribute to the flood of sensationalism which was beginning to flow from the American press. When, at the denouement, he wished to show Marcia Hubbard's confrontation of her husband in an Indiana law court, he was not content to allow so important a scene to grow out of his own unaided imagination, but journeyed to Crawfordsville to watch a similar case be tried.

In later life, he would cast back over the remembrances of his youth for his materials. The situation for *Fennel and Rue* (1908) had been one of the farcical moments in his early success as a novelist. He had been overcome by a combination of deep sympathy and deeper pride when a young lady wrote him a letter in 1885, pathetically begging him to send her the final installments of *Indian Summer* which was appearing serially in *Harper's.* She was a dying invalid, her letter ran, with but a few days to live, and she could not bear the thought of never knowing the story's end. Howells wrote her his humble gratitude that he was able to lighten her last hours, and tried to get the advance sheets for her. But the girl proved to be a fraud, a young lady suffering only from an attack of curiosity, and, twenty-three years later, the story of her hoax appeared as *Fennel and Rue.*

If Howells could not see the life he wanted to put into literature, or hear its sounds with his own ears, he would rely upon the testimony of others. The genesis of *The Lady of the Aroostook* was in a situation Samuel Pierpont Langley reported to him, describing how a New England schoolmistress found herself on an ocean voyage in what would now be considered the glorious state of being the only woman passenger aboard, but which then seemed filled with certain social problems. On working out the story, Howells succeeded so well that Langley declared he would vouch for the authenticity of Lydia Blood's character before any critics. The train wreck in *The Quality of Mercy* was taken from reports of a catastrophe of February 5, 1887, when a passenger train of the Vermont Central Railroad ran off Woodstock Bridge. The details of the crime reporter's discovery of the embezzlement were derived from the account of Sylvester Baxter, whom Howells had written asking for details of reportorial procedure in such cases; the description of Quebec was adapted from the notes which Howells had asked his sister to "jot down" so he could report those aspects of the city most likely to strike a visitor. He had not, as a child, been at home when his house had been "raised," so he asked both Hamlin Garland and his brother to send him their eyewitness accounts of that generous frontier ceremony, for use in *New Leaf Mills,* and he told Garland later that he would find his account of the house-raising in it.

And so he went through the American life around him, either

observing it himself, or depending upon the observation of others, searching its feature, catching its gait, its accent, a little of its ugliness, some of its beauty, much of its homeliness. While he would agree with Henry James that the exhortation to write only of what one knew should not be taken too literally, he himself rarely strayed from reporting what his "fleshly eyes" could see. While he knew that within every man there is the possibility of all men, that in self-knowledge there is knowledge of the race, he only rarely allowed himself to see within to the core of the savagery that is part of the human animal. This was not the task he set himself; he limited himself to that which he could do and which he knew needed doing—to portray middle-class life honestly in its homely, common, average features. Henry James thought he did this remarkably well. "You have had the advantage," James wrote him, "of sitting up to your neck . . . or at least up to your waist—amid the sources of inspiration." And, James said with some wistfulness, "you have piled up your monument just by remaining at your post."

It was fitting that Basil and Isabel March, the characters Howells invented to represent himself and his wife, should have been the protagonists of the novel which brought to climax and fruition his method of autobiographical fiction. The Marches, along with Howells, reached their full maturity in *A Hazard of New Fortunes*, the novel written when the author's knowledge of his society had been expanded by his immersion in the greatest social crises of his age: the Haymarket riots and executions. The move Howells made from Boston to New York, a move which an historian of our literature has called the symbol of the transfer of cultural dominance from the Hub City to Manhattan, was the hazard of fortunes which Basil March made. Like March, Howells had sat at the feet of a beloved old German tutor in Ohio, and this tutor became Lindau, the old socialist about whose head raged the great debate over principle which was the theme of the novel. And it was no coincidence, but the logical outcome of his life-long belief in the empirical method of fiction, that *A Hazard of New Fortunes*, growing as it did out of its author's own intensely and agonizingly personal experience during his country's economic and political turmoil, became his most significant work.

5. The Autobiographical Method: De Forest, Harte, Eggleston, Garland, Twain

With Howells, the group that became known as the "realists" agreed that the way to write truthfully was to write of the life one knew, and whenever one of their segments of clarified autobiography appeared, it was assured of the praise of Howells and the powerful magazines for which he wrote. De Forest's pioneer work, *Miss Ravenel's Conversion*, gained its strength from the knowing account of the Civil War which only someone who had campaigned in it could write. Many years after its publication, De Forest issued the original letters which he had sent to his family during the great cataclysm. The description of the chaotic battle of Port Hudson, the scenes at the hospital where, for the first time, Americans were permitted to see the realities of war, to watch the hideous drop of amputated legs and the numb wonder of the dying, these and scenes like them were reworked with little change from the letters which the young captain De Forest had written when the impressions were vivid within him. Like De Forest, his Western contemporary, Bret Harte, thought, at least, that he was drawing his characters and actions from the life about him, and claimed that every person in his stories had their living counterparts. Eggleston, in the Midwest, had written his best book, *The Hoosier Schoolmaster*, as a sentimentalized but nonetheless fairly accurate impression of his own and his brother's experiences with the rude farmers of Indiana and their ruder children. A generation after he wrote it, an Indiana paper printed the death notice of one Hoosier who had achieved his greatest fame by being the prototype of "Jeemie Phillips," who lost the spelling bee in Eggleston's novel. Ten years after Eggleston had met Taine through the pages of *Art of the Netherlands*, Hamlin Garland made the impressive acquaintance of the French critic through the pages of *The History of English Literature*, and diligently copied word for word Taine's analysis of the duties of a writer in an age of science. He made Taine's theory the basis of his lectures on literature in Boston in 1884, and then, hat in hand, he waited upon the man who was doing most to turn these theories into fruitful practice. He felt the thrill of discipleship surging through him when the kindly Howells smiled upon him, the day of their meeting at the "dean's" vacation home in Auburndale, and when Howells talked to him about the simple honesty of autobiographical fiction, Garland knew he must write the story of his own life. When *Main-Travelled Roads* appeared in 1891, tortured triptychs of farm life on the mid-frontier as Garland and his family had lived it, Howells could devote a large part of his "Editor's Study" to hailing it as the creation out of burning dust of the truth about human experience on the American soil.

The ultimate worth of any literary method, however, is not in the production of the good, but of the best. The works of De Forest, of Eggleston, of Garland, even of Howells are of the class of honest second-rate, occasionally pressing close to greatness, never quite pushing past to glory. But in Mark Twain, the group produced the timeless figure, one of the four or five giants of American letters. And Mark Twain, like the others, wrote according to the realists' creed and achieved his stature when transmuting the ore of his personal experience into the gold of reminiscence, autobiography, and autobiographical fiction. From the beginning Twain knew his way to lie in reporting and interpreting what he saw and heard. The Mississippi and the West provided him with all the characters he would ever encounter again: whenever he met a stranger, he knew he had met him before—on the river. And so he spun his greatness out of his experience, and when he tried to do otherwise, he wrote well, but not greatly.

Although Howells encouraged the lesser side of Twain's genius when it turned to inventions like *The Prince and the Pauper* and *A Connecticut Yankee*, his first and highest praise was reserved for works which Twain created out of his remembrance. He was first brought close to the great Westerner by the autobiographical *The Innocents Abroad*, with its large amount of "real life" in it and its fidelity to the experience of its author.

Twain was raised by this criticism to the heights of exultation, and for the rest of his life he yearned to taste the rum of his friend's approval. When he had made his initial success with his travel books, he had promised to use his eyes, to see clearly with them, and report accurately. He never lost this faith in the eye as the organ of truthful perception. Truly a son of Missouri, he believed what he saw. Although he wasted very little of his energies discussing the techniques of fiction, the little criticism he did write was largely on this one theme—that the author who tells what he has seen is taking the first necessary step towards literary value, and that when he invents, he is apt to be mistaken, or sentimental, or silly. This was the sum of his attack on Fenimore Cooper, who simply had not been there and therefore simply could not know. And Twain, furthermore, was not bothered in the least, until the very end, by the possibilities of illusion, of deception by the senses. The metaphor with which he attacked Professor Edward Dowden illustrates his commonsensical attitude towards the testimony of the eyes and ears. People like Dowden, he wrote, would have us believe we are mistaken when we look at a body of water and say it is blue, since, they say, you can dip up a glassful and show it is white. But, replied Twain, the water looks blue, and it is blue.

So he wrote most of his best work about life as it looked to him, and therefore as he believed it was. After the careful reporting of *The Innocents Abroad*, he continued his recreation of personal experience with *Roughing It*. And then he made the first bridge between autobiography and autobiographical fiction in *The Gilded Age*. The amount of personal history in this book was enormous, ranging from minor detail upward through the entire story of a family and an era as Twain had seen it develop. The Hawkinses, cursed with the hopeless hope of quick, undeserved riches, and a post-war America threatened by the same corruption, were the Clemens family and the America of Twain's youth and manhood. Washington Hawkins had much of Mark himself in him, the elder Clemens were the models for the elder Hawkinses. Lafayette Hawkins, he told Howells, was his seldom-do-well brother, Orion. Colonel Sellers was copied directly from his cousin James Lampton. When the Hawkinses, on their way to a new home on the frontier, witnessed a Mississippi steamboat explosion, Mark reproduced, in the novel, the catastrophe he had personally witnessed and which he later described in *Life on the Mississippi:* even the little French Midshipman was there in the fiction, as he was in life, heroically refusing aid as he died so that others might better use it. *Life on the Mississippi*, which has come to be classed, along with *Huckleberry Finn*, as the greatest work of a great author, was a return to straight autobiography. While Joe Twichell had suggested its theme on a walk one day in Hartford, Howells gave Twain, who by then had become close to him personally as well as artistically, the impetus which set him writing one of his two masterworks. In searching for contributors who would write simply of the things they knew well, Howells turned to Twain and asked him to write of his old times on the Mississippi. Twain then sat down and did the first, and best section of the book, which appeared as a series in the *Atlantic* in 1874, and Howells told him enthusiastically that he could taste the mud in it.

Before and after *The Prince and the Pauper*, his allegory in praise of progress, Twain kept close to personal reminiscence and out of it brought *Tom Sawyer* and then *Huckleberry Finn*. In making these two stories, he selected and arranged and hence interpreted much of his rich and varied experience at Hannibal. In Tom Sawyer, he created his own image and placed it outside himself, breathed his own life into it, and with that breath, all the romantic weaknesses and sentimentalism which he knew were the qualities of every boy, but of the boy that was Sam Clemens more than most. Huckleberry Finn and his evil father were recreations of Tom Blankenship and his parent, the town drunkard of Hannibal. Nigger Jim was one of his uncle's slaves in whose memory Mark Twain fashioned the most warmly rounded Negro character in our literature. When Mark wanted to tell of river humbuggery, he did not have to go outside his own experience to make the epitomes of all duping falsity in the Duke and the Dauphin, for as a boy he had seen and reported the same swindling rascals. Their names were different, of course, and the swindles they practiced, but their spirits were the same, and undoubtedly their strangely contrasting bodies as well. They had come down the river in 1852 and had advertised the performance of a "celebrated troupe." When the suckers had paid their silver, the curtains parted to disclose the frauds posturing absurdly in a "burlesque of a farce, the dullness of which was not relieved even by the disgusting blackguardisms with which it was profusely interlarded."

As well as the squint of fraud, Twain knew well the narrowing look of pride that he drew in Colonel Sherburn's eyes as he faced the mob in *Huckleberry Finn*, and he knew the look of death in the eyes of the drunkard Boggs whom the Colonel had warned to get out of town and then had murdered when his warning went unheeded. For this drama had been enacted on the streets of Hannibal and he had watched "Uncle Sam" Smarr, the prototype of Boggs, gasping out his last breath after William Owsley had shot him down.

It was out of this kind of recreated personal experience that Mark Twain's masterworks came, the best flower of the realistic method of fiction–writing of the life one knew.

6. Local Color: The Great American Novel

The immediate result of the positivistic theory of literature was an accent on personal experience; the corollary was a conviction that the writer should concern himself with surroundings which he knew completely, with truthful depiction of the people of his own region, with direct observation of their ways of life, with faithful rendering of their cadences of speech. If it was a provincial area in which the writer was raised, if it was a little known way of life to which he had been accustomed, so much the better, for then to the benefits of instruction would be added the charm of novelty. So in the age of Howells, the range of the American continent came into its literature. Young writers came to know that they need not migrate physically to Europe or the East, or imaginatively to the past. All they need do was to look about them and find their materials in the lives they had lived in the region they had lived them. What do we have here in America for materials? Hawthorne had asked, and he and Henry James, in turn, had answered: little or nothing. But Howells replied, and the writers around him echoed, "we have the whole of human life remaining, and a social structure presenting the only novel opportunities left to fiction."

In writing of native materials, of course, there were opportunities to reach a public, as well as to carry into practice a theory of the function of literature in an age of science. And the realization that there was a market for their regional fiction was the most powerful impetus for the realists, an impetus they could feel without the slightest sense of cheapness or commercialism, for they knew that their craft was dependent upon a relationship between them and their readers. Since they viewed "good" and "truth," as we shall see, not as absolutes, but as changing relationships, they naturally looked upon "good literature" not as pursuit of abstract, perfect form, but as a communication between book-maker and book-buyer. And while they rarely debased their craft trying to strike the fancy of the multitude, every one of them knew that without readers there is no writing.

Fortunately, there were readers for regional writing, for America was becoming intensely self-conscious at exactly the time the realists began to write about its various aspects. Americans wanted to know what their country looked like, and how the varied races which made up their growing population lived and talked. It was the age of the first geodetic surveys, the first mappings and surveyings of the West by government agents like John Wesley Powell who brought back descriptions of the amazing canyons of the Colorado; it was the age at the very beginning of which the rails of the first transcontinental railroad had bound East to West. What kinds of people leading what kinds of life are at the other end of those bands of iron? the Eastern reader asked. Men and women like yourselves, but dressed differently, speaking differently, with different social ways, the Western regionalists answered; fantastic deserts, mile-deep canyons, mountains high enough to bear snow the year round, forests with trees as wide as man can stretch and wider, villages where the only woman was the town whore, camps where the only currency was gold-dust. Writers of the South told of swamps where the cypress grew out of green-scummed water and the moss grew down into it, and of cities where the obsessive blood-consciousness of its inhabitants testified to the mingling of the races. Western authors narrated the tales of plains where a man could be lost in the dust or ruined by a hailstorm; of cities where fortunes were made or lost in a day's trading on the beef or grain exchanges. The literary map of America, so long a small corner of light in the east, with a glimmer on the southern coast, began to be totally illuminated, north and south, east and west, until by 1900 there was no section which had not found some writer, and usually several, to describe its features and speak with its voice. Bret Harte and Mark Twain brought in California, Nevada, and Missouri; Eggleston the hills of Indiana; George Washington Cable and William Harben the Delta country and North Georgia; Mary Noailles Murfree the mountains of Tennessee; Sarah Orne Jewett and Mary E. Wilkins Freeman the back country of New England; Harold Frederic the upstate valleys of New York; E. W. Howe the village life of Kansas; Hamlin Garland the towns and plains of the Dakotas and Wisconsin; Henry Blake Fuller the cement cliffs of Chicago; Henry Harland the tenements of Manhattan. By 1912 Howells could look back upon a literary search which had involved many of the nation's critics since the Civil War and draw the conclusion that there could never have been any such thing as THE American novel, for it had been written bit by bit, through the provincial, parochial fiction which enabled the American to "know his environment from himself."

Given the growth of the country and of its intellectual resources, this vast, sprawling "American Novel" of the local colorists would have been written regardless of critical disapproval or approval. But it took its particular form from the ceaseless prodding, pushing, shaping of William Dean Howells. From his first days of editorship of the *Atlantic*, he encouraged writers to give him stories about people and places they knew, without worrying about plot or incident. When books came across his reviewing desk which contained truthful characterizations in clearly observed settings, he cheered for them. When such stories were submitted to him, he accepted them and asked for more; when they were slow in coming in, he went out and got them; when the pieces he received were lacking in these elements, he would ask the contributor to get more sense of "*locality*" into his stories and articles.

As early as 1867, he saw that John De Forest was making a start in the direction of studying a local life "little known to literature" with some of his descriptions in *Miss Ravenel's Conversion* and asked him if he would do more stories of Southern life for the *Atlantic.* De Forest could do no short pieces for him, but he wrote two more books about the South and its manners, *Kate Beaumont*, and the ridiculously melodramatic *The Bloody Chasm* in which a Northern officer woos and wins a Southern belle by wearing a chest-length beard to conceal his identity. De Forest looked about him for other localities in which to set his stories, still in an attempt to satisfy America's growing curiosity about its provinces, and hit upon the Grand Canyon country. His romance called *Overland* was the first book to take advantage of this magnificent setting, and was a forerunner of the Western "action story" destined to become so popular in the twentieth century. But De Forest had nothing more to say; by 1879 he mourned that he could not understand why he did not "sell monstrously." And finally he retreated into gloom and expressed nothing but contempt for the nineteen-twentieths of people in America to the portrayal of whose lives and manners he had at first dedicated himself.

Meanwhile others had taken up the method and the materials and had received the powerful editorial encouragement of Howells. Bret Harte's *The Luck of Roaring Camp* had appeared, and although Howells saw the essential sentimentality of many of the stories which made up the collection, he also felt the fresh winds from the western mountain slopes with which Harte was aerating American literature, and he invited him to enter upon a contract to provide the *Atlantic* with more of his California tales. Harte tried to supply them, and, when they turned out to be second-rate, tried to appease Howells by writing that there were in them, at least, "bits of local color that are truthful and new to most Eastern people." Harte came east with his family and Howells introduced him to Boston literary society where he was lionized, then regarded with some suspicion, and finally despised. For he had unfortunate weaknesses—for drink, for borrowing and not repaying, for contracting and not fulfilling. Howells was somewhat dismayed by the fecklessness of his protégé, but bore it with a good temper which contrasted strongly with the downright hatred Mark Twain developed for his co-regionalist. True, Howells knew that Harte was the kind of a man who could charge seventy-five dollars' worth of silk underwear to a friend's account, but he also remembered that Harte was one of the first writers of the growing school of local colorists, and for this, he wrote his cousin, Rutherford B. Hayes, Harte should be rewarded with a post as consul to Crefeld, Germany.

Even in sentimentalists like Henry Ward Beecher, Howells found small grains of the gold of local color, and tried to encourage the author to get more of it into his fiction, more of the "felicity in expressing the flavor and color of New England life." When Cable showed this kind of faithfulness to the people and places of Louisiana, Howells hailed him publicly in the *Atlantic* and privately in letters which told Cable of the pleasure the whole Howells family took in his work; in his household, Howells told the little man from New Orleans, they were talking nothing but the Creole dialect he had caught so well in his short stories and in *The Grandissimes*. Howells continued to implore Southern writers to turn away from Poe, and to base their works on life. Remember, he told them, "there is no greatness, no beauty, which does not come fresh from truth to your own knowledge of things." And when writers like Mary Noailles Murfree and William Harben wrote of Southern life from their own observation of it, he beat the drums for them. Mark Twain thought Harben's pictures of the South a bit grim, but, answered Howells, Harben "didn't make North Georgia; he only made a likeness of it. Don't shoot the artist."

In Sarah Orne Jewett, who had treated a vastly dissimilar environment, Howells had found the same method and the same values. He took delight in the "very tint and form of reality" in her collection called *Deephaven*, and hoped publicly that she would turn her ability to observe and characterize "to the advantage of all of us in fiction." She listened to this advice, and created the etchings of New England life some of which were collected under the title, *The Country of the Pointed Firs*, stories in which the transition from fiction to nonfiction is so slight as to be imperceptible. A tale like "The Courtin' of Sister Wisby" was typical. It began with the simple description of the author walking through a New England countryside, observing the swell of the hills, the colors of the fields, and then, the country-woman who would serve as a narrator. The author reported the hang of her clothes, her stoop as she picked her "yarbs," and her dialect as she told about the medicinal properties of "mullein" and "poke-weed." More than half the "tale" was concerned with this faithful transcription of country life; then the old woman told her story of the "courtin" of the strong-minded sister by the deacon, and how, after some difficulties, she allowed herself to be won.

Howells was excited, one day in 1878, by the appearance on his desk of another contribution which seemed to him an addition to his readers' knowledge of their country. It was called "Dancin' Party at Harrison's Cove," and pictured the folkways of the mountaineers of Tennessee. On its title page was the vigorous name "Charles Egbert Craddock," and Howells accepted the story from the unknown contributor, asked for more, and invited him to Boston. "Mr. Craddock" came, a twisted, crippled, vibrant woman named Mary Noailles Murfree, who won his instant love. Her story appeared with seven others in the volume called *In the Tennessee Mountains;* the collection was one of the prime forces in the development of the American short story of local color.

The movement, nurtured by Howells, found its major spokesman in Hamlin Garland, the young Midwesterner who, as we have seen, had already been impressed enough with the positivistic theories of literature to have made a summary in his own adolescent hand of the "work upon English literature by M. Taine." And when he came to Boston and found the example and personal encouragement of Howells, he wrote his only substantial work of fiction: *Main-Travelled Roads*, the book that almost singlehandedly exploded the myth of the West as the

Garden of America, the happy lair of noble primitives surrounded by the soft beneficence of a friendly nature. It was a work, Howells saw immediately, which expressed the sad spirit of the rural Northwest from the experiences of one who had been part of what he saw. Following Howells' precepts, Garland wrote out of his own experience and about the region he knew best, and for the particular brand of realism which dealt explicitly with the provincial environment out of which an author came, he coined the word "veritism." This kind of realism, he wrote in *Crumbling Idols,* had become the significant movement in American letters, and under its other name—"local color"—the most profitable direction literature could take.

But Garland was not able to cling to his ideal. He had chosen an unfortunate decade for his enthusiasm, a decade which quickly was to turn to the "horrid tumult of the swashbuckler swashing on his buckler," and he made the mistake of trying to hit the popular fancy with a kind of fiction in which he deeply disbelieved. To Howells' pain, and his own intense dissatisfaction, he began writing Western romances. Howells tried to get him back to his ideal; as early as 1892, he told Garland that the stories he was beginning to write were romantic and badly motivated. When Garland's *They of the High Trails* appeared, he wrote that "the flush of wild adventure replaces the coloring of his prime." He begged Garland to be true to the ideals of his youth, his dreams of an unsparing and unflinching "veritism," but Garland told him, at fifty, that his work was done. Finally, however, he returned to the most basic kind of "local color"—to autobiography, and gave America its definitive studies of life on the near-frontier. And Howells was able to sigh with happy relief and give his aging disciple the first unqualified praise in twenty years when he was able to say, three years before his death, that *A Son of the Middle Border* was the realization of Garland's youthful ideals, "perfectly true to life and beautiful with right feeling."

Garland's generation of regional American writers, those who began publishing in the 'eighties and 'nineties as distinguished from the older generation of realists whose first works were dated in the late 'sixties or 'seventies, knew that Howells and Mark Twain had won the fight for them—that they need only be faithful to the aspects of American life they knew and they would win sympathy, encouragement, and publication. Alice French, who wrote local color under the name "Octave Thanet," was most grateful for Howells' criticism in *Harper's* which gave her the faith in study, and patient observation, and the will to become an artist. Henry Harland kept asking himself, when writing his stories, how would Howells like them, and would Howells think them a step in the right direction. Henry Blake Fuller tried to express his gratitude to Howells in an extended metaphor: Did Howells remember, Fuller asked him, how he first came to New York in 1860? And did he perhaps recall his dismay at finding himself in a new and unfriendly city? And was he, perhaps, rescued by some competent and friendly policeman who set him on a safe curbstone? Well, he assured Howells, the same thing happened to him, a sadly detached modern writer in the literary jungle, and he wanted to thank the head of the force for having taken the trouble to give him his bearings.

7. Techniques for Truth: The Dramatic Method

Writing from one's experience, about an area of American life that one knew well—these, then, were the two basic axioms in the realistic formula for writing truth in fiction. The truth the realists were trying to tell, it must be repeated, was the truth of externalities rather than internalities, truth about the way things looked and the way people acted, an outside kind of truth. But it was still a difficult kind of truth to write in a society which was increasingly coming to prefer fiction about how readers would like the world to be in their middle-class fantasies rather than the way it was. In order to tell this kind of truth—"hard, and dry . . . but immensely wholesome and sanative"—the realist, again under Howells' leadership, adopted a mode of story-telling which can best be termed "the dramatic method." As in a play, the author was to set the stage, give his characters their lines, and then disappear behind the wings, depending upon the intelligence of the audience to draw whatever conclusions seem necessary from the given actions in the given surroundings. The author, according to this theory, should no more step out of his narrative to confide in the reader, to point out who is villain, who is hero, what is the moral of his tale, than the dramatist should come out from the wings to confide to the audience what his intention was, and what they should believe. All intervention on the part of a writer, in brief, all outward semblance of subjectivity, was renounced. In its place came a kind of novelist's license to pretend to the same kind of objectivity as that of a scientific observer.

While for Henry James, the revelation of this artistic method came from Ivan Turgenev, Howells already had been weighing the advantages of the dramatic method three years before the great Russian was available to him. In 1869, he perceived that Berthold Auerbach allowed his story *Edelweiss* apparently to "tell itself." From the beginning, he said, the novel "goes alone" and "one does not think of the author till the end." And when Turgenev finally was translated into English, three years later, Howells read him at the suggestion of T. S. Perry, and immediately was struck by Turgenev's careful abstention from a seeming intervention in his stories. "He seems the most self-forgetful of the story-telling tribe, and he is no more enamored of his creations than of himself . . . you like them or hate them for what they are; it does not seem to be his affair." And by the following year, Howells had completely formulated his theory of dramatic presentation in fiction and had served notice that he would hold future novelists to this criterion. "The novelist's business," he wrote, "is to paint such facts of character as he finds so strongly that their relative value in his picture will be at once apparent . . . without a word of comment." Turgenev, he repeated again, leaves "all comment to the reader." And then he concluded: "Everything necessary to the reader's intelligence should be quietly and artfully supplied, and nothing else should be added." In the same issue of the *Atlantic*, he ran G. P. Lathrop's article on the modern novel which was an evaluation of the progress of the form from the confidential, subjective to the objective and dramatic method; there was still too much of the former in contemporary fiction, Lathrop declared, and he blamed this state of affairs on the continuing vogue of Rousseau and Goethe. Howells agreed with him, finding it to be the principal fault of the otherwise admirable George Eliot that she "plucks her people apart between their speeches, and anatomizes their motive and intention, while they pause to take breath at a comma."

8. Dramatic Method and Organic Form

"*. . . the art of not arriving . . .*"
—Howells

The moment he began practicing this dramatic theory, however, Howells felt the strain which allegiance to the dramatic form was placing upon his art. For he actually was dedicated only to one small part of dramatic technique—letting the characters speak for themselves, as in a drama. But the other aspects of dramatic form: unity of action, beginning, middle and end, well-made form in which all contributes to a total effect, tight sequence of causality—these were alien to what came to be his conception of the novel as that art form which presses close to the realities of life itself. He had decided that the form of autobiography, or fiction which was near-autobiography, was the best form for approximating the sprawling, never-beginning, never-ending dynamic process of organic inter-relationships. He wanted only to use the technique of seeming to let the reader make up his own mind so that the novel would appear to be more like life where we have an apparent freedom of choice after we have collected the sensory facts upon which to base our conclusions. But he only gradually realized this trap of tight form into which his adoption of the dramatic method led him, and spent the first dozen years of his artistic development sometimes writing loose autobiographical fiction (*Their Wedding Journey*), more often writing tightly constructed stories (*A Chance Acquaintance*), and then wondering why the latter seemed to lack objectivity, and refused to have the appearance of "going it alone" such as he admired in the works of Auerbach and Turgenev. But he came to see that the little fragment of dramatized human experience that he thought was his metier was too limited a form to imitate life, and he gave his allegiance to a more organic theory of novel structure, carrying over from dramatic technique only the refusal to step from the wings and confide in the reader.

This avoidance of careful form certainly was the attitude of Mark Twain, for whom a "story," in the sense of a unified series of events linked together by causality, was simply an impossibility. It was, further, something which he had no desire to write. He was interested first in people and then in places, and was concerned with incident only when it revealed character or explained locality. His sole method of getting action into his fiction was to move his characters about physically; the only way he could introduce new people was to shift his main character into the environment of new personalities, and either carry them along with him as he progressed farther in space, or leave them behind and pick up others. It would have been inconceivable to coop the prince up in London: no, he arranged it so that, with Miles Hendon, the prince got out and started wandering. After making an immense journey in time, the Connecticut Yankee soon did not know what to do with himself at Arthur's court, and Twain didn't know what to do with him either; so he sent him off for a tour of the provinces, and then, in a kind of fabulous desperation, over to France. *Huckleberry Finn* would never have become America's greatest story of the Mississippi if Huck had stayed in town with Miss Watson; it was as essential for Huck to keep moving as it was for him to breathe; but it was also as necessary for Mark to keep him moving as it was for him to write; and the last time we see Huck, he is on his way again, off this time to the spaciousness of the West.

Mark Twain had already gained success as the author of travel literature by 1870, and was therefore early predisposed to a form of fiction so close to the texture of his first triumph. And, like Howells, he had formed a lasting admiration for the early Spanish realists who had started the novel on its career in the West by adopting, as a method, the recitation of the episodic adventures of a rogue, or picaro, who moved from one self-contained adventure to another. But coincidentally, at the very time when Twain and Howells, the one unconsciously, the other quite consciously, were searching for a mode of narration fit for the American scene, there appeared among them to hold a unique place in their affections a true American picaro named Ralph Keeler, whose own life was the kind of extended adventure which was the stuff of the Spanish picaresque. He had run away from a foster home in Buffalo at the age of eleven, had worked his way down the Mississippi as a cabin boy, and up it again as a minstrel in one of the river's show-boats, had been educated by a kind priest, had wandered abroad to vagabond through Europe on a total original capital of $181, and, back in America, after the Civil War, settled briefly in Boston where he earned his living as a typesetter, and his only real fame by becoming warmly intimate with Aldrich and Howells and Twain. "You wretch," Howells would write him lovingly, and would beg him to come back as quickly as possible so he could drink toasts to his perdition. But Keeler could not stay in Boston any more than could Huck Finn, and so he sailed to Cuba, in 1878, to report the insurrections which were beginning to shake that Spanish possession. He disappeared overboard one dark night, probably, his friends thought, with a Spanish dagger between his ribs, and when he died, Howells remembered, he took a good deal of light and joy out of the world with him. But he had left a record of his earlier wanderings in a series of articles which Howells had printed in the *Atlantic*, and then had reviewed with keenest interest when they appeared in book form as *Vagabond Adventures* in 1870. For Howells found it proof that the best way to capture American life in fiction would be to use the picaresque narrative. And he encouraged Twain to follow this mode, reminding him, and the reading public, that his fiction was in the best tradition of the novel, "the good old sort, like De Foe's . . . and like that of the Spanish picaresque novelists, Mendoza and the rest" whose easy, almost formless tales flowed "from incident to incident."

But in his own early fiction, Howells was wooed away from loose structure to tight form by his preoccupation with the dramatic technique of objective presentation, and tried to write small things in which the hand of the author, moving his characters about the settings he had chosen for them, was all too obvious. It was probably his large early admiration for Turgenev which led him to write only of four or five people, away in their corner, with little of the great world impinging upon them. For all of the

Russian's works involved a small cast of characters moving through a few stage-like settings. *Smoke*, for example, has its "cast" of hero, heroine, the heroine's loyal aunt, the dissolute princess and her decadent husband, and the mysterious stranger from the princess' past; these are the only "speaking parts" in the novel. The settings are similarly restricted: several scenes at Baden-Baden, a "flash-back" to the princess' home in Moscow, and an epilogue at Litvinov's country estate. The same economy of character and setting was true of *Liza, A Lear of the Steppes, Spring Freshets*, and *Fathers and Sons*, all of which Howells read and admired inordinately. So it is not surprising that in the years which followed his introduction to Turgenev, the years when he was searching for ways to be life-like, and yet had not lived enough to cast largely about him into the atmosphere of his country, Howells wrote a series of novels in which a few people act and react upon one another, seemingly cut apart from the rest of society. For two years he even set his hand to writing pure drama, and made his "novels" into plays: *The Parlor Car* (1876), *Out of the Question* (1877), and *A Counterfeit Presentment* (1877). And his other works of this decade, if not overtly in this form, had the same kind of smallness about them.

Fortunately, he broke his self-forged bonds, and while he continued to cling to the dramatic technique of allowing his characters to speak for themselves, he renounced his allegiance to the dogma of dramatic compactness and unity. Whereas in 1877, he told Charles Dudley Warner that he hated to read stories in which one had to drop the thread of one person's fate and take up another's, and that he disliked to write stories where there were more than a few people kept before the reader, by 1882 he had already begun and by 1886 was well into a series of densely populated novels where characters appeared and disappeared with something of the same random quality of the actual world, and one of them, an author, remarked: "I don't know that you are bound to relate things strictly to each other in art, any more than they are related in life." While in 1873, Howells was attracted by the fineness of Turgenev, in 1886 he was completely captured by the vastness of Tolstoy. Earlier, he had confessed to liking "a finished story"; later, he said of George Bernard Shaw that he "has surprised the prime secret of life, the art of not arriving, and, after not arriving with him, you like it." In 1873 he had written the neatly symmetrical *A Chance Acquaintance* where every action was calculated to work towards the novel's thesis, every setting chosen to point up the action which takes place within it; in 1890 he wrote *A Hazard of New Fortunes* whose absence of symmetrical arrangement was part of its superiority to his earlier work.

And the principal novels of this later period form one large testimonial to his gradual escape from the restrictions of the dramatic technique. *A Modern Instance*, *A Woman's Reason*, *The Rise of Silas Lapham*, *The Quality of Mercy*, *The World of Chance*, and *The Story of a Play*, all written between 1882 and 1898, form a species of continuous novel, an American *Human Comedy*, in which the end of one work is the beginning of another, characters come and go, meet and separate with the same apparent irrelevance, so full of deeper meaning, which Howells was sure was a part of the life process itself.

He had first experimented with the technique of linking his novels towards the end of his "dramatic" period. In *A Fearful Responsibility* (1881) he revisited Venice, the scene of his earlier work *A Foregone Conclusion*. In the first novel, Ferris, the American Consul to Venice, was one of the principal characters, and as much of a "hero" as Howells ever permitted himself to draw. *A Fearful Responsibility*, however, told the story of another little group of Americans abroad, and the earlier tale was given a fleeting glance through the eyes of new characters, and then dismissed, for "By this time a change had taken place in the consular office. Mr. Ferris, some months before, had suddenly thrown up his charge and gone home. . . . Mrs. Elmore had never liked Ferris. . . . She believed he had not behaved quite well towards an American lady,—a Miss Vervain." A minor tragedy had developed through to its climax and then subsided, to be remembered only as a fleeting and mistaken impression in a prudish woman's mind. Howells must have felt the success of this overlapping of fictional portraits, and must have sensed how well this method caught the interrelated confusions, the logical paradoxes of life, for with *A Modern Instance* he began a picture of New England society which was only completed after eight more novels had been written.

In *A Modern Instance*, he told the story of the decline of Boston journalism as well as of the unhappy marriage of Bartley Hubbard and Marcia Gaylord. Bartley was first associated with the staid *Chronicle Abstract*, but he left it to go with the *Events* which he helped to debauch to yellow journalism by his own lack of taste and morality. Its editor had proposed a piece of "outside work" for him, a series of interviews with "leading manufacturers and merchant princes at their places of business." During his rapid rise, Bartley was helped by Clara Kingsbury, a likeable and philanthropic Boston socialite. Clara reappeared in *A Woman's Reason* when she once again played the role of Good Samaritan, trying to rescue Helen Harkness who was thrown on her pitiful woman's resources after the death of her father, thereby giving Howells the opportunity of exploring the state of woman's fitness in the nineteenth-century world of sexual inequality.

On Bartley Hubbard's list of subjects for his "Solid Men" series had been one Silas Lapham, the paint king, and it was with his interview with the title character that *The Rise of Silas Lapham* begins. After collecting his data for the article, Bartley hurried home to his wife, Marcia, and found her already admiring a set of paints Lapham had sent in appreciation. In the course of Lapham's moral rise and financial fall, his daughter married Tom Corey, son of the Brahmin, Bromfield Corey, one of whose good friends was Clara Kingsbury. Their minister was the Reverend David Sewell, a constant and kindly visitor to the Corey home.

Sewell's kindliness, and the trouble into which it plunged him, provided the story for *The Minister's Charge*. He had taken a young boor, Lemuel Barker, under his care, and found him a job at a boardinghouse—the same one in which Helen Harkness had taken lodging in *A Woman's Reason;* Lemuel met here one Mr. Evans, editor of the *Saturday Afternoon*, who had also been a character in *A Woman's Reason.* Late in the narrative, Sewell took an evening off from his worries about Lemuel, and went ". . . to see an old parishioner of his . . . who among his eccentricities had the habit of occupying his house all summer long, while his family flitted with other people of fashion to the sea-shore." The "old parishioner" was Bromfield Corey, and he told the news of Tom Corey and his wife, Penelope Lapham Corey, the daughter of the ex-paint-king.

In *Annie Kilburn*, Howells shifted the locale of his fiction from Boston to the New England mill town of "Hatboro," and told of Annie's struggles to find a common ground with the oppressed millworkers. She found help in her work from the local minister, the Reverend Mr. Peck, from Dr. Morrell, and from the town's lawyer, Ralph Putney. Arrayed against her were the storekeeping Gerrishes, J. Milton Northwick, and other respectable members of the Hatboro community. One of them was the toady, Percy Brandreth, whose answer to the problems of capital and labor was to put on a production of *Romeo and Juliet* to raise funds for a "social Union"—a club for workingmen where soft-drinks and sandwiches would be served in an effort to prevent the workers from drinking away their wages. Among his other odious characteristics, Percy was an avid hunter of heiresses.

J. Milton Northwick's subsequent history provided the basis for *The Quality of Mercy*, for Northwick eventually succumbed to the temptations of his position as treasurer of the Ponkwasset Mills, owned by Eben Hilary. A reporter from the Boston *Events* was sent on the trail of the sensational story; the *Events*, it appeared, was continuing the yellow career it had started under the leadership of "a certain Bartley Hubbard," and the reporter first went to the town tavern to pick up scents of his story, inquiring about the town's minister. "I guess he ain't very friendless," the tavern mistress told him in the down-East dialect Howells could report so well. "He's about the most popular minister, especially with the working folks, since Mr. Peck . . . the one who was run over by the cars at the depot two or three years back." Peck, she told him, mistakenly, had started the tavern as a "sort of co-operation" at first. "And then the co-operation petered out," the reporter continued smartly, "and then you took it and began to make money. Standard history of co-operation." (It had *not* been Peck's idea; he had opposed it vigorously as a sop in place of justice; and he had died, and all that was left of him was the misconception of his aims in the hazy recollection of a barmaid.)

The rival and more principled newspaper, the *Abstract*, also sent a reporter, Brice Maxwell, to cover the Northwick case, and in the course of his investigation Maxwell met Louise Hilary, daughter of the president of the mills, and close friend of Annie Kilburn, now Mrs. Morrell. And some of Hilary's old friends came from Boston to comfort him, among whom was Bromfield Corey.

In *The World of Chance*, P. B. S. Ray, a young journalist and critic of the drama for an upstate paper, came to New York City with the manuscript of a new novel under his arm and a letter of introduction to the publishing house of Chapley and Brandreth. He was interviewed by a junior member of the firm, Percy Brandreth, who was attracted by the title of the novel—"A Modern Romeo"—for he "once took part in an amateur performance of *Romeo* . . ." And, of course, he had obtained his position by marrying Chapley's daughter.

Meanwhile, Brice Maxwell, the other journalist whose fortunes had been interwoven with those of the other characters of this spacious imitation of New England life, had married Louise Hilary, daughter of the president of Ponkwasset Mills, and had written a drama; the tale of how it came to be created and produced was told in *The Story of A Play*, and it received its first enthusiastic review from a young critic on a small paper in upper New York State. The young critic's name was P. B. S. Ray.

And so the mural ended, not really ending at all. There was no ending just as there was no beginning, no border, no cutting of the interweaving lines; the picture simply runs off the edge of the canvas. The Hilarys, Coreys, Athertons, Laphams, Sewells, Northwicks, Hubbards, Rays, Brandreths went on, are going on, will go on, and Howells, in creating them, was creating something very close to the texture of life itself. He could not have done this through the medium of the well-formed dramatic novel. But he had come to perceive that "the more art resembles life, the less responsive it was to any hard and fast design; the nearer he pressed to an imitation of reality, the less he could constrain his characters by a preconceived plot he had arranged for them to enact; the more successful he was in making characters with truth in them, the less they would obey any other dictates than 'their own natures," the more they would "create the story," and not consent to be "created for it." And so finally he came to talk about the novel, not as an artifact, but as an organism, and used the same terms as Emerson and Thoreau and Coleridge had used for their "organic" theory of poetry. His "work of art," he declared, "was a growth from all his thinking and feeling about it," and would eventuate in a climax as a tree would ripen its fruit only after having struck its roots in the ground, "coming of the age to bear, and then some springtime budding, putting out leaves, breaking into blossom."

Mark Twain put it more simply. In 1873 he had written *The Gilded Age* with Charles Dudley Warner, and the pair had started a story line involving the mystery of Laura Hawkins and her father, and then dropped it. You'll have to forgive us for never having alluded to him again, the authors told their public with charming candor, but he just simply wouldn't fit in anywhere. And in the realist's program to create imitations of American life, the well-made plot did not fit in either.

9. "Symbolism" and "Use of Symbol"

Art which comes as close as possible to life, fiction which is truth and tells men about themselves so that they may observe themselves and draw reasonable conclusions about the conduct of their lives, this was the goal of the realists. The autobiographical method, the use of local color, the dramatic technique of narration combined with looseness of plot, absence of fable, and a structure which was organic rather than superimposed—these were the means of achieving this desired "life-likeness." But this hyphenated word carries a sting in its tail, jolting the observer with the realization that, after all, art can only be *like* life and can never *be* life. Literature is not life, reading is not living; written words are feeble imitations of spoken sounds, spoken sounds still feebler representations of what humans can see and hear and feel, of redness and ripeness, of warmth and hate. These unassailable facts raise questions about the nature of the realistic movement in American letters: were these realists so bewildered by the glories of science that they could not see the difference between science and art, between recording and interpreting? If they did not see these differences clearly, what did they believe the purpose of art to be? Why bother? Did they think literature had nothing to say about the difference between good and evil? Did it, for the realist, have nothing to tell us about the *meaning* of our existence?

In trying to answer these questions, we shall find it necessary to use some words which have to do with the removal of experience into communication, the rendering of life in literature, the meaning of which may not be a matter of common agreement: "sign," "symbol," and "convention." "Signs" are the bodily movements, gestures, the sounds we make, or the written transcription of those sounds which stand for something other than themselves, which "point" to an object in the world of experience. A "symbol" is a sign, too, but a sign which represents something rather more complex than the simple sign. While all language is "sign," most "signs" tend to become "symbols." The sign "table" points to a flat object with four legs; but who can hear it spoken or see it written without thinking of food, and human gathering? And "cross," "flag," and "rose," have so many reverberations of conscious and unconscious response that we may safely say that these are truly "symbols." To use a symbol, then, is to tell us some complicated things by telling us one simpler thing, and all writers use symbols, some more than others, of course, but all without exception finding them indispensable for the purposes of even the most elementary kinds of communication.

But if all writers use symbols, not all writers are *symbolists.* And this distinction marks the different techniques of the American romantic and the realist. Convinced of the existence of either a supersensory world, or of the need for exploring the realm of the subconscious, the romantic symbolists tried to express these otherwise incommunicable truths through the use of concrete objects which represent the outcroppings into the physical world of the metaphysical or the subconscious. The White Whale became, for Melville, an expression of all his feelings about the infinitely complex nature of good and evil, fate and free will. When Hawthorne saw a scrap of material shaped like an "A" in the Custom House at Salem, he felt it was a "mystic symbol" from which a "deep meaning . . . streamed forth," communicating itself to his sensibility but eluding the analysis of his mind. And he used the scarlet letter in his romance as means of expressing the paradoxical nature of sin. On the other hand, limiting himself to the physical world of things and our rational perceptions of them, the realist used his symbols to reinforce or to give emotional dimension to some meaning already within the frame of his narrative. An example of this more limited use of symbol was Twain's summation of the dangers of corrupt sentimentalism, in *Huckleberry Finn*, by showing us the wreck of the *Walter Scott*. Howells constantly used symbols in this way. In *A Foregone Conclusion*, he showed his Venetian priest finding in a walled garden a refuge from the world, a representation of his own sentimental withdrawal from reality. At the moment he awakens to an understanding of the hopelessness of his position, the fountain in the garden ceases to flow. Howells employed similar devices in all his works, and most effectively, as we shall see, in *The Rise of Silas Lapham* and *A Hazard of New Fortunes*.

When a literary method makes constant use of symbols to try to extend its stories beyond the horizons of the immediately knowable and communicable, or deep into the equally indistinct regions of the human subconscious, we can call the method "symbolism," and we shall use the word "symbolism" only in this sense. For the other, more limited way of using symbols, to reflect not outside the story to a metaphysical or psychological truth, but inside the story, to reinforce some meaning already in the frame of the narrative, we have no term. Perhaps we can employ the awkward phrase "use of symbol" to distinguish this method from "symbolism." The romantics were "symbolists"; the realists "used symbols."

Now, when a pattern of symbols is used so often in a culture that its mere presentation is sufficient to evoke a predictable pattern of response from the reader in that culture, we can call this pattern of symbols a "convention." A convention is simply an agreement between readers and writers that certain groups of symbols will receive certain responses whenever they are used. They are the rules of the game of fiction to which certain cultures tacitly agree so that the business of communicating the complex ideas and emotions of fiction may be carried on. Literature is made up largely of the calculated manipulation of these conventions. There are the conventions of the "point of view," for example. If the book is written in the third person, the reader agrees to the "rule" that the narrator may be everywhere at once, and see or hear all that he chooses to see and hear. If the work is written in the first person, the reader agrees to allow the author to become that person for the duration of the story. These are some of the large and obvious "conventions" of fiction. But there are subtler agreements reached tacitly between reader and writer, and some of these were different in the age of Howells and will have to be understood if we are to appraise nineteenth-century realism justly.

With these distinctions and definitions in mind, we return to the questions concerning the achievements of the realists in the realm of human values. Did they not see the difference between art and life, between sign and thing? The answer is partly that, by and large, the realists did not concern themselves with such ontological differences. The least self-conscious of artists, they were unworried by the distinction between "symbol" and "thing." They used, in their writing, those usual symbols and conventions that were natural to them and to their environment. They rarely went to literature, or to any but native mythologies, for their symbols and images; they went to the living speech of their times, to the symbols which were the common property of them and their readers. Hamlin Garland had noted, instinctively, Herbert Spencer's admonition that the best writing was that which was most instantly apprehended by the reader; Mark Twain disliked poetry because it was too difficult, and wanted his own work to be easy to swallow: "My books are water; those of the great geniuses are wine. Everybody drinks water." Howells quoted with admiration the statement of Edmund Burke that "the true standard of the arts is in every man's power; and an easy observation of the most common, sometimes of the meanest things in nature, will give the truest lights. . . ." The strength of the realists lay in this artistic unself-consciousness and lack of pretension. How to make something like life itself? Observe closely, and report honestly in the words which your experience in living has taught you are the symbols that are closest to the things you have observed.

10. Impressionism and Realism

But Howells held a unique position among this loose coterie of unselfconscious artists; for as their guide and leader, as the only professional critic among them (even though he hated criticism, he became a critic nevertheless), he was forced to consider the problem of the ways in which art was different from, as well as like, life. Mark Twain could believe that fiction was, perhaps, doing something which the camera might eventually do much better. But Howells realized that the art of fiction was the art of symbols and conventions. He saw that in order to be like life, fiction must be different from the usual flow of human perceptions; because of the necessary gap between the symbol and the thing itself, a writer who attempted to truthfully describe everything that "happened" to one commonplace person sitting at his desk for one hour would soon find himself engaged in an endless task, and a thankless one, for the reader would have no conception of what actually had occurred. What the writer must do, Howells saw, was to select and arrange those symbols and conventions that would give a truthful *impression* of life as it appears to the average man of good sense in the culture for which he was writing. He insisted that these symbols *not* be selected and arranged in favor of this or that preconceived theory, or to preach some sermon, or to grind some metaphysical axe. But selected and arranged the material must be, in order to tell the truth. In order to be truthful, art and fiction must be "more real" than any isolated aspect of reality, because they must be more general, because they must by their selection and arrangement, create a world of fiction whose truth is more truthful because it is more universal, than the ordinary world of random sense experience.

"Impression" became a key word in Howells' critical vocabulary from the very beginning of his attempts to find his way towards a theory of fiction. So often does it occur in his writing, and in the writing of Hamlin Garland, that one realizes the strong bonds that existed, not between the literary realists and the painters who went by the name, but between the literary realists and the group of artists known as "impressionists." Howells and Garland both felt that the techniques of this school of painters was like their own—the ignoring of photographic representation in favor of emphasizing those visual aspects which could suggest the truthful aspect of the complex whole. Howells was attracted by literary impressionism as early as 1870 when he noted that Björnstjerne Björnson, in tales like *Arne*, could represent a situation or a character by "a few distinct touches," and could make "one expressive particular serve for all introduction and explanation." He used the language of painting, in the same year, to find fault with the pre-Raphaelitism of Hans Christian Andersen which caused him to "spend so much time upon the beautiful rendering of particulars in his pictures, as to lose his control over the whole effect." "The whole effect" was the concern, Howells believed, of both writer and painter. And the author who would catch this total truthfulness must, like his fellow who worked in oils, highlight certain significant details, suppress others, rescue from obscurity the incident which is typical, tone down to recessive gray the color which is sensational, but unrepresentative.

And the "whole effect" of American life was, for Howells, an effect of the cheerful, small round of ordinary life. It is incontestable, he thought, that life, by the very definition of "normal," must consist largely of usual commonplace events. For if the abnormal occurred with enough frequency, it would become "normal," and new aberrations would be considered abnormal. So a corollary of the belief that the writer should select his material to present a truthful impression of life was the conviction that he must concern himself with normality and abnormality, with the common and the uncommon, in somewhat the same proportion as they occur in living. Howells' lifelong concern with the right proportion led Frank Norris to say that Howells never dealt with anything other than "tea-cup tragedies," forgetting that in his works are accidental deaths, a suicide, a clubbing, a shooting. Not a long list of deeds of violence, and certainly nothing to compare with what might be found in one chapter of many a modern work. But the life Howells lived and knew, the life of peaceful, middle-class America in its most optimistic period, certainly included no greater proportion of abnormalities, and Howells believed that a literature which was untrue to this proportion of the tranquil to the violent would be untrue to life. "Realism," he told an interviewer, did not mean "preoccupation with the common things of life" to the exclusion of the abnormal, for it "makes all things its province, the uncommon as well as the every-day affairs of human existence; tragedy, disaster, and crisis as well as the small round of daily events." But it was in the right proportion of the "small round of events" to the climaxes that they lead up to and away from that Howells saw the essence of the realistic method. "Realism," he said again, "holds that they [the daily events], and not the momentary arrests of life, should be the most important in the fiction that aims to reproduce that life with faithfulness."

This view, of course, did not impress a new generation; and an age captivated by the discovery of psychoanalysis has been deeply, almost exclusively occupied with the abnormal as a clue to the operation of the human mind; the psychology of the "id" has been the part of the Freudian theory most interesting to moderns, and readers and writers have turned to the primitive as that condition in which the human could be most truthfully observed. Nowhere could we find a better definition of the difference between the age of Howells and the succeeding age of Americans. For if Howells had had the terminology at his disposal, he would have answered that the "super-ego" is what makes humans human; for him, "man" meant, by definition, "civilized man" who had patiently and laboriously climbed from the abyss of barbarism, by the hard paths of manners, conventions, decorums, and laws. Howells' affinity was with the eighteenth century, and he was the inheritor of none of the sentimental primitivism which also had its inception in the age which was primarily the Age of Reason. When William Henry Bishop asked him about the uses of moments of stress in fiction, Howells told him that man under dominance of passion, stripped of his reason, was not man at all, but animal. "Supposing there were a fire in the street," he said, "the people in the houses would run out in terror or amazement. All finer shades of character would be lost; they would be, for the nonce, alike in their common animal impulse. No," he continued, "to truly study character, you must study men in the lesser and ordinary circumstances of their lives."

The normal and the usual, then, would be selected in proportions that would indicate the true balance of life between tension and relaxation. If the life one observed produced a freak or a coincidence, the writer should edit it out of his fiction; for in fiction, he said at the very beginning of his career, and maintained this position until the end, "the true artist will shun the use even of real events if they are of an improbable character." He defended John De Forest from the charge of rearranging his materials about the war, declaring that such rearrangement constituted a definition of art. Thomas Bailey Aldrich, he thought, could be attacked on many grounds, but not on failing of an absolute fidelity to nature, for "it is well to remember that a novel is not a true narrative." These were statements made in the early 1870's, and he held to the ideas they expressed throughout his life. "Every writer of fiction," he declared, "creates the world where his characters live . . . giving their habitat stricter limits than his own." He had insisted, earlier in the quotation, that "of course . . . it is vital to him to believe he is representing the world where he lives himself." But by giving his created world the stricter limits that come from selection and arrangement, Howells felt, and the writers of his age felt with him, he was creating a "microcosm," a "miniature" in which the drama of the whole race plays itself "in a moment, in a corner, as it plays itself through all the history of the world."

11. "Morality" in Realism

"I could not have palpitating divans in my stories. . . ."
—Howells

Selection and arrangement so that the truth might be told about American life. But to what purpose? Was the writer to become, as Taine suggested, only an observer, no more commenting upon the rightness or wrongness of human actions than the scientist would blame or praise the reactions of chemicals in his glass retorts? In posing these questions we press close to crucial matters; for the incursions of science into the realm of human values has been one of the primary concerns of our times. But in trying to find their answers, we must distinguish carefully between two completely different meanings of the word "morality" when used in this connection. Using the word in one sense, the nineteenth century feared the realistic movement had too little morality; using it in quite another, moderns have charged it had too much. And by and large the most strident indictment has been on the latter count; for morality, in Anglo-American culture, has come to be peculiarly identified with only one of the deadly sins, and "morals," or lack of them, have been associated with good or evil action in only one phase of human conduct—the sexual. And even here, the meaning of "morality" has become yet more restrictive. Far from meaning what is "good" and what is "bad" in the conduct of the sexes towards each other, it has come to mean simply the treatment of these relations with what the observer considers suitable frankness, and "moralist" has become a pejorative; an author who treats sex with the proper degree of openness is considered emancipated; an author who seems reticent in these matters is dismissed as a "moralist," usually a "Victorian moralist" and a prude.

This has certainly been the fate of the age. By 1895 Howells was falling from favor, and by 1928 he had completed the fall, and during the descent of his reputation no more damaging accusation has been made than that of his prudery. "Sissy," "bourgeois," "dull," "timid," "respectable," "narrow,"—these epithets have been applied to his general choice and treatment of materials, and hovering over all of them is the aura of a Puritanism which considers sex the only field for moral investigation. This trend of derogation on "moral" grounds started at the beginning of the 1890's, and its increasing tempo was an index to the corresponding weakening of the beliefs which formed the intellectual structure of the age of Howells.

From the standpoint of our age, of course, Howells *was* a prude; not a hopeless one, but nevertheless a man of easily offended sensibilities; were he to appear among us we would dismiss him as impossibly neglectful of the physical involvements of love. The best possible summary of his personal attitude towards relations between the sexes is contained in his own description of one of his early introductions to sex, an incident which is not only important for what it tells, but for the fact that Howells himself told it. A seamstress in the Dayton of his youth had been seduced by one of the prominent local citizens, and her betrayal was common knowledge. Many, however, took pity on her, among them Howells' mother, and she not only employed the girl, but invited her to live as one of her family. Howells was then twelve, obviously tormented by the stirrings of adolescence, and he acted in a way that remained an ache in his memory to the end of his days. He began a persecution of the girl in the cause of "social purity," as he later called it ironically, refusing to pass her a plate at the table, or take one from her, avoiding her whenever possible; refusing to speak when avoidance was impossible, taking upon himself the role of "society incarnate" in the attitudes which he knew society took towards such as she. The poor girl finally broke down and begged to be told why he treated her so, and left the young moralist with a bitter shame which he never forgot.

The incident tells us the worst about Howells; his telling it, his willingness to show it publicly and his bitter distaste for the part he played in it tell us the best. The worst about Howells and sex was that he was no deviate from the social norm with its taboos on public discussion of the body and its functions. There are no plural breasts (as Malcolm Cowley puts it) in any of his works (or for that matter few, if any English or American novels of general circulation in the period, including those of James and Twain). And he partook personally of much of the unwillingness of his times to face the naked facts, either literally or figuratively. He remembered seeing as a boy a painting of nudes and felt that a youth might well shrink ashamed from it. His longing was always for the "cleanly respectabilities" and he was self-admittedly "very Victorian" in his preference of decency over indecency. When twenty-three and beginning to go out into the society of Columbus, Ohio, he fell in love with a pale girl in a blue dress, but promptly fell out of love when he saw her at the next party in a low-necked gown. When he wrote fiction, he felt that his books should be suitable for the entire family, and he was delighted that he need not fear to see his son curled upon the lounge reading the "love-makingest" parts of one of his novels; for this reason alone, he said, he could not have any "palpitating divans" in his stories. And sometimes, though not frequently, he allowed an author's frankness to be the occasion for a critical rebuke.

But it is from the perspective of the present that these appear the thoughts and actions of a prude; when seen against a background of their times and atmosphere, they appear in not so unpleasantly pure a light. We need hardly be reminded that this was an era, in America and in England, of almost complete public suppression of references to the body. Whitman paid for his boldness with almost thirty years of obscurity; just before the beginning of this age, Hawthorne went to Italy and recorded his conviction that the modern sculptor should either clothe his figures or let the art perish. When Oliver Wendell Holmes wrote a scene around a dining table in *Elsie Venner*, he had a young man "of the more dashing sort" daringly ask one of the girls present if she would like a bit of the "–under-limb"; for the word "leg," even when used in allusion to a bird, would remind a lady too bluntly of her own body with its unmentionable appurtenances. Even the ankle was considered a daring public topic, and the view of one a cause of indecent titillation. "It is a confounded pretty foot," exclaimed a young gallant in the sentimental novel *Ruth Hall;* "I always put my coat on in the front entry, about the time she goes upstairs, to get a peep at it." From these low-water marks of moral temper, the age proceeded to recede even further into the veiling of physical facts by either euphemism or suppression. When Dr. E. H. Clarke lectured in 1873 and alluded to physiological differences between the sexes which made different kinds of education advisable for boys and girls, Oliver Wendell Holmes questioned the propriety of a public treatment of so delicate a subject. In the next decade, Howells wrote a notice of Zola's *La Terre*, and his editor asked him if he didn't think they had been a little daring in printing it, and added that it would be well to draw the line a little this side of such absolutely disgusting books.

And what of Howells' two great contemporaries, Mark Twain and Henry James? There is plenty of evidence that Mark was more than happy to profit by the magnificent drive that bawdiness has always lent to humor; he would report hearing a lady lecturer who stood behind a small table "with slender legs and no drawers" and then add, "The table, understand me." Or he would make a speech in praise of woman, and offer her the toast: "She mends our clothes, she sews on our buttons, she bears our children . . ." and then, as an afterthought, "ours as a general thing." But *not in literature.* He was, as Bernard DeVoto has said, almost "lustfully hypersensitive" to any allusion to sex in print. There is only one suggestion of an illicit relationship in all his works, and the act had occurred before the opening of his narrative, and only its results are visible. Out of his thirty-nine notebooks, DeVoto reports, there are only three entries that deal with sex, and one of them does not contemplate its use for fiction. And this man who had known Mississippi River towns and mining camps of the West could say of his native Hannibal, with a straight face, that matters of the flesh "were not even dreamed of in that society, much less spoken of and referred to as possibilities."

Howells stood between his two great contemporaries, Mark Twain and Henry James, so unlike each other save in two respects. One was their firm friendship with him. And the only other quality Twain and James shared was a willingness to avoid the physical aspects of sex in literature. James, the antithesis of Twain, with a cosmopolite's easy acceptance of human difference and human weakness, understood equally with Twain and Howells the necessity of writing for an audience with a location in cultural time and space, and with peculiar areas of sensitivity. His was not as wholehearted a capitulation. He chafed under the restrictions which Howells and Twain accepted without question. There was some bitterness in the words he put into the mouth of an editor in "John Delavoy": ". . . With the question of sex in any degree . . . we have nothing whatever to do. If you want to know what our public won't stand, there you have it." But James never treated such matters in his fiction save with suitable indirection and ambiguity. When Paul Bourget mentioned to him a situation in which a young woman committed suicide because she was sure her mother had taken lovers, James knew that to "make something of it" he would have to "modify it essentially" as he could not, and did not "particularly want to, depict in an American magazine, a woman carrying on adulteries under her daughter's eyes." He recalled another potential "germ" of a story that he had heard at a dinner party, an incident involving a young lord who, despairing of his hopeless love for a married woman, became engaged for convenience. The husband of his love had then died, and he was faced with the problem of what to do about his fiancée. One way of resolving the story, James thought, might be to have the fiancée agree to a *vie à trois*, with Lord Stafford marrying her and having Lady Grosvenor as a mistress. But this was a solution, he realized, which he could adopt only if he "were a Frenchman or a naturalist." Being neither, he had to drop the idea completely. He made the point about the necessity of keeping one's audience in mind more specifically in his early ruminations over the tale that was to become *The Wings of the Dove*. The environment for which he was producing this story, he knew, had to be kept in mind; if he were writing "for a French public," he could simply have Kate Croy be the mistress of Merton Densher and "it would be a question of his taking on the dying girl for a time—having a temporary liaison with her." But this would not do, he saw, for an Anglo-Saxon audience. "One can do so little with English adultery," he felt; for it is essentially unaesthetic, so "undermined by our immemorial tradition of original freedom of choice, and by our practically universal acceptance of divorce." And when he wrote the final draft of *The Wings of the Dove*, he made it clear enough that the attachment between Merton Densher and Milly Theale was a spiritual one.

Against this background, Howells' "prudery" does not seem to glare so intensely. He rarely allowed indecency or even scatology to interfere with his literary passions and his critical recommendations. At a time when the editor of one of America's two leading intellectual magazines was saying that Zola could not be noticed in his publication, Howells was not only noticing him, but reading everything of his he could lay his hands on; and his final judgment was that Zola was intensely a moralist. For Howells was wise enough to see that morality is not simply a matter of sex but of all the relations involved in man's struggles to achieve social maturity, and Zola's books, he said, were "alive with his sense of what was wrong and false and bad." He greatly admired Defoe, and thought *Roxana* "one of the best written books in the language." He wrote Robert Herrick that his women seemed to him "wonderfully well done—the worse, alas! the better." And when he complained of Herrick's treatment of sex, it was not because Herrick treated it, but because he seemed to say that the overcoming of reason by passion would not be followed by retribution in the real world, and this, as we shall see, violated Howells' deepest beliefs about the meaning of the actual world of experience. He meanwhile encouraged Garland to recognize man's brute instinct for woman, because he felt, in his waning years, that sexual relations constituted an important ground "through which the pioneer must break his way"; and then he added: "but it may be it is time the way were broken." And he repeated this prediction in one of the last book reviews he wrote —of William McFee's *Casuals of the Sea.* Here he restated the necessity of a widening point of view in fiction, saying that the novel would be shocking if one viewed it in the "old-fashioned" way; but the modern reader, he said, simply asks "why . . . look at it that way."

And looked at not in "that way," but in the light of a modern willingness to understand events in terms of their contexts and relations, Howells' prudery seems not so damning. And the testimony of readers and reviewers during the first twenty years of his career helps further in placing his reticence in proper perspective. Difficult as it is to believe, it is nevertheless incontestable that Howells often shocked his contemporaries! For example, in *A Chance Acquaintance* Howells portrayed a Boston snob who fell in love with (and embraced) a pert and lovely Ohio girl who then refused marriage because she knew she could never be happy with so class-conscious a member of the Brahmin caste, and some reviewers were intensely displeased with this conclusion. One wrote that the work was "so provoking . . . that it is impossible to come to any other conclusion than that Mr. Howell[s] wrote his novel experimentally." A critic for another magazine admitted that the ending was truthful, and inevitable; nevertheless the reviewer added that he (or could it have been "she") "could not help feeling that we are deliberately cheated out of a marriage festival and that pleasurable emotion which one feels at sight of a bride."

Several years later, Henry James alluded to the discussion aroused by *A Chance Acquaintance*, which featured "young Arbuton's famous repudiation of the object of his refined affections," and went on to say that an episode in Howells' most recent work would probably provoke as much controversy. This episode in *A Foregone Conclusion* was the climax of the one-sided romance of the beautiful American girl, Florida Vervain, and the Catholic priest, Don Ippolito, when the girl, horrified by the tragedy of his position, took the young cleric's head in her hands, and pressed it to her bosom; James predicted that "Miss Vervain's seizing the young priest's head and caressing it" would cause much discussion; and the same month, the *Nation* reported that it already "has had the good fortune to create something like a scandal." When Howells' *Lady of the Aroostook* appeared in 1879, *Scribner's Monthly* was shocked and disgusted by parts of it. Today we find nothing but purity in the story of a young girl who finds herself the only female passenger on a transatlantic sailing, but the contemporary reviewer talked about the "error of taste," the "disagreeable fullness," and the "want of healthy mental action in a writer who habitually takes such a gloomy view of external nature." And the reaction to *A Modern Instance* is even more revealing of the way in which we may misjudge the effect of an author upon the Victorians. The novel, the first complete treatment of a broken home in serious American fiction, traced the decay of Marcia Gaylord's marriage to Bartley Hubbard, and Howells convincingly portrayed the breakdown of a union based only on physical attraction. One Grace D. Pattan of Bangor, Maine, was moved to write a letter to the editor of the New York *Tribune* about it. "The whole thing from beginning to end is revolting," the angry lady wrote. When an anonymous letter answered the irate reader from Maine, it admitted the novel's "pitiless reality," but defended the "sordidness" of the book on grounds of its social value. But a critic in the *Century* agreed with Miss Pattan. "Man gains a knowledge of anatomy by stepping aside into the dissection room," this reviewer declared, "but the great majority of readers could forget anatomy, especially morbid anatomy, and be the better for it." And then, a little plaintively, the critic demanded if it were not possible that Howells was giving the public entirely too little of "the sweet fragrance of blossom time?"

The appearance of *The Minister's Charge* apparently provoked another small outburst of protest. One of the loudest voices in the cry was that of the *Literary World* which indignantly protested its own liberality but claimed that this time Howells had gone too far. "We are ready to admit the democratic principle in fiction," its spokesman wrote. "We believe that no phase of life is too common, too rude, or too vulgar to be seriously considered by the novelist. But," he went on, "Mr. Howells in *The Minister's Charge*, is more than democratic, he is anarchical." By this time Howells was complaining that "every 'half-bred rogue that groomed his mother's cow' reproaches me for introducing him to low company." And it would seem that the "reticent" Howells was regarded as *avant-garde* and outspoken by his contemporaries.

Part of the reason for this strange reaction has been observed: it was an age of concealment, an age in which it took very little frankness to be regarded as vulgar and anarchical. But one feels that there must be other reasons for such pained outcries at what seem to us the mild and inoffensive novels of Howells. Perhaps there were literary conventions in operation at the time to which a modern reader is insensitive, since his are a different set of symbols relating to sex—different, but still conventional, for in no area of the representation of life does convention operate more strongly. In dealing with this most basic of human drives, surrounded by all of the tabus a culture erects around it, the writer is playing with emotional explosive; it must be handled with the greatest of care or it breaks out of its walls and blows up over the entire story, blurring other nuances and details. It is obvious, further, that save in textbooks, the sexual act can rarely be described accurately in letters, but must always be conveyed by more or less indirection. The tendency to less indirection has been marked in recent years, and formed, as we have seen, one of the newer paths which Howells admitted literature would have to explore. But nevertheless, in the modern novel, the indirection is there. It is a convention between reader and writer that sexual acts should be represented by certain euphemisms, certain metaphors, or even certain omissions. "Sleep with," "be intimate with," "know" (in the biblical sense)—the list is interminable. Comparisons of states of mind of the protagonists with certain elemental conditions implying the penting and release of wind, water or fire is one of the metaphorical conventions. Or perhaps the author conducts the reader up to certain points of intimacy and then begins a new paragraph or a new chapter; the reader agrees to the convention that between the end of the last sentence and the beginning of the next, a sexual act has been completed. It is another modern convention that a small amount of such sexual activity is sufficient to represent the "normal" sex life of the characters in a story, a life which we know is much more full of sexual expression than even the most outspoken modern novel. It is surprising how long a way a little fictional sex goes; it sets up such strong emotional vibrations that it forms an undertone for the entire book, and a half-dozen such encounters spread over three hundred pages is sufficient to make the reader see all else in the work through the red spectacles of luridity.

Now, the conventions in Howells' time were far more strict, as we have seen. The society he knew transformed all its expression of sexual activity into decorous outward symbols. And authors, in order to talk about sex, had to use these symbols in order to talk about it publicly at all. What was the outward symbol of mating during this era? There is strong reason to believe that the meeting of the lips of the opposite sexes, the kiss, in fine, as Henry James would say, was the symbol for the Victorian which had the area of emotional reverberation associated with the act of sex itself, and the giving of the lips by the woman, the taking of the kiss by the man, seems to have been regarded as the act of reception and possession which joined the flesh as one.

This is difficult to prove, of course. But the evidence for it is strong. Take a novel published by a first-rate English author as late as 1908, when Howells was already suggesting that a more outspoken treatment of sexual relations was in order. It is a novel peculiarly pertinent because its theme is the attitude of society towards sex. It was E. M. Forster's *Room with a View*, and in it, old Mr. Emerson "with the face of a saint who understands," tells the muddled heroine: "love is of the body; not the body, but of the body. . . . Ah! for a little directness to liberate the soul!" Yet in this work, with this theme, what crucial incident did Forster choose as the pivotal situation of his plot? It was obviously a situation to which Forster knew both his characters and the contemporary society which they represented would react with all the sensitivities associated with the full act of sexual possession. And what was it? In the hills above Florence, an English girl had been separated from a group of sightseers and had come upon a young man to whom she had previously felt both attracted and from whom she had also retreated in alarm: "George had turned at the sound of her arrival. For a moment he contemplated her, as one who had fallen out of heaven. He saw radiant joy in her face, he saw the flowers beat against her dress in blue waves. The bushes above them closed. He stepped quickly forward and kissed her.

"Before she could speak, almost before she could feel, a voice called, 'Lucy, Lucy! Lucy!' The silence of life had been broken by Miss Bartlett who stood brown against the view." And from this point on, Forester treats the situation as of that compromising kind which, if known, would arouse in Lucy's proper fiancé the anger of the jealous male.

The care with which the two major American authors of the period immediately preceding Forster's novel had avoided this symbol supports the contention that it was an act which, when reported in literature, had serious sexual overtones. The kiss is rare in the works of Henry James, and rarer in those of Mark Twain. For Twain and his Hannibal society the touch of the lips had all the strangely uncomfortable associations of intimacy;

Dixon Wecter reports that in an unpublished work, "Huck Finn and Tom Sawyer among the Indians," Huck was overwhelmed with embarrassment at the endearments between brothers and sisters of a family with whom he was travelling, and could not keep from blushing for two or three days when he recalled their kissing; but he mentally apologized for them because they were uncivilized, and just "didn't know no better." This recalls Huck's repulsion at the embracing of Mary Jane Wilks by the Dauphin who poses as her uncle. As always, these fictional incidents were autobiographical and represented the feelings of a man who had been raised in a family where no warmer gesture than a handshake was ever exchanged save on the occasion of the death of the second son, Benjamin.

In the light of this convention, the reaction to Howells' work becomes more understandable; the society for which he wrote obviously expected the outward symbol of sexual possession to be treated with circumspection, and, if portrayed at all, to be followed by marriage. But in Howells' novels, the ring did not always follow the kiss. Kitty, in *A Chance Acquaintance*, rejected Arbuton and incensed the reviewers; Florida Vervain embraced the priest, and the critics cringed; Marcia Gaylord and Bartley Hubbard did not make a go of their marriage, and poor Miss Pattan of Bangor was prostrated with lacerated sensitivities. In *Letters Home*, Howells developed a love affair between the hero and a girl obviously beneath him in everything but sweet good will; and he rejected sentimental morality by marrying him to an educated heiress—this despite the fact that the first love affair had proceeded to the stage of frequent embraces.

Howells played somewhat daringly, then, with the outward symbol of sexuality; and in many ways he seemed to have selected those incidents of courtship which affected the subconscious sensitivities of his readers, just as the convention of the kiss played upon their conscious; that he himself was probably but dimly aware of the full meanings of the actions he chose to depict is not the point; what is important is that he sensed the right thing to have his men and women do that might convey the undertones of the physical basis for their attraction. What might have moved Miss Pattan, for example, even more than the general theme of

A Modern Instance, was the tremor of meaning aroused by descriptions like that of the lovelorn Marcia, sinking to her knees with a yearning that was almost a sickness, and kissing the doorknob which was still warm from her departed lover's hand. Or the scene in *Silas Lapham* has been pointed out as another example of the instinct with which Howells chose the right sexual symbolism. Seated upon a trestle in her father's unfinished house and anxious to attract the handsome Tom Corey, Penelope Lapham began to play with the curled shavings of wood that lay at her feet, thrusting the point of her parasol into them; then the scene continued:

"She found another shaving within reach of her parasol, and began poking that with it, and trying to follow it through its folds. Corey watched her a while.

" 'You seem to have a great passion for playing with shavings,' he said. 'Is it a new one?'

" 'New what?'

" 'Passion.'

" 'I don't know,' she said, dropping her eyelids, and keeping on with her effort. She looked shyly aslant at him. 'Perhaps you don't approve of playing with shavings?'

" 'Oh yes, I do. I admire it very much. But it seems rather difficult. I've a great ambition to put my foot on the shaving's tail and hold it for you.'

" 'Well,' said the girl.

" 'Thank you,' said the young man. He did so, and now she ran her parasol point easily through it. They looked at each other and laughed. 'That was wonderful. Would you like to try another?' he asked."

Now all the foregoing is not meant to suggest that by the standards of our own times or any other era, Howells was outspoken. Far from it. What it does suggest is that within the framework of the conventions and symbols of their times, Howells and the writers around him worked honestly with the materials of the visible, conscious world of human relations with which they were familiar. The life they wanted to portray was the expressed life, rather than the unexpressed, and their business was therefore with the outward social signs of sexual behavior which their admittedly restrained society produced. In 1904 an interviewer asked Howells if perhaps "the superficial treatment of love in current American fiction . . . was but a realistic reflection of the facts." And Howells answered: "Yes. One might put it that way." It must be remembered, too, that the age was interested in truthfully depicting the normal, the average, the general, not the eccentric. And most important of all, we must be reminded that they saw that it was not the simple portrayal or failure to portray the body and its drives which made ultimately for morality or immorality, but the way in which this material was handled. Restraint or lack of restraint could be either moral or immoral, depending upon the author's treatment. Howells' protest against the flood of historical romances which were submerging realism at the turn of the century was directed largely against their "immorality"—despite the fact that they always got their lovers married at all hazards; this was untrue to human experience, Howells declared, and was therefore a "ludicrous immorality." And this intelligent reaction strikes the proper note upon which to embark upon an investigation of the second, and more important kind of "moral charges" advanced against the realists.

12. Pragmatism and Realism

The charge of a lack of morality was made most cogently at the height of Howells' career by Hamilton Wright Mabie. Howells, the leader of the realistic movement, Mabie declared, took positivism as his philosophy and the scientific method as his model, and made the unholy marriage of science and art. For if art tries to become the tool of science, content to show what life looks like and not what it means, it abdicates its most important function—showing us what is good and evil in human actions. Was this charge true? Did Howells and the American realists relinquish the moral function of literature? If we can discover the answer to that question, it may help us to understand the wrenching of our own souls, caught between the testimony of our senses and the promptings of our hearts.

The answer lay in the sea-change of positive philosophy as it came to America. For American authors, and then American philosophers, felt that hope is the emotion that can save and despair the sin that can eternally damn; and hope and faith have set a trap for despair in the metaphor of the "laboratory"; for were there no faith that, given the same things under the same conditions and operated on by the same forces there will follow the same results—were there not this faith there would be no experiment. This kind of belief in the meaning of the world of things was a necessity for the American realist. He felt that the factual world he was portraying was a world that could be believed in, a world, with all its imperfections, which was permeated with morality; and he believed that the purpose of his fiction was to portray that morality and, by picturing it, to help men to understand it.

In describing this moral scheme in their fiction, De Forest and Twain and, above all, Howells were constructing the imaginative forerunners and counterparts of the general philosophical attitude known as pragmatism. Pragmatism, "a new name for some old ways of thinking," was coined by Charles Sanders Peirce in 1878 and lay almost unnoticed until William James brought it to public attention in 1898; by then it was evident that the term was a convenient designation for a collection of tendencies that were already widespread in American culture, and that the times were ready for its reception as the label for the dominant American philosophy.

Part of the reason the time was ripe for it at the end of the century was that for thirty years the novels of the realists had been reflecting their society's growing pragmatic "sense of what life honestly and deeply means," its way of "seeing and feeling the total push and pressure of the cosmos." This sense, first of all, turned away from "abstraction . . . from bad *a priori* reasons, from fixed principles, closed systems, and pretended absolutes. . . ." To expose the "bad *a priori*" that the savage and the untutored were necessarily noble was the motive behind Eggleston's realistic portraits in *The Hoosier Schoolmaster* and *The Circuit Rider.*

The falsity of the assumption that the agrarian life of the West was inevitably the good life was the subject of Hamlin Garland's *Main-Travelled Roads* and *Jason Edwards*. The "pretended absolutes" of the South's chivalric ideals were the targets for John De Forest's criticism in *Miss Ravenel's Conversion*, for Tourgée in his reconstruction novels, for Mark Twain in *Huckleberry Finn* and *Life on the Mississippi*. A criticism of unexamined "fixed principles" and closed systems of morality was the motivation for Howells' fiction. Misguided Puritan devotion to duty was the principle he challenged in *A Fearful Responsibility*, *Dr. Breen's Practice*, and *An Imperative Duty*. Romantic codes of behavior between the sexes were the fixed principles he attacked in *Indian Summer* and *Letters Home*. The Gospel of Wealth of the Gilded Age was the pretended absolute he challenged in his "economic" novels: *Annie Kilburn*, *A Hazard of New Fortunes*, *The Quality of Mercy*, and *The World of Chance*.

Pragmatic philosophy, after rejecting the Absolute, went on to affirm experience as the test of truth, and, indeed, as truth itself. Peirce had pointed out that our beliefs adjust themselves to the outside world of fact, to the broad course of experience. James later emphasized that pragmatism represented the empiricist attitude, "looking away from first things, principles, 'categories,' . . . and of looking towards last things, fruits, consequences, facts." Herbert Spencer, he said, called out reverence, in spite of his weaknesses, because the "noise of facts resounds through all his chapters." The noise of facts had been resounding, too, for thirty years in the novel. At the very outset of his career, Howells had proclaimed the rights of the "earth of things" to the attention of the artist: "We shall never have a poetry of our own till we get over this absurd reluctance from facts, till we make the ideal embrace and include the real, till we consent to face the music in our simple common names, and put Smith into a lyric and Jones in a tragedy." From then on, he and the realists devoted their craft to an attempt at representing, through the impressionistic technique, the truth about the "earth of things" they knew best—their contemporary America.

Rejecting the absolute, embracing the flux and change of experience, the pragmatists faced the probability that "truth independent . . . truth no longer malleable to human need; truth incorrigible" was nowhere to be found. The true and hence the good are not states which men can seek and find and, having found them, in which they could rest secure; rather they are processes which are constantly changing. Ideas, said James, become true "just in so far as they help us to get into satisfactory relation with other parts of our experience." This was the idea of the true and the good which De Forest and Twain had been describing in their novels. That which works, taking into account the ignorance of the freedmen and the difficulties of reconstruction—that will be the right way, Dr. Ravenel declared. Not the code of the South, but the code which worked for him and for Jim, was the code Huck Finn found the true one. The kind of behavior which made for the least pain to the humans involved—that will be the right sexual behavior, Howells said in his fiction; and in his criticism, he warned that "the same thing may be admissible at one time and deplorable at another."

Above all, it was in temperament, the true mother of philosophies, according to William James, that the realists had been most clearly pragmatic. Theirs had been the middle ground between a crass naturalism which would see man as the hopeless sport of external forces and an idealism which would turn its gaze away from the changing world of fact to a world of eternal essence. We can study God only by studying His creation, was the essence of James' position. Howells had been studying His creation for a generation. The buoyancy of William James let him feel that the world could be made a better place by the application of human reason to its problems; this was the same hopefulness which motivated the development of satiric realism. And this buoyancy, for both literary realist and philosophical pragmatist, was no saccharine acquiescence in the world as it was. Instead it was a mediation between a pessimism that, in the words of James, thinks "the salvation of the world impossible," and an optimism which "thinks the world's salvation inevitable." James called this middle ground "meliorism," an attitude which "treats salvation . . . as a possibility." The realistic novelists were all meliorists, and a sense of the possibilities of a world which can be made better by the commitments of reasonable men informs their fiction from *The Gilded Age* to *A Hazard of New Fortunes.*

No wonder, then, that by 1907 William James could say that pragmatism suddenly appeared to be everywhere. For the speculum of the novelist had caught, reflected, and intensified a culture's growing sense of what life honestly and deeply meant. The premises of pragmatism as they came to be expressed by William James had been the premises behind realism in fiction.

13. Rejection of Moralizing

The pragmatic mode of fiction practiced by Howells and his followers began with a rejection of any absolute standards of good and evil. The basic axiom of the realistic view of morality was that there could be no moralizing in the novel. Howells consistently attacked preaching and sermonizing, and the imposition of a pre-formulated moral scheme upon the characters of a fiction and upon their actions.

Those authors who sermonized, Howells would not suffer; those who tried to make their literature servant of their neat ethical schemes he accused of treason to their calling. In 1867 he shook his head in dismay at the didacticism of Henry Ward Beecher's *Norwood* and at the "ruthlessness" with which the author preached; in 1915 he wrote Paul Kester that the best thing about his novel was his refusal to take sides overtly, and his willingness to let his characters and their actions speak for themselves. And between these two dates, Howells consistently objected to literature which preached a sermon and hence became dull, which is to say, became not literature. "His moral would have been good if his art had been true," Howells said of Charles Reade, and what he meant was that Reade should keep his *a priori* ideas of good and evil out of his books, and let the books speak for themselves. Galdós, whom he introduced to the American public, he called a transitionary rather than an achieved artist, for his novels were "tendencious," a word he used again and again to indict the weaknesses of didactic fiction. But Ibsen, for him, was the greatest artist and the greatest moralist of all, for he never preached, never polemicized but simply presented the nettles of social behavior as he found them growing, not dried and labelled for the ethicists' collection. Howells had nothing against sermons, as sermons; he simply objected to them when they masqueraded as fiction. For like the other arts, Howells felt that literature could, nay must, help those whose life is depicted only "indirectly"; for when fiction became "hortatory," it was in the danger of becoming "dull, that is to say, suicidal."

14. *The Gilded Age*, *Huckleberry Finn*, and *The Rise of Silas Lapham*

"Morality penetrates all things . . ."
—Howells

The morality of the realists, then, was built upon what appears a paradox—morality with an abhorrence of moralizing. Their ethical beliefs called, first of all, for a rejection of any scheme of moral behavior imposed, from without, upon the characters of fiction and their actions. Yet Howells always claimed for his works a deep moral purpose. What was it? It was based upon three propositions: that life, social life as lived in the world Howells knew, was valuable, and was permeated with morality; that its continued health depended upon the use of human reason to overcome the anarchic selfishness of human passions; that an objective portrayal of human life, by art, will illustrate the superior value of social, civilized man, of human reason over animal passion and primitive ignorance.

The first axiom—that social life has value—was an unquestioned article of faith during this period; when it came to be seriously questioned, the age of Howells was at an end. For that age had a faith in the physical world and its meaning, a faith that, in the endless complexities, in the cracks and joints of materiality, there was a moral force which held the palpable together and gave it its meaning. Indeed, this was Howells' own metaphor: "Morality penetrates all things, it is the soul of all things." He wrote these words at the time he was reading Tolstoy, for his introduction to the great Russian in 1886 was like a religious experience to him. What had been dark and dim before—the reason for his absorption with the common, the familiar, the low—suddenly was illuminated.

And notwithstanding all his wild flings at the iniquities of man, Mark Twain, too, had this same faith in the essential morality permeating his social structure. A scene he and Warner wrote into *The Gilded Age* is almost a definition of this complex moral vision of the realist who believed he was writing a species of "objective" social history, but at the same time was writing a commentary upon that history which was based upon its essentially moral meaning. True to the realistic method as we have seen it, Twain and his collaborator took this scene from life. A woman named Laura D. Fair had, one day in 1870, bought a revolver in a shop near her home in San Francisco, had taken the ferry across the bay to Oakland, had waited until the train discharged her middle-aged lover who was returning with his recently reconciled wife and children, had stalked him until he was aboard the ferry and seated with his family about him, and then had walked up to him and put a bullet into his chest. She was tried for murder, pleaded momentary insanity, and finally was acquitted. Twain was so repelled by this example of mass unreason that he wrote the major subplot of *The Gilded Age* around Laura Hawkins, betrayed by her middle-aged lover, Colonel Phelps. Just as Laura Fair had hunted down her victim, Laura Hawkins followed Phelps to a New York hotel and shot him down under the same unambiguously premeditated circumstances. The Laura of fiction was tried and freed on the same grounds as the real Laura. There was a great scene of rejoicing in the courtroom as the women swarmed about the successful defense attorney and embraced him in a scene, the authors said, which went down in the annals of New York as "the kissing of Braham." From this point on, we must watch the fictional handling of the incident carefully. The authors described what followed: the judge rapped his gavel, and reasonably declared that the accused must be placed in an institution since it had been found that, while in a deranged condition, she had taken a life. Laura was led away to a hospital for the criminally insane, and sank back upon the cot as the door shut upon her terrible despair. But then the authors cried "wait!" And they stepped aside to tell the "dear reader" that this is what would have happened had they been writing a novel; for, they declared, the author of a novel would have had to arrange his material towards this reasonable and moral outcome; however, they were not, they said, writing a novel, but were writing history, and so they would have to reluctantly report that Laura Hawkins did not go to the insane asylum, but was driven home in a carriage amid the cheers of her admirers and left free to follow her career as a momentarily popular heroine.

Let us stop for a moment and consider the implications of this extraordinary little piece of artistic "business." The authors seem to have said, first, that fiction has an obligation to morality and to reason; that it must show the readers the way the good life should be lived. Then they declared that their work is not fiction, but history, and what they were describing was the history of their own society, a society ruled not by reason but by unreason, and therefore one in which good and evil were not followed by some kind of reward or punishment.

But we must go further before we accept this superficial analysis. For the plain fact is that Twain and Warner were not writing history, but were writing fiction. Laura Hawkins was like Laura Fair, but was not Laura Fair; her story was taken from life, but it was life selected and arranged. And to what did this arrangement eventually lead? To a scene where Laura Hawkins, reaching the depth of human misery, feeling herself worse than worthless, sells herself to be scorned and mocked by the vulgar in an almost empty auditorium, and wounded deeply with the knowledge of her own uselessness, totters off the stage to die. So in their novel which, like all realistic novels pressed close to the actual, there was still the arrangement of the "real" for moral instruction. Indeed, it was the essence of satiric realism that it should so scoff at the iniquities of society, that it should try to show Americans wherein their lives were leading to error, not because the realists hated the life they were criticizing, but because they loved it, and therefore wanted to reform it. When, at one point, Howells asked Twain for another satire on European travel, Twain replied that he could not give him one, for he hated it; and, he went on, one has to like something before one can satirize it. Believing in the essentially "moral" and "right" nature of their American society, although ready at the drop of a tort to spring to the attack of that which they loved so that it might be brought nearer to perfection, Twain and Warner could not do otherwise, in writing their "history" of the Gilded Age, than to arrange its details to show that "wrong" actions, individual and social, lead to unhappiness and ruin.

This same moral purpose, based upon a belief in an essentially moral society, operated in all of Twain's fiction, even, as we shall see, in his late and presumably "disillusioned works," and it is the force that holds together the episodic structure of *Huckleberry Finn*, the meaning that fills in and seals the joints of the rambling narrative, just as, for Twain and Howells, it held together the structure of their nineteenth-century world, making it a comedy instead of a nightmare. *Huckleberry Finn* is, on one level, a moral attack on social unreason, an indictment of social sentimentalism and a demonstration of the virtues of social empiricism. The frame of the picaresque story is the contrast between the method of reason, embodied by Huck Finn, and the method of sentimental romance, personified by Tom Sawyer, between hard-headed Huck who could be counted upon to do the right thing, and romantic Tom who could be counted on to do the wrong, and do it with a great flourish. The contrast was introduced at the beginning, when Huck described how Tom would transform the world of reality into a world of phantoms, of sheep who are maidens in distress, farmers who are knights, rusty lamps which are passports to the supernatural. And then the narrative was rounded at the end by the reintroduction of Tom who "assisted" in the ultimate freeing of Nigger Jim. This long section, covering about a third of the book, has often been called disproportionate and anticlimactic; but in one sense its very extravagance is a commentary upon Tom's "unrealism." When Jim had been betrayed by the Duke and the Dauphin, and locked up in a flimsy shack, Huck wanted to steal the key, which was hanging within easy reach, let Jim out, and then shove off down the river. But Tom Sawyer had read the *Count of Monte Cristo*, and would have none of the plan. "It's too blame simple," he said. "What's the good of a plan that ain't no more trouble than that?" He told Huck *his* scheme and Huck admitted, "I could see in a minute it was worth fifteen of mine for style, and would make Jim just as free a man as mine would, and maybe get us all killed besides." Tom nearly did get them killed, and it almost seemed as if Nigger Jim would go back to captivity when the scamp revealed the total uselessness of his dramatics, for he had known all along that Miss Watson had freed Jim in her will. This was Mark Twain's commentary upon the social inutility of sentimentalism, the wrongness of the romantic failure to face the facts of practical living.

Twain's masterwork was, then, based on a rejection of a false absolute. It also proposed as the test of a "good" action the results of that action in bettering the immediate human situation. It was, in short, a work based upon the prevailing pragmatic assumptions of the North after the Civil War. This is worth emphasizing, because *Huckleberry Finn* is, in one sense, a story of revolt against society, a tale of Huck's flight from the restrictions of civilization. It is all too easy, therefore, to read this same kind of revolt into its moral scheme as well. But in its morality, the book is not a work of revolt, but of acquiescence in the fundamental premises of the dominant American society of its time.

To see this clearly, we must become aware of the two circles of moral judgment which operate in the act of experiencing the novel. One was a morality of pragmatic humanitarianism; its premise was the right of the individual to the pursuit of happiness, regardless of the individual's color. The other was the *a priori* code of the slaveholding South which regarded the Negro not as a human being, but as a commodity; and in this frame of reference, the injunction "thou shalt not steal" became a principle which would make it a crime to aid a runaway slave. Huck feels himself completely within this Southern frame of reference, and can therefore experience only a sense of guilt when he helps Nigger Jim to escape. The reader, however, exactly reverses each one of Huck's judgments upon himself, because the book is written and must be read in the other, the general American pragmatic frame of reference.

This reversal occurs most obviously when, on the raft, Jim

started daydreaming. "He was saying," Huck reported uncomfortably, "how the first thing he would do when he got to a free state he would go to saving up money and never spend a single cent, and when he got enough he would buy his wife, which was owned on a farm close to where Miss Watson lived; and then they would both work to buy the two children, and if their master wouldn't sell them, they'd get an Abolitionist to go and steal them." Huck was shocked beyond measure. "It almost froze me to hear such talk. He wouldn't ever dared to talk such talk in his life before. . . . Thinks I, this is what comes of my not thinking. Here was this nigger, which I had as good as helped run away, coming right out flat-footed and saying he would steal his own children—children that belonged to a man I didn't know, a man that hadn't ever done me no harm."

Huck thereupon decided to give Jim up to the authorities, and immediately felt "easy and happy and light as a feather right off." But when a canoe-load of white men approached, Huck put them off with a wonderfully clever ruse; and when they went and Jim was saved, Huck said: "I got aboard the raft feeling bad and low, because I knowed very well I had done wrong, and I see it warn't no use for me to try to do right; a body that don't get *started* right when he's little ain't got no show." Huck, having adopted the ethics of slavery, was convinced he was a great sinner; every time he helped Jim, he was saddened by this sense of guilt. But, of course, each time he was saddened, the reader was cheered; each time, operating under a false code, he thought he did wrong, he did right, by the true code of humanitarianism. And this irony would only be possible if Mark Twain could feel sure that the society for which he was producing *Huckleberry Finn* was a society that, by and large, accepted the code of humanitarianism. And that is why *Huckleberry Finn*, like *Miss Ravenel's Conversion*, like *A Hazard of New Fortunes*, has a happy ending. Mark Twain believed that the moral principles of his society could triumph; the slave, after all, had been freed.

Twain was never called upon to formulate his moral code explicitly; but Howells was, and often; and he finally summarized his beliefs concerning the moral function of fiction. There were three levels of immorality in novels, he felt, and we note that nowhere does he speak of immorality as simply the violation of the conventional sexual code. The least pernicious, the most venial sins of the novel are the tickling of our prejudices, the lulling of our judgments, or the pampering of "our gross appetite for the marvellous." These are "not so fatal, but they are innutritious and clog the soul with unwholesome vapors." More immoral is the novel which flatters our passions, and "exalts them above the principles." This kind of novel, he said, is "poisonous," and while it "may not kill" it will "certainly injure." But the mortal crime is committed by the novelist who imagines "a world where the sins of sense are unvisited by the penalties following, swift or slow, but inexorably sure, in the real world. . . ." He produces novels which are "deadly poison: these do kill."

The cataloguing of fictional immorality was based upon the conviction that in the real world, in Howells' world of nineteenth-century America, there was a relation between wrong action and the results of that action; between deed and penalty or reward; the whole structure of his belief depended upon a real world which was fundamentally moral. We may translate "sins of the senses" to mean any usurpation of human reason by human unreason or passion—by the passion of pride as well as love, the passion of possessiveness and acquisition as well as the passions of an unreasoned devotion to an abstract "duty." Any one of these passions, Howells firmly believed, prevented the leading of the good life, individually and socially; and if a novel was to tell the truth about life, it would have to mimic a world in which the supremacy of such passions was penalized by human unhappiness. Sometimes he showed these penalties in operation: the lifelong unhappiness of a professor who, in *A Fearful Responsibility*, acted under false and outdated senses of chivalry and duty, the miserable death of Don Ippolito after the usurpation of his rational faculties by a dreamworld of sentimental unreality, the misery of a Marcia Hubbard who allowed reason to be overcome by physical attraction, the greater degradation of Bartley Hubbard, who placed selfish ambition above the emotional health of the society for which he provided news. More often, with typical optimism, his comedies showed the triumph of reason over temporary aberration: the partial satisfaction of Grace Breen in marriage after she had come to terms with her puritanic obsession with duty, the good life Colville found after rejecting the falsities of sentimentalism which had engendered his attachment to Imogene. And finally in 1885, Howells gave this optimism its final expression in *The Rise of Silas Lapham.*

The moral scheme envisioned in this work was ill-served by the simplicity of the book's structure; for in keeping with his earlier dedication to the small, the well made, the unified, Howells wrote the book about a house, the building of which becomes, in almost every respect, neatly symbolic of the moral rise and material fall of its builder, Silas Lapham, the man of industry and commerce. Lapham had turned his native force and energies into the production and marketing of "the best paint in the world," and had devoted his life to its success and his. He told its merits to Bartley Hubbard, the young reporter who came to interview him, with "the intonation of a prayer." And when Bartley asked him for "your life or your money," it was not in jest that Lapham replied that he guessed no one would want his life without his money. He pursued his success, not selfishly, but simply as "someone who had lived to himself" without the knowledge of social good and evil. He defended his advertising which had spread "Lapham's Mineral Paint—Specimen" on every board-fence, bridge-girder, dead wall, barn, and rock in the region; as long as there was no objection from the people that owned the barns and fences, he didn't see "what the public" had got to do with it. He drove his fine trotter down the Boston streets, feeling his sense of triumph as the mare left everything behind her on the road. "And as he grazed a hundred encountered and rival sledges" in his passage, he made his first announcement to his wife that he was going to build a house on the water side of Beacon.

As the first timbers went up, Lapham and his wife stood enjoying it until they sensed someone at their elbow, and it turned out to be Rogers, the man over whom Lapham had rolled on his way to the top, appearing at the moment when the house, the symbol of Lapham's worldly success, was going up. Mrs. Lapham immediately made the identification, and said she would never live in the building, for it represented Lapham's violation of moral law. At this point, the theme of the novel was explicitly stated: "Happy is the man for ever after who can choose the ideal, the unselfish part in such an exigency" (as Lapham's choice in buying out Rogers); and then Howells bluntly told us "Lapham could not rise to it." The remainder of the tale is concerned largely with Lapham's moral education, his achieving the moral ability to "rise."

To what? To a sense of the morality which binds the social world together, making it imperative that we live for others and not for ourselves. In this moral world, happiness follows when we have pursued the course that will make for the most well-being for the most people. For the world of purely personal relationships, Howells had already explored this morality, which David Sewell, the minister, called "economy of pain," in *Indian Summer*. And for the subplot of *Silas Lapham,* Howells chose the same triadic misunderstanding between lovers, one of whom wants to sacrifice herself, and make three people miserable, instead of just one. The building of the house became a symbol for this relationship, too, for Irene, the young and empty-headed daughter, deceived herself into believing herself beloved while sitting upon a trestle of the house with Tom Corey, and playing her unconscious but nonetheless pointed sexually symbolic game with the wood shavings left behind by the carpenters. The shaving from the house, a sliver of the major symbol, became the symbol for the sliver of personal morality which is part of the large morality of social living.

For as the shaving is to the whole house, so is the complexity of the personal ethic to the social. And it is the socal ethic which Howells tried to understand through writing *Silas Lapham.* The "rise," if it is a rise (and there were many, including one English reviewer, who were puzzled by the title, since the story apparently told of a financial disaster) was a rise from barbaric isolation to civilized social conduct, the only means of achieving, if not happiness, at least inner peace. The ability to rise above self-interest to the interest of another, the ability to rise above the interest of another, no matter how close, to the interest of a group, the strength to rise above even the interests of a group to which you have ties of proximity and affection to the interests of the larger society of which you are impersonally a part—these were the successive stages of the salvation of modern man, Howells told us in *The Rise of Silas Lapham.* The first stage was easy—for Lapham. The first stage is personal, with deeply personal emotional rewards granted the simple altruist; and both deed and reward are exceedingly simple to render in the emotional and personalized method of fiction. There was Rogers, a man with a wife (like his own) with hopes (like his), and the act of empathy demanded only the little imagination of which he was capable. But it is not in this easy, first act that social salvation lay, Howells knew, but in an act of the imagination so great that it has yet to be captured in American literature, perhaps cannot be captured in our literature until there are enough of us capable of performing it ourselves. No wonder that poor rough Silas Lapham and the essentially frail structure of well-formed narrative in which he was embedded were not quite capable of giving it full expression.

What is this act of the imagination? It is really the logical demands of the basic faith, the religious faith we may even call it, of Howells and his age in the value of their material world of social appearances. In this world, the acts of devotion of man to man are, by definition, acts of devotion to the only way in which they could conceive of God. Tom Corey, at one point, the crucial point in the story, alluded to the moral act which Howells believed the most significant of his century—the war for the preservation of the Union and the freeing of the slaves, and asked of the action of the common soldier in it: "What has ever been conceived of omnipotence, of omniscience, so sublime, so divine as that?" And the minister, David Sewell, replied quietly: "Nothing." And then he said: "God has never been imagined at all. But if you suppose such a man as that was Authorized, I think it will help you to imagine what God must be." At this point Lapham took his cigar out of his mouth, placed his forearms on the table and said simply: "There's sense in that." This moment, at the Coreys' dinner party, was the hub around which the structure of the novel turned. It was the end of Lapham's dreams of success in Society and the beginning of his realization of the demands of society. As he worked out his salvation, he remembered the minister's words and Sewell became, for him, the preacher of the true religion. When his daughters become involved in a sentimental tangle of meaningless self-sacrifice over Tom Corey, he suggested that his wife visit Sewell whose looks, Lapham said, he liked "about as well as any man he ever saw." And when she did, Sewell threw the light of common sense upon the "traditions which are the figment of the shallowest sentimentality."

Just before the visit to Sewell, Lapham and his wife had been driving the trotter, the same mare in which he had taken so much individualistic pride at the beginning of the story, and this time, preoccupied by their discussion of their children's problems, he ran into another carriage, and the "voice in front of him" shouted, "Where the devil you goin' to?" And Lapham began, from this point on, to understand that the world is a scene of an ethical struggle between a tempting devil and a redeeming God. When an opportunity arose for Lapham to recoup his losses by letting some property buyers beware, his wife said: "It does seem too hard . . . that you have to give up this chance when Providence had fairly raised it up for you." And Lapham replied grimly: "I guess it wan't *Providence* raised it up." It was as near as modern man can come to the devil, for the series of temptations placed in his progress were subtly worthy of the archfiend. At first, it was made possible for Lapham to sin by omission—simply *not* to say something; then the buyers of his worthless property showed themselves willing and eager to be duped since the funds involved were not their own; and finally, Rogers wanted to permit himself to be used as the instrument of evil; sell me the property, he said; what I do with it afterwards is no ethical concern of yours. But Lapham rose to this final temptation saying: "If you think I'm going to help you whip the devil round the stump, you're mistaken. . . ." And that night, he paced up and down while in the next room his wife listened to him and thought of the scriptural words: "'And there wrestled a man with him until the breaking of the day. . . . And he said, Let me go, for the day breaketh. And he said I will not let thee go, except thou bless me.' " Lapham, at the end, a ruined man, could tell the minister solemnly that he had been blessed and had come out of the hell of selfishness; in his homelier words: "Seems sometimes as if it was a hole opened for me, and I crept out of it."

The nature of the successive temptations of Lapham illustrates the complexities of the problem of social ethics as they spiral out of the simplicity of individual right and wrong conduct, and this complexity when seen against the essentially oversimplified fictional structure is the reason why the novel is so oddly dissatisfying despite its many merits. After unselfishness involving single personalities, an altruism easily visualized, its rewards immediately, intensely, personally warming, comes the welfare of groups, human groups, but with individual faces blurred, individual reactions diluted by immersal in the mass, and the strain on the imagination becomes greater. But then, after the group to which one is tied by bonds of proximity, comes the social body as a whole, something without name, without wife or child, without eyes to cry and heart to suffer, and yet, Howells believed, the most important concept constructed by man in his climb from barbarism to civilized life. It was the well-being of this impersonal personification that Lapham was called upon to place above the well-being of a man's invalid wife ("You want to sacrifice her to a mere idea!" shouted Rogers), and his factory workers ("I don't know what's going to become of the hands in the middle of winter," said Mrs. Lapham). For the Englishmen who wished to buy the land were agents of a community ". . . of an association of rich and charitable people," as they suavely put it, and by insisting that the transaction would hurt no one but those that could afford it, appealed to "that easy-going, not evilly intentioned, potential immorality which regards common property as common prey, and gives us the most corrupt municipal governments under the sun—which makes the poorest voter, when he has tricked into place, as unscrupulous in regard to other's money as an hereditary prince."

This then was the nature of the ethical truth about his society which Howells held in 1885, and which he tried to propound through his novel—a truth difficult of dramatic and imaginative realization because of the almost complete absence of personality in the social organism; it takes an enormous feat of the imagination to envisage this entity and be concerned for its welfare; one must feel the organic complexities and inter-relationships which throb in a modern society; and yet, in order to make concrete such complexity, Howells had chosen, as we have seen, a small, tight, almost allegorical construction where scene reflects character, and symbol reflects moral purpose with almost mechanical consistency, and makes us feel smallness and constriction, instead of greatness and expansion and complexity. The vehicle was simply not up to the burden it had to carry; it was a vehicle suitable to the moral load of the individual social problem of *A Woman's Reason*, or the problems in personal love of *Indian Summer*, or the individual moral dilemmas of *A Modern Instance*. But it could not involve the reader imaginatively in a whole society.

The next few years after *Silas Lapham* were crucial for Howells, personally and artistically. In his next works, written under the stress of this crisis, he expanded and loosened his forms so that they were capable of bearing the burden of larger social implication. How he did this is the story of the turmoil of a man who, in his maturity, had all his easy acceptations shaken to their roots, and of a comic age which began to doubt the premises of its comedy.

CHAPTER IV

CRITICAL REALISM

1. Industrialism and Corruption

"The high moral ones cost more . . ."
—Twain and Warner

"I have done with preaching for the present. Later I may have something to say. Now I feel sure of nothing, not even what I've been saying here." This was the Reverend Julius Peck in *Annie Kilburn;* it was Howells speaking as well. For its mood in 1887 expressed the change in the tone of the age and of its serious writers. It was the end of the self-assurance of a representative man like Howells that eighteenth-century moderation and reason, adapted to the contemporary American scene, would inevitably make it better; it was the gradual disillusion of the age's genius, Mark Twain, in the certainty that the triumph of the empirical method was all that democratic America needed to perfect its democracy. The disillusion spelt, for Twain, the end of his greatness, for with it deepening upon him, he was capable only of a sombre afterglow. But it established Howells as the representative man of his times, for the change in tone led him to the next stage of his development wherein he turned from the working out of the fates of a few people in their corner of the world to the problems of a whole society, and from the carefully constructed dramatic form to looser and more organic structure. And in this transition he created a major mode of American fiction, one which dominated much of the American literary scene in the twentieth century. "Critical realism" is the name given to this literature which truthfully reports warped and maladjusted social relationships so that men may study and improve them. The story of its development is bound up with the economic turmoil and strife of America during the 1880's and 1890's, a turmoil which changed Howells from an optimistic believer that existing American institutions had produced a satisfactory way of life into a humble and agonized doubter, whose doubt deepened not into despair but into creation, into the making of a series of pioneer novels unswerving in their criticism of things as they were.

It was natural that the realistic movement should have moved into this phase, given the state of American society at the end of the century. The realists were always social satirists, their comedy directed at the vices and foibles of the society they found about them. But through the 1870's and 1880's there were growing rumblings of trouble which went deeper than the surface of manners and were symptomatic of the basic disturbances which finally erupted in a series of strikes, bombings, and executions which left Howells and his America so shaken that their molecules were permanently rearranged.

The tremblings of the American political and economic earth clearly corresponded to those in the parent Western culture which had been developing the pressures of industrialization. Militant trade unionism, socialism, "communism," anarchism, nihilism had begun to attack laissez-faire capitalism from the left, and growing monopolies had begun its destruction from the right. Pierre Joseph Proudhon in *What Is Property?* gave the world the word "anarchy," a word which was to generate in its time all the fears and hatreds the twentieth century has attached to "communism." Karl Marx issued his Manifesto in 1847. The socialist International Workingmen's Association was formed in 1864 and transferred its headquarters to New York in 1867. Foreign-born Socialists "found sympathy and assistance among some native American intellectuals who had imbibed the ideas of Fourier and Owen in the forties and fifties."

In 1862, in the coal fields of Pennsylvania, the Molly Maguires had begun their campaigns of terrorism in answer to the dreadful working conditions and the oppressive anti-unionism of the owners. The next twenty years saw the formation of the Knights of Labor and its extension into a national union, the organization of the Social-Labor and Greenback-Labor parties, the New York General Strike of 1872 and the Great Railway Strike of 1877, the publication of Henry George's *Progress and Poverty*, and Henry Demarest Lloyd's first article against Standard Oil which had been incorporated in 1870 and became the first "trust" in 1880. These assaults on the established order from the left had their counterparts on the right. John D. Rockefeller spoke of his monopoly as the beginning of a new economic order: "The time was ripe for it," he said. "It had to come, though all we saw at the moment was the need to save ourselves from wasteful conditions. . . . The day of combination is here to stay. Individualism has gone, never to return."

The tremendous expansion of American industry which the Rockefeller empire symbolized, operating for the last time without public interference, had created those incredible political corruptions of the Grant era, the age of the Great Barbecue at which unscrupulous businessmen gorged themselves, throwing fragments of the feast over their shoulders to waiting politicians. When the organizers of the Union Pacific contrived to milk the public through its dummy purchasing organization, the Crédit Mobilier, they found it easy to accomplish the bribery of sufficient congressmen through the "sale" of stock to them at gift prices. The weapons Gould and Vanderbilt carried with them in the Erie War were satchels full of greenbacks with which they bought up New York State's senators and assemblymen, bidding up the price of legislators so briskly that, according to the social historians of the era, some districts felt disgraced when their representatives sold themselves for less than the prevailing market quotation. By 1871 when a citizen's committee caught up with them, Boss Tweed had milked the city of New York of an estimated twenty million dollars. The same year a state legislator in Kansas arose in his seat, put seven thousand dollars on the table before him, and announced that the sum had been placed in his hands the evening before by United States Senator Samuel C. Pomeroy in return for his vote.

The realists had not allowed these doings to escape their satiric vision. *The Gilded Age* was primarily a comment on the speculative spirit of the age; but its authors gave more than passing attention to the carnival of corruption in their nation's government. After Colonel Sellers and Washington Hawkins had succeeded in getting an appropriation of $200,000 from Congress, they received not a penny of it, and went to their agent in Washington for an explanation. That worthy blandly presented them with the cost of getting the bill through: an itemized list of congressmen and senators bought at ten and twenty thousand dollars apiece, with "a high moral Congressman—the high moral ones cost more"—going at thirty thousand dollars. But the general feeling of the work was far from bitter; in the end, Senator Dilworthy was unmasked by an aroused press, and the Tennessee land fraud was defeated, just as in the private moral world of the novel the characters met the kinds of fate which the authors believed a fundamentally moral social world would prescribe for them. There was no sense of defeat or despair; instead there was a species of robust enjoyment at the very extravagance of the vice which they were exposing, for theirs was a certainty that it was a blight susceptible of vigorous treatment and cure by the application of reason to human affairs.

This was the tone, too, of John De Forest, a tone which would change, as did Twain's in the late 1880's, but which was then the buoyant optimism which could regard the iniquities of the Grant era with the constructive zeal of the reformer. De Forest's contribution to the nascent stirrings of a more deeply critical realism was *Honest John Vane* (1875), a little parable in which the title character, spurred on by the excessive demands of his beautiful but unsympathetic wife and by the importunings of Darius Dorman who had financed and managed his successful campaign for Congress, finally accepted a thousand dollars' worth of stock in the "Subfluvial Scheme" to build a tunnel between New Orleans and the Great Lakes. After this fall, Vane became the errand boy for every lobbyist and special interest seeker in Washington. But finally, "That vast, industrious, decent American public, which wire-pullers usually regarded as having no more intelligence or moral principle than one of the forces of nature, showed unmistakably that it possessed much political virtue and some political sense." The public demanded an investigation, got it, and "the popular storm soon blew the doors open."

The novelists could rest content that extraordinary corruption was a temporary and eradicable feature of American government, and that a certain amount of easy morality was to be expected of the fallible human being whose foibles they regarded as the proper subject of their attentions. Eggleston had described how "a curious effect of political aspirations . . . was to shut the eyes that they could not see, to close the ears that they could not hear, and to destroy the sense of smell"; but a little later he alluded with nice ambiguity to the good old days "when Congressmen were so honorable that they scorned bribes, and were only kept from killing one another by the exertions of the sergeant-at-arms." So it would remain for another generation—the generation of Lincoln Steffens and David Graham Phillips—to make fictional capital out of corruption in government.

2. Sentimentalists Preferred Blondes: Labor and Capital in the Novel

But the writers of the age of Howells could not rest easy when faced by the much more personalized and dramatic inequities produced by the growing strife between capital and labor. And it was, at the beginning, not the plight of the laborer that aroused the sympathies and affected the sensitivities of the novelists, but the problems of the employer and the individualistic workingman when confronted by the coercion of the labor organizer. This functionary quickly became the stock villain of the early novels dealing with the labor movement. By 1889, *Frank Leslie's Illustrated Newspaper* could count upon the reader's recognition of the stereotype, and use it as a front-page cartoon: the full-page drawing was entitled "The Troubles of Labor"; it pictured a "walking delegate" (the contemporary term for any labor organizer), large of paunch, pendulous of feature, dressed in top hat and pin-stripe trousers; over his fat stomach hung a heavy gold chain with large watch and diamond fob; in one hand was an expensive cigar; the other was upraised in imperious command "stop work" to an unwilling group of laborers who glowered at him over their shovels.

Such was the portrait of one stereotype; but an even more frequent caricature of this scapegoat was an unkempt, dirty foreigner, from either the Mediterranean or Slavic countries, who duped the good-looking, well-mannered Anglo-Saxon workers with his imported sophistries. Thomas Bailey Aldrich's *The Stillwater Tragedy* (1880) was the first to describe the problems of labor in these terms. It concerned the workers in a stone-cutting company who made no trouble until a swarthy Italian named Torrini "and two or three others came over here with foreign grievances." "How is it," asked the hero (with the very English name of Shackford) of a workman (with the Irish name of Denyvan, sufficiently northern European to account for his decency, yet enough removed from the Anglo-Saxon to account for his dullness), "How is it . . . that you, and sensible workmen like you, have permitted such a quarrelsome and irresponsible fellow to become a leader in the Association?" Denyvan answered that Torrini was "a born horator" and besides was "up to all the parli'mentary dodges." By 1890, "Torrini" had become "Berensky"; the latter was the walking delegate in Ellen Olney Kirk's *Walford* and his dark hair was "matted and tangled," his whiskers long and unkempt. Spencer (again we note the nationality of the name) called him not "a working man" but a "talking man," and, worst of all, a "fiery socialist."

The most celebrated of all the early works to use this theme was John Hay's *The Bread-Winners.* Hay had been Lincoln's assistant private-secretary, Hayes' Assistant Secretary of State, and was to become Secretary of State under McKinley and Theodore Roosevelt. He had dabbled in essays and poetry, and in 1884 anonymously published the novel which gave the age its most strikingly repulsive stereotype, in Andrew Jackson Offit. The name, Hay declared, was "an unconscious brand" showing "the person bearing it" to be "the son of illiterate parents with no family pride or affections, but filled with a bitter and savage partisanship which found its expression in a servile worship of the most injurious personality in American history." Hay's treatment of the stock situation where innocent workmen were duped and misled by wily and self-seeking organizers was classic. His portrait was simpler in its outlines, blacker in its blacks, whiter in its whites than any other that made the pretense of being serious fiction. The use of darkness of feature to denote evil and fairness to symbolize good was as old as the Puritan identification of the dusky savages in the New World forests as devil's henchmen; using this symbolism for their parables of good and evil, Hawthorne had fashioned his Hester, his Pearl, and his Miriam with raven tresses, and had made his Hilda a fair-skinned blonde; Melville had created a dark-haired Hautia who was Sin, and a fair Yillah who was the Good. This convention Hay debased for the purpose of special pleading. Andy Offit was as black and greasy as they came, with "a face whose whole expression was oleaginous . . . surmounted by a low and shining forehead covered by reeking black hair. . . . The parted lips, which were coarse and thin, displayed an imperfect set of teeth, much discolored with tobacco. The eyes were light green, with the space which should have been white suffused with yellow and red. It was one of those gifted countenances which could change in a moment from a dog-like fawning to a snaky venomousness." Contrasted to this force of blackness were various representatives of the Nordic light: Sam Sleeny, for example, whose "shapely build, his curly blond hair and beard, his frank blue eye, first attracted . . . envious notice . . . a workman whose daily life was a practical argument against the doctrines of socialism. . . ." And when a labor spokesman tried to remonstrate with his picture of the growing union movement, Hay replied that if his work had succeeded in preventing one honest workman from joining a labor organization, he felt it had been worth while.

3. Howells' Early Attitudes Towards Society

And *The Bread-Winners* was very nearly dedicated to William Dean Howells! To be sure, Howells was glad enough that the inscription had not been made, but nevertheless he gave the book guarded praise. With the passage of years he was to see that its outlook was antiquated, but he defended it at the time of its appearance, and not only because of his usual loyalty to a friend, or his gratitude for Hay's assistance in securing him his consulate. For during the 1870's and the first half of the next decade, Howells rested in generally conservative contentment that American laissez-faire economics and Jeffersonian democracy had produced a satisfactory way of life for most of its people. When he was twenty-three, he sat at the door of a hotel in Lowell, Massachusetts, and watched the work-worn mill girls stream by with no emotion within him other than acceptance of the order which made their ten-hour day and abominable working conditions. He voted the straight Republican ticket, even when it meant supporting Ulysses S. Grant; "Many of us who will vote for General Grant," he wrote, "are still not sensible of being animated by any higher motive than the desire of self preservation." There was a hint of what he meant by these words in an earlier article in which he brought up, if only to ridicule, charges that Horace Greeley was a Fourierist and an advocate of free love. "Our social and political system," he declared, might not be "all that patriotism could desire, but it abounds in fortunate individual results." And so he went along with that aspect of the Gospel of Wealth and that residuum of Puritanism which combined to produce the myth of Horatio Alger: virtue equals prosperity. He gave high praise to a "new observer" of certain "Dangerous Tendencies of American Life" which led the poor to blame their economic environment for their miseries during the depression. Howells repeated with admiration the observer's suggestion that the poor, in hard times, should drink less and live more frugally. It is not surprising that early in 1886, he "invited" American novelists who would get the "whole effect" of their happy environment to concern themselves with "the more smiling aspects of life which are the more American."

Then, on May 4, 1886, a bomb exploded in Haymarket Square, Chicago.

The explosion and its aftermath did not so much create new attitudes in a man like Howells, although this might seem the case from a recital of the evidence for his basic complacency in the years before the Haymarket Affair; instead, the crisis acted as a chemical agent, precipitating tendencies already held in the warm solution of his sympathies. As a child he had tasted the bitterness of overwork in his father's print shop, and had felt the torturing uncertainties of perpetual indebtedness. Quiescent during his early maturity, these memories came back to him in full force when his political and economic eyes were finally opened. He had, too, a continued sympathy for the Negro and for "all the pain" which a man with black skin must endure, "however proudly" he tried "to hide it or lightheartedly forget it"; and this sensitivity for the problems of a class submerged because of color he later transferred to the groups oppressed because of their hopeless poverty. Even amid the sunny pleasantness of *Their Wedding Journey* he had paused to put himself imaginatively in the position of "a friendless German boy, setting foot for the first time on this happy continent." Then, strangely enough, Howells used for the first time his oft-quoted phrase about America: its "smiling aspects"; and at this point used it ironically, for he exclaimed: "What a smiling aspect life in the New World must wear to the young eyes of this hypothetical immigrant!" And a page or two earlier, he had described one of these "smiling aspects": the sight of "two jaded women . . . with their lean hands clasped outside their knees . . ." who ". . . sat and stared, silent and hopeless."

As editor of the *Atlantic*, Howells printed the most searing reproach to laissez-faire commercialism to appear before Henry D. Lloyd's attacks on the Rockefeller monopoly, J. R. Coleman's "The Fight of a Man with a Railroad," which told of the fruitless quest of a citizen for justice against the arrogant employees of a public carrier who had ruptured him for life after a dispute about his ticket. And although Lloyd's article attacking Standard Oil did not appear until March, 1881, a month after Howells had resigned from the editorship, exigencies of printing make it certain that Howells had edited the article and given it its feature place in the issue.

In these years the first seeds of his later socialism were implanted, and stranger than strange was the source from which they came; for he later ascribed them to his distant cousin, the quietly conservative President of the United States, Rutherford B. Hayes! Hayes had called his attention to socialism as an active force in modern life, Howells told an interviewer, and "referred to our national postoffice as an example of practical socialism, adapted to the old Jeffersonian system of government. . . ."

Throughout the fiction of these earlier years, too, there ran a thread of social criticism. One of his characters in the closet drama, *Out of the Question*, said of the depression and its concomitant human misery: "We're all part of the tangle; we're all of us to blame, we're none of us to blame." By 1884, he was beginning to look upon life "as a very serious affair," and in *The Rise of Silas Lapham* and *The Minister's Charge* there were signs of a growing consciousness of the more sombre side of his civilization: a character in the latter novel suggested that the city workhouse was the first blind stirring of a movement that would end with a "State which would support and employ all its citizens." Undoubtedly the personal tragedy of his own family, haunted by the sight of a hopelessly invalided daughter gradually sinking towards inevitable death, humbled him with a sense of the insufficiency of Gilded Age assumptions of the equivalence between one's deeds and one's deserts.

And then came The Bomb.

4. The Haymarket Affair

"*. . . horizons indefinitely widened . . .*"

The overture to the Haymarket drama had been playing for twenty years before 1886; the discords of the strife between organizing capital and organizing labor had made the public suitably jumpy; the squeals of the newspapers and magazines about the conspiracies of socialists, anarchists, and "walking delegates" had been supplemented by the deeper resonances of anti-labor novels like *The Stillwater Tragedy* and *The Bread-Winners*, and together the whole orchestra of fear and hatred had prepared the American audience for the rising of the curtain on the Chicago tragedy.

The agitation for the eight-hour day which started the series of events leading to the final disaster was connected in the public mind with attacks upon the dearest beliefs of Americans: religion, freedom, and prosperity. Such a reduction in hours, one spokesman for industry said in 1872, would violate that portion of the scriptures which held that man must earn his bread by the sweat of his brow, and eight hours was patently not long enough to work up an honest Christian sweat. Edward Everett Hale felt such limitations to be unconstitutional, for "the Bill of Rights in most states would be enough to show that a legislature must not interfere with the rights of a man to sell in market his own labor, and as much of it as he chooses." The *Nation* at first satirized the eight-hour movement, then turned serious as it asserted: "Everyone would be glad if progress could be maintained with less labor than at present, but most persons are apprehensive that if the day's work should be reduced to eight hours, a serious check would be given to our prosperity."

The Haymarket rioters were not only associated with this unpopular concept, but were further and more damningly connected with those three labels which were linked together into one terrible if illogical hyphenation: unionism-socialism-anarchy. "In American labor history the tumultuous years of the middle eighties have long been marked as exceptional," and this tumult evoked widespread disapproval of labor organization in the press of the day, and a revulsion against socialism and anarchism which were regarded as natural outgrowths of trade unionism. Socialism was the red herring of the 'eighties, and there seemed to be no attempt to distinguish between the radically different philosophies of socialism and anarchism. The day after the Haymarket bombing, for example, the *Nation* reported that in Cincinnati "Socialists, to the number of 600, are organized, armed with effective rifles," and that "they control . . . the manufacture of dynamite bombs. . . ."

It was at a meeting devoted to agitation for the disturbing doctrine of the eight-hour day that the first of a series of conflicts began between Chicago workers and Chicago police—a series which ended with the bombing on May 4. On May 3, five hundred strikers (the *Nation* called them "7000 or 8000 anarchists, workmen, and tramps") stoned and clubbed a group of strikebreakers in front of the McCormick Reaper Works. The police opened fire on the mob, and, although accounts differ, it was generally agreed that one striker was killed and several wounded. The following day a meeting of protest was called at Haymarket Square. Sam Fielden, an acknowledged anarchist, had begun to speak with what the *Nation* called "the most incendiary utterances," when Inspector Bonfield, at the head of 125 men, marched on the crowd. From behind the speaker's wagon, a bomb was thrown; its explosion killed one officer, Matthias Degan, wounded six more so critically that they died within the next six months, and injured a number of others, variously estimated from twelve to seventy.

When word was flashed to the country, the public demanded vengeance and the newspapers called for blood. In *One Woman's Life* (1913), Robert Herrick later described Chicago on the night of the bombing, when bands of enraged citizens roamed the streets in search of anarchists. What followed was "an illuminating demonstration of what a city and its forces of law and order are capable when in the grip of fear, suspicion, and a lust for revenge." The Indianapolis *News* held that the "Chicago police would have been justified in wholesale slaughter." The Louisville *Courier-Journal* demanded that "the blatant cattle" be "immediately strung up." Chicago authorities answered the cry for vengeance by rounding up eight anarchists. The eight were tried for the murder of Matthias Degan, convicted in August, 1886, and, after several unsuccessful appeals, Louis Lingg committed suicide in his cell, and Albert Parsons, Adolph Fischer, George Engel, and August Spies were hanged on November 11, 1887. The others were sentenced to long prison terms. On June 26, 1893, Governor Louis Altgeld pardoned the surviving anarchists, bluntly declaring that the evidence at the trial had not proved the defendants guilty, and Altgeld's findings have not been seriously challenged by any historians.

But at the time of the trials and the execution, the duty of almost every American seemed clear. Our way of life was endangered by foreign radicals; these men might not have been directly guilty, but their political philosophy called for the use of force in abolishing our institutions; therefore, as James Russell Lowell declared and John Greenleaf Whittier seemed to agree, "the ruffians" were "well hanged."

There quickly arose the miasma of hysteria in which it was all but impossible for any man to speak sanely without risking livelihood and reputation. Even a polemicist like Michael Foran, who wrote his novel *The Other Side* to "call attention to some of the iniquities of the wage system," felt it necessary to disown "chimerical ideas, such as socialism," before he felt he could gain his book any kind of reading; and he was sure to have his hero denounce violence which leads to "anarchy and terror." Even more revealing of the atmosphere of the year was the reaction of Steele MacKaye, the handsome and dynamic actor-manager, the idol of the New York stage, and one of its foremost dramatists, who was equally crowded between his sincere humanitarianism and the irresistible pressures of public opinion.

MacKaye was deep into a new play when he read of the trial and conviction of the anarchists. He was convinced that an injustice had been done, and he privately denounced the verdict with what Howells described as "wrathful fervour," and cited "instances . . . of police brutality." Publicly he played it safer, opening his appeal for clemency with the "let's-not-make-martyrs-out-of-rogues" gambit, and called upon the American people to refrain from throwing around the anarchists' mania "the seductive glamour of heroism"; but he nevertheless quite bravely protested against their execution as "a national folly and a national disgrace." And while he was being deeply moved by contemporary events, he began reshaping his current play, which carried marked overtones of the crisis in American life. It was a drama of the French Revolution at the stage of the Terror; he entitled it *Anarchy*, and opened it out of town with that name; but then, "to avoid trading" upon the plight of the Chicago radicals, he brought it into New York with the title *Paul Kauvar* and the subtitle "Or Anarchy."

The theme of the play, as MacKaye declared, was contained in Kauvar's assertion: "The torch of liberty which should light mankind to progress, if left in madmen's hands, kindles that blaze of Anarchy whose only end is ashes." And whenever the word "anarchist" was spoken, it was associated with phrases like "slaughter hundreds of defenseless women," "outrage little children," "ravishing the poor," "shouting fraternity and committing fratricide," and with adjectives and appositives like "libertine," "assassin," "vulture," and "toad." The effects of this kind of melodrama upon a public inflamed by headlines like those of the Indianapolis and Louisville papers can be easily imagined. At the end of the first New York performance the audience "roared and rose" as if it were "one enormous being, deep-lunged and myriad-armed," and a contemporary reviewer declared that "the wildly enthusiastic crowd in front made one think that a pandemoniac delirium had usurped the place of reason." What the American public needed least was a play which encouraged the usurpation of reason by hysteria, but that is what Steele MacKaye gave it under the subtle but hydraulic pressures of opinion.

At a meeting in the home of Judge Roger A. Pryor, the counsel for the Haymarket defendants, MacKaye caught the eye of the short, squat, gentle dean of American letters and leader of the movement towards realism in fiction. William Dean Howells, a most unlikely candidate for martyrdom, past editor of the *Atlantic*, successful novelist, under contract to a conservative publishing house at ten thousand dollars a year which seemed to him, at the time, like all the money in the Harper treasury, had made up his mind to protest the treatment of the Chicago anarchists and was, at the time of his meeting with MacKaye, deep in the struggle. The exact occasion for the transformation of Howells from conservative to radical, the exact moment of his sudden anguish, cannot be determined. He said it came "through reading their trial" and this reading necessarily was at some time between the summer of 1886 and the summer of 1887. In this year he came to the realization that an America which could present only smiling aspects to the realist was no longer; that if a writer were to portray truthfully he would have to portray a society which could create a submerged social class and then had "civically murdered" four men who were calling attention to the plight of that class.

Howells plunged unreservedly into the desperately unpopular fight to save the convicted anarchists. He presumed upon the slightest of acquaintances with their defense counsel to commend him for taking the case, and told him that he had never believed the men guilty of anything but their opinions. A week before the execution he addressed a letter to the editor of the New York *Tribune*, declaring he had petitioned the Governor of Illinois to show mercy to the convicted men, and urging others to join him in the plea. He turned to John Greenleaf Whittier as the most likely aid in his struggle against injustice, remembering his efforts in behalf of the victims of black slavery, but Whittier refused him and later made the substance of their conversation public, adding to the scorn heaped upon Howells by the press. On the day of the executions, Howells wrote Francis Browne, the editor of the *Dial*, expressing his torture at the "hideous . . . damnable . . . abominable . . ." scene, and two days later, the tone of his letter to his father was the weary enervation of a man who had been through hell. He told Garland that he could well believe that one did not bring oneself to an open espousal of a cause like that of the anarchists without "thinking and feeling much," and having one's "horizons . . . infinitely widened" in the process.

This mild man, virtually alone among American intellectuals, conducted his open rebellion against prevailing public opinion with gallantry and courage. He was excoriated as heartily as if he had proven himself "a dynamiter." He feared that his stand might cost him his position with the house of Harper. While in retrospect, and in the pages of a biography of the founder of the firm, he insisted that no pressures had been put upon him, there is good reason to believe that this was hardly the case. H. M. Alden, the editor of *Harper's*, had, as we know, protested against Howells' notice of Zola; but then, a year after the death of the anarchists, Alden was provoked to write another warning; far worse than the charge of immorality, Alden told Howells, was the accusation that he had written a letter to be read at an Anarchist's Memorial Service, expressing sympathy with Spies and his companions. This statement, Alden wrote him firmly, should be contradicted at once, and he asked Howells' permission to publish a peremptory denial. With this the attitude of his employers a year after the hangings, one may imagine their feelings about so unpopular a stand by an author closely associated with them. And the testimony of Howells' family is that he feared he was staking his reputation and livelihood on his actions.

During these crucial years, his faith in the *status quo* shaken, Howells fell under the influence of Leo Tolstoy, Laurence Gronlund, and William Morris. From Tolstoy he derived his new social gospel: Christian socialism; from Gronlund he took the pattern of his expectation about the way that socialism would come: from the gradual integration of industry into one gigantic "accumulation" which would then be taken over by the people through their instrumentality, the State; from Morris he took his basic indifference to mechanization and his corresponding hope that the New World would be a world of handicrafts. But more important, he began a line of critical theorizing, and a new method of fiction which were the natural developments of his earlier theory and practice, but which took their shape from his passage through the crucible of a national injustice.

5. The Invalidation of *Criticism and Fiction*

The "smiling aspects . . . changing for the worse"

A peculiar circumstance has stood in the way of a full understanding of this change in Howells. A single phrase has succeeded in damning him in the eyes of subsequent critics and writers: "the smiling aspects" of American life. In every history of American literature, these words have been quoted as the summary of his myopic and uncritical optimism. And yet, at the same time, he has been called "the prophet of 'critical realism.'" The explanation of this paradox lies in the details surrounding Howells' composition of the volume of essays entitled *Criticism and Fiction*, where this phrase appeared, and from whose context it is generally taken.

The history of *Criticism and Fiction* began with Howells' series of monthly critical essays in *Harper's*, a series which appeared as the regular department called "The Editor's Study." The department had been suggested to Howells by Alden in a conversation at the beginning of 1886, at the same time that he concluded a contract with the firm calling for "at least one short novel every year, with at least one farce, and as much more as I could or liked in the various kinds I was supposed to be expert in." He understandably balked at committing himself to a several-thousand-word monthly essay in addition to this staggering amount of work. For he regarded it as forming a break in his chosen and dedicated career as a novelist; and he later felt that he had been right in the objection, and that the burden had prevented him from achieving his full potentialities as a novelist. Nevertheless, he agreed to do the job, and he regularly turned out his monthly stint until 1892. In the last essay he announced the intended publication of the volume *Criticism and Fiction* which the "ill-advised Study-presence" was going to distill from his monthly ministrations of "gall and wormwood."

Criticism and Fiction, then, was avowedly a product of the scissors and pastepot. Howells made the book up of reprints from articles he had not wanted to write in the first place, and which he regarded as a vexing distraction from his main job of writing fiction. When it came to wielding the scissors, therefore, it is not surprising that he used them with haste; and this haste explains why much of the book is vague. It also precludes acceptance of the work as a unified piece of writing.

The general technique he used was to clip passages from the "Studies" which dealt in general terms with either criticism or the art of fiction. He then arranged those excerpts dealing with criticism under the Roman numerals I-XIII, and those dealing more with the art of fiction under the numerals XIV-XXVIII. And he reprinted these excerpts with only the very minor changes needed to take them out of the magazine and into a book—the transformation of the editorial "we" to the personal "I" and the elimination of references to the "Study." The amount of new material written for the book was negligible, and consisted almost entirely of short transitions which he supplied, in eleven passages, to bridge the jump from section to section. Elsewhere he began new thoughts and new divisions without transition.

This policy of organization, in itself, made for a lack of direction and impact. But more prejudicial to the coherence of the work was his surprising custom of taking paragraphs out of essays written at widely spaced intervals and about widely different subjects, piecing them together—sometimes with a word or two of transition, sometimes without—and placing them all together under one Roman numeral heading. There are seven such jerry-built essays and one of them is the essay in which appeared his remark about "the smiling aspects."

When we see how *Criticism and Fiction* was composed, when we observe that it was a compilation of snatches of articles written over a period of five years, we are immediately struck by the necessity of weighing the various judgments passed in it on the basis of the dates on which they were first written. This would be true even of a five-year period in an author's life during which his ideas were subject only to the normal fluctuations of mood and fortune. But these five years, as we have seen, were the most important and soul-shaking in Howells' life. It would be wise, then, to review the judgments he passes in *Criticism and Fiction* and see whether they preceded or followed the critical date in his life. Here, first, is the celebrated "smiling aspects" passage:

> It used to be one of the disadvantages of the practice of romance in America, which Hawthorne more or less whimsically lamented, that there were so few shadows and inequalities in our broad level of prosperity; and it is one of the reflections suggested by Dostoievsky's novel, The Crime and the Punishment, that whoever struck a note so profoundly tragic in American fiction would do a false and mistaken thing. . . . Whatever their deserts, very few American novelists have been led out to be shot, or finally exiled to the rigors of a winter at Duluth; and in a land where journeymen carpenters and plumbers strike for four dollars a day the sum of hunger and cold is comparatively small, and the wrong from class to class has been almost inappreciable, though all this is changing for the worse. Our novelists, therefore, concern themselves with the more smiling aspects of life, which are the more American. . . .

This, then, is the paragraph which has been so vexing. It originally appeared in the September, 1886, issue of *Harper's*. In the same number there was a note under the "Monthly Record of Current Events" which says: "Our record is closed on the 15th of July." Since a department of late news such as this would be held until the latest possible deadline for the magazine to go on the presses, it is safe to say that a contribution such as "The Editor's Study" must have been in the forms before July 15. Was this before or after Howells changed his views as a result of the Haymarket Affair? It was two months after the anarchists' trial began, but at least one month before the verdict was handed down on August 20, 1886. Howells said that he became convinced of the victims' innocence "through reading their trial." This terminology would make it appear that he was talking about the transcripts of the completed case. That he might have been moved by the injustice during the trial is unlikely. For until the verdict, the injustice had not been committed. And any newspaper account he might have read, and certainly the lurid report in *Harper's* itself, would have done nothing to make him sympathize with the anarchists. On November 18, 1887, he wrote that "the last two months" had been full of "heartache and horror" for him because of the "civic murder committed last Friday in Chicago." This would place his personal crisis as late as August, 1887. It is safe to say, then, that some time between the late summer of 1886 and the summer of 1887, Howells went through the kind of agony of spirit which would have necessarily modified his opinions concerning American life. There is, then, no question of "why did Howells write this atypical statement?" For the answer is that he wrote it before the event which changed his outlook and which, therefore, made it atypical. The question is, rather: "Why, when he was using his scissors, did he not cut away this vexing statement?"

The new question can be answered when we examine the nature of the successive contexts in which this paragraph appeared, and when we note two significant changes which Howells made in the passage in its later forms.

In the original appearance of the passage in *Harper's* for September, 1886, Howells discussed the bitter and tragic life of Dostoievsky, and then added the paragraph under consideration. When it came to the issue of *Criticism and Fiction* in 1891, Howells clipped a passage from the February, 1890, "Editor's Study" which had originally discussed the differences between American and English novelists. To it he added a description of the differences between the physical and social settings of the two countries which had originally appeared in the October, 1890, issue of *Harper's*. To the essay then formed by these two, he added the "smiling aspects" passage. It is clear that in the hasty process of building essays out of prefabricated materials Howells felt that the "smiling aspects" section fitted in nicely with the new essay about the differences between English and American fiction. But even then, he felt compelled to make two changes in the text of the original, and these changes loom large in the perspective of the fact that in no other instance did Howells make significant additions or alterations in the wording of the original material. The first change was made where the original read: "We invite our novelists, therefore, to concern themselves with the more smiling aspects." This he altered to: "Our novelists, therefore, concern themselves with the more smiling aspects." He changed the sense from one of exhortation to one of observation. And then, after the words: "the wrong from class to class is inappreciable," he added: "though all this is changing for the worse."

When the Library Edition of *Criticism and Fiction* was issued in 1910, a peculiar circumstance enabled this "smiling aspects" passage to assume greater importance in the format of the work than originally intended. For in his mellow age, Howells' lifelong antipathy for things English began to fade, and in this mood he decided to excise most of the derogatory remarks about contemporary English criticism and English fiction. Such an excision meant the removal of the passages from the February and October, 1890, "Studies" and left the "smiling aspects" standing alone and naked in all its obvious insufficiency.

Another passage in *Criticism and Fiction* which needs to be reviewed in the light of its original dates of composition is the concluding essay XXVIII, which somewhat vaguely advocates humanitarianism in literature. Howells here declared that the humane impulse is always present in fiction, especially in America where the height that the race had reached was an eminence which enabled "more men than ever before to see how the vast masses of men are sunk in a misery that must every day grow more helpless." "Art," he declared, must make friends with

"Need." The art which "disdains the office of teacher is one of the last refuges of the aristocratic spirit."

Strange words from the man who in 1886 invited his fellow writers to concern themselves with the more smiling aspects of life! But not so strange when we see that the dates of composition of these words all postdated August, 1886. And it is when reading this last essay that one feels the full regret at Howells' method of composing the little volume which became the measure of his critical insights for subsequent generations. Hidden beneath these inadequate and poorly connected sentences are the deeply felt and sincerely conceived beliefs of one of the most sympathetic figures in American literature. But after examining this essay, and other sections of the volume, one is compelled to reject it as a hastily contrived product of the scissors and the pastepot, and to look elsewhere for the best expression of his critical opinions.

6. The Theory of Critical Realism

Dispersing "the conventional acceptations . . ."

And one need not look far, for these opinions were written vigorously and unceasingly, in a steady flow of reviews, articles, essays written until his death, all of which add up to the mature convictions of a realist for whom reality lost not its meaning but its familiar outlines of sunniness, and became instead a more sombre and more shadowed thing. Once *Criticism and Fiction* has been rejected as the definitive statement of Howells' mature beliefs, the task of charting his development as a literary critic who was also a social critic becomes simpler; once the vexatious ghost of the "smiling aspects" is laid to rest, the picture of Howells is resolved into one of a man who, during much of his life, had been an optimistic believer that existing American institutions would go on producing satisfactory results, but who changed, under the impact of a national tragedy, into a serious critic of those institutions; and while his social and political horizons were widened "indefinitely," his literary horizons were also extended to include realistic literature with a more definite purpose than the enabling of mankind to "know itself and others" better; the purpose was to disperse "the conventional acceptations by which men live on easy terms with themselves," and to make them "examine the grounds of their social and moral opinions." In brief, Howells developed the theory of critical realism.

In September, 1887, he made a first tentative formulation of this theory which inspired the writing of his "economic novels," *Annie Kilburn*, *A Hazard of New Fortunes*, and *The World of Chance*. The writer, he said in 1887, should make men "know one another better, that they may be all humbled and strengthened by a sense of their fraternity." This humility will tend to "make the race better" and in so far as the arts tend to make men better and kinder are they to be regarded as "serious interests." There was here still some vagueness, some lack of direction; but none of this is apparent a year later when he devoted an entire "Study" to the mission of critical realism. This was the essay from which he snipped a paragraph for the conclusion of *Criticism and Fiction*. The point of departure was a discussion of the new Christmas literature which, he declared, "appeals to no sentimental impulse, but confronts its readers with themselves, and with the problem which it grows less and less easy to shirk." The problem which this literature had to make its readers face is not only "turkeys to the turkeyless" but the "ineffably better" task of making the reader "take thought somehow in our social, our political system to prevent some future year, decade, century, the destitution which we now relieve." Leo Tolstoy, he declared, was the foremost of the writers of Christmas literature, because "the whole of his testimony" was against "the system by which a few men win wealth and miserably waste it in idleness and luxury, and the vast mass of men are overworked and underfed." Then he made it clear that he was using "Christmas" in the sense of "Christian," for "all good literature is now Christmas literature." He went on to explain that "the old heathenish axiom of art for art's sake is as dead as the great Pan himself, and the best art tends to be art for humanity's sake." Then, in its context of the foregoing paragraphs, the following statement, so ineffective in its final setting in the book, became pointed and meaningful: "Art, indeed, is beginning to find out that if it does not make friends with Need it must perish. It perceives that to take itself from the many and leave them no joy in their work, and to give itself to the few whom it can bring no joy in their idleness, is an error that kills."

A month or so before he had written these deeply felt words, Howells had explained to Edward Everett Hale that *Annie Kilburn* had been written "to set a few people thinking," and then he wrote him several months later to say that he was tortured by the problem of making words into deeds, and that the words were running into the story which was to be *A Hazard of New Fortunes*. And while his own pen was turning in the direction of a critical realism, he tried to encourage all those evidences of the same stirrings which he found in the writing of his contemporaries. He found Harold Frederic's work not only vigorous and forceful, but full of a groping towards a new economic as well as artistic truth. Hamlin Garland's *Main-Travelled Roads* was, he told the readers of *Harper's*, "full of the . . . life of the men who hopelessly and cheerlessly make the wealth that enriches the alien and the idler, and impoverishes the producer. If anyone is still at a loss to account for that uprising of the farmers in the West, which is the translation of the Peasants' War into modern and republican terms, let him read *Main-Travelled Roads* and he will begin to understand." By 1893 he had reached the conclusion that "any conscientious and enlightened fiction" in some way points the need for and the way toward socialism. He found it despicable not "to hit the fancy of our enormous commonplace average," but to "hit the popular fancy and not have done anything to change it."

Ibsen, in the drama, Howells thought, was trying to do exactly what the writer of fiction should try to do in the novel—give us the "truth about ourselves, hard and dry indeed, but immensely wholesome and sanative." And then he wrote the best single definition of critical realism: "dispersing the conventional acceptations by which men live on easy terms with themselves, and obliging them to examine the grounds of their social and moral opinions." He defined this method of fiction more personally and dramatically in his summary of the merits of the Chicago novelist, Robert Herrick, whose work, he said, gave the reader "something to think about: himself, for instance, and his relations with other men very like himself in their common human nature. If his thoughts are not altogether pleasant, it will appeal to his sense of justice to declare why, and it ought to set him about seeing how he can make his thoughts pleasant."

In the waning years of his life, Howells looked back upon American literature from his new perspectives, and saw each of its successive stages as implicated with one form or another of man's aspirations to make the world he loved better and nearer to his heart's desire. Realism, he felt, *critical* realism began when "people began to see that life and the pursuit of happiness had their difficulties even in the universal liberty we enjoyed." And the artist became aware that "in the day that is and is to come the life stories must be homelier, simpler, sadder." And at the age of seventy-five, Howells faced a ballroom full of banqueters who had gathered to do him honor, and he told them about critical realism. He told the assembly which included William Howard Taft and the novelist Winston Churchill, as well as William Allen White, that "literature which was once of the cloister, the school, has become more and more of the forum and incidentally of the market-place." In becoming of the forum, he said, it was "actuated by a clearer motive than before." Then he had some words to say about poetry, which, for the moment, seemed to him a generic representative of all literature. The poets of the "romantic age" in America, the age immediately before the Civil War, belonged to an idealistic period "when men dreamed of human perfectibility through one mighty reform." But with the freeing of the slaves, said Howells, the poet's dream was broken, and through its rifts "the faces of underwaged women and overworked children stare at us; and it does not seem as if it were a sufficient change that now the faces are white and not black." And now, he continued, the true poet must do what he can to help the reader see those faces: "For equality, which is justice writ large, is now the hope of humanity and its service is the condition which has effected itself even in the mystical sources where the inspirations of art have their rise."

The reports of the banquet have it that Howells' speech was greeted with a great ovation; presumably William Howard Taft was among those who rose to their feet and applauded. Possibly they thought they were cheering the mild dean of genteel American letters. If they had listened to Howells carefully, if critics and readers since had listened to him and had read the novels of the crucial and climactic years of his life, they would have realized that they were hearing the theory and observing the practice of a realistic literature whose function is to depict society truthfully so that men might reform it.

In proclaiming this theory, Howells did not discard any of the elements of his former philosophy of fiction; and in keeping his previous beliefs, with their good-sense and moderation, he saved himself from falling into the trap of propaganda. A propagandist or special pleader he himself never became, and he tried to keep others from becoming. For his new vision of a "critical" realism simply reinforced his older conceptions of literary value, rather than displaced them. Throughout the criticism of his maturity and his age, he clung to his basic beliefs: that the writer be perfectly free to choose his own mode of writing; that the mode best suited to an age of empiricism and science was the novel rather than the romance; that once having chosen the novel as his mode, the writer is dedicated to a re-creation of life by selection and arrangement from the materials he knows. What he now called upon himself and his fellows to do was to turn their attention to areas of society which Americans desperately needed to know more about if they were to save their just and democratic society from devolving into an iniquitous plutocracy. But in immersing itself in these newer areas of American experience, realism was to keep to its fifth basic tenet: to abjure imposed morality and "moralizing"—to let the story speak for itself.

The romantic mode, when it had attacked social problems like slavery, Howells felt, had often degenerated into sentimentalism and idealized the victims of society, painting them "impossibly virtuous and beautiful." The truth was, Howells knew, that the poor were no better than the rich, and were very likely to be worse; the duty of the realist was to make the world "consider them not because they are beautiful and virtuous, but because they are ugly and vicious, cruel and filthy, and only not altogether loathsome because the divine can never wholly die out of the human."

Refusing to be taken in by the Victorian fallacy of the virtuous poor, Howells was able to see that labor unionism might develop into a substitute tyranny. He had told John Hay that "the workingmen *as* workingmen are no better or wiser than the rich *as* the rich, and are quite as likely to be false and foolish." He remembered his feelings as an *Atlantic* editor when one of his contributors brought him interviews with thirty workingmen from three states; he had been dismayed by the dullness and stupidity of their thinking, and predicted that if people like them ever got the upper hand, America could say good-bye to liberty, for it would be ground down by a new despotism. And this economic realism persisted in him even through his days of conversion to socialism. While his conversion led him to temper these doubts with a warm understanding of the difficulties of the workingman in a laissez-faire economy, he nevertheless carried this basic skepticism with him. He refused, for example, to be moved intensely by strikes, asking himself why he should be "in the wage-takers' camp rather than the wage-givers' if they are themselves ready to go over to the enemy as soon as they have money enough." The union and the trust may have each made the other inevitable, but Howells came to feel that "in their fatal existence the sense of individual responsibility is lost." In *Annie Kilburn*, Ralph Putney, the lawyer who specialized in lost causes, sighed over the unwillingness of the workers to vote the reforms they desire, instead of "persecuting non-union men" that have as "good a right to earn their bread." And Howells repeated Putney's words, declaring that "In one thing the labor side *is* wrong. It has the majority of votes, and can *vote* the laws it wants, and it won't, but prefers to break the laws we share."

Together with this clear-headed, unsentimental appraisal of the actualities of the rise of labor, another, less praiseworthy perhaps, but very human motive operated to prevent Howells from losing perspective: his own wryly admitted love of comfort. He anticipated by "three or four years" George Bernard Shaw's famous statement that one could not live as a socialist in a capitalist country, and long anticipated him in "practice as well as precept." At the time of the revolution in his political and economic beliefs, he wrote his father reassuringly that the Howellses and the Twains were all of accord: "theoretical socialists, and practical aristocrats." While this might have been an unsavory or even an immoral position for a prophet, it was not an unwholesome one for a writer. It prevented him from degenerating into either pamphleteer or fanatic. In fact, he succeeded in dramatizing and objectifying his social concerns so well, that his disciples sometimes feared that he had left out his message. Hamlin Garland felt that *Annie Kilburn* was too inconclusive a treatment of the problems of labor; Howells replied that the book was all of a piece, an illustration for the need of justice instead of charity.

A man like Garland could feel that the Single Tax offered the best hope of salvation for humanity, but Howells could only nod his head sadly, if sympathetically, at any such naive hope for a simple cure of the complex evils of an industrialized civilization. He wanted a critically realistic literature which showed the problems in all their complexities till "something like science brings the time when His will shall be done on earth as it is done in heaven," not one which would blueprint the author's plan for the future. His own Utopias, *A Visitor from Altruria* and *Through the Eye of the Needle*, were frankly romances of never-never lands where he could present a mythical society which might have developed had the original ideals of the early Christian communes been carried into practice. And even these visions of perfection, he said, had something of a nightmare in them.

But stronger than these forces which prevented him from sinking into propaganda was his basic optimism which still sustained him despite the bitterness of the years of his inner torments. Indeed, it was probably because he remained essentially optimistic that he was able to develop critical realism; for, after all, criticism implies hope—hope that the cause for criticism may be removed by criticism; and the reformer is undoubtedly the supreme optimist to believe that his small plaintive pull will move the stolid bulk of society's inertia. In America the democratic processes had begun, and there were possibilities that they might continue. Even during the crucial years of his social agony, even, perhaps, during the very months when the cry of the Haymarket victims was beginning to penetrate the insulated fastness of his middle-class certainties, he had observed that with all its many imperfections, life in America was different from, and better than, life in other countries; when compared to the lot of the Russian, for example, it was "almost a better world by comparison." While it was still "far from justice," it was "infinitely nearer it than the Russian," and had "but to recognize that equality and fraternity in everything" was the hope of the race. He never lost this perspective, even during the dark years when he had slipped into a mood of seeming despair. He was able to recapture, in age, the same homesickness he had felt as a youth when abroad. In 1860 he had written home to remark on the beauties of America and Americans, and in 1897, he struck the same note when he excoriated the pomp of the German court and contrasted it with the "sincerity and reality" of the American scene. While a series of articles he wrote from 1894 to 1897 averred that America was becoming a plutocracy, he concluded in the last of them that "we may not think the republic is that best thing that can ever be, but we feel that it is the best we can have for the present, and that anything better must be something more rather than something less of it."

When a correspondent wrote him, in 1903, to ask the difference between the American realistic novel and its European counterparts, Howells' answer was charged with this hopeful bitterness against a society which had not reached its potentialities, but which still might. Anyone, he believed, who had seen the poor of both the New and the Old World knew the difference between a people which still might hope, and a people whose "misery is of such ancient date that all hope has died out of it."

This bitter optimism, this hope which had lost the complacency of an earlier time and was the hard-won reward of a painful education in social and personal misery—this was the major legacy of Howells to the next century. It prevented him from losing himself in a despair whose literary issues are often sterility or the flight from life into art. Howells, and a group of American writers whom he helped to nourish, neither abdicated the creative role, nor sought to erect a religion of art or technique. For the newer sombreness of the American writer increased his uncertainty without destroying his faith, and reconvinced him of the complexities of social existence and the consequent difficulties of the task of understanding it and portraying it truthfully. The reformer Howells portrayed in *The World of Chance* rejected even community socialism as a sterile withdrawal from the problems of society. "I don't believe in communities," said David Hughes. ". . . A community is an aggrandized individual." Even worse, Howells thought, was the eremiticism of a Thoreau; his flight to the Pond was no solution, Howells declared, for men are never going to find the answer to " 'the riddle of the painful earth' " by "building themselves shanties and living on beans and watching ant-fights. . . ." Much as he loved Tolstoy—and his admiration for the great Russian had something religious about it—he nevertheless criticized him for "the gloom of his mood" in which he groped "for a hopeless reversion to innocence through individual renunciation of society instead of pressing forward to the social redemption which the very ecstasy of error must help to effect." The message of Howells to the next generation was not renunciation, but espousal, the embracing of a world so that it might be made better than it was.

7. *Annie Kilburn*

". . . the social as well as the individual conscience . . ."

Howells said what he had to say, in the best way he could say it, in four novels: *Annie Kilburn*, *A Hazard of New Fortunes*, *The Quality of Mercy*, and *The World of Chance*. *A Hazard of New Fortunes* was the dominant work of this group; *Annie Kilburn* was a preparation for it; the others were anticlimactic elaborations of themes sounded better in the master work.

Of the three minor works, *Annie Kilburn* was the most intensely felt, for it was the novel which Howells mentioned in the same breath with his hope that he could "someday . . . do justice" to the "irreparably wronged" Haymarket anarchists. He tried to make it a dramatic plea for justice instead of charity, a plea to replace the philanthropy of the Gospel of Wealth with the equality of a nascent Christian socialism. Annie Kilburn was a

New Englander, who had returned from Italy, convinced that she must make her life mean something by helping others. The pressure of this obsessive Puritan "dutiolatry" (which Howells had explored in *Dr. Breen's Practice*), her forebears, like Eben Hilary, in *The Quality of Mercy*, had relieved by their immersal in the cause of Abolition; but now that this fight had been won, men like Hilary had relaxed in contentment, while his son, and women like Annie Kilburn, saw in industrial slavery a new field for their deeply philanthropic instincts. The superficiality of Annie's view of American society was nicely paralleled by her unhappy imposition of Italian art upon the New England scene; she replaced the simple design for a war memorial with an elaborate museum piece from another age and another land. With the other well-meaning citizens of Hatboro she thought the problem of capital and labor could be solved by charity; in this case, the establishment of a "Social-Union" for the millworkers where they might come for innocent recreation and sandwiches and ice-cream—at a nominal cost. But the minister, Julius Peck, tried to tell them that the laborer needed not their alms, but their love, and "justice . . . which stirs in every honest man's heart when his superfluity is confronted with another's destitution, and which is destined to increase in power till it becomes the social as well as the individual conscience." In the society of the minister's vision, the words of Christ will have become economic as well as religious gospel. But Peck realized that he could do little good among the well-to-do suburbanites, and decided to live among the mill hands and share their misery as well as give them his love; but on the way to his new life, a railway car crushed him to death.

In the struggle between members of his congregation over his literal reading of the doctrines of Christianity, Peck found his greatest enemy in the storekeeper, Gerrish, whose description deserves comparison with the earlier picture Howells had drawn of a businessman in *The Rise of Silas Lapham*, and the difference between the two portraits is an index to the change in Howells' outlook between 1885 and 1887. Lapham, though ill-mannered, uncultured, and a driver of shrewd bargains, had a native Yankee earthiness and a basic honesty which had finally transformed him into the hero of the novel. But observe the businessman in *Annie Kilburn:* a petty monster of middle-class ugliness and greed, mouthing the sentimental clichés and hackneyed phrases of his newspapers, hated and feared by his cowed sales-girls whose emotions would occasionally break out in an hysterical impudence. When Mrs. Munger asked him if he thought the workers should be admitted to the benefit performance of *Romeo and Juliet* (a performance for the *workers'* benefit, it must be added) Gerrish's answer was a summation of the social philosophy out of Andrew Carnegie by Horatio Alger: "I came into this town a poor boy, without a penny in my pocket, and I have made my own way, every inch of it, unaided and alone"; naturally, he went on, by applying his energies and abilities to the task, he became wealthy; and just as naturally, the millworkers had not become wealthy, because they had not lived righteously and energetically. So, said Gerrish, "I do not believe—I do *not* believe—in pampering those who have not risen, or have made no effort to rise." He ended the discussion by declaring he would contribute to the Social Union only if the separation of the virtuous well-to-do from the lazy poor were maintained.

The enlightened conversation had been prefaced by a general discussion of labor troubles, and Gerrish told Mrs. Munger, whose face was constantly arranged as if for "indefinite photography," that the real crime was committed by employers who allowed unions to exist, and did not simply discharge any worker who would join one. And even worse was the arbitration of industrial disputes. " '. . . What is arbitration?' asked Mr. Gerrish, levelling his ruler at Mrs. Munger. 'It is postponing the evil day.' 'Exactly,' said Mrs. Munger without winking."

The bitterness of *Annie Kilburn* diminished into the cooler analyses of *The Quality of Mercy* and *The World of Chance.* Millionaires were victims of the chance world of amoral commercialism, Howells decided, as much as were laborers, and so he devoted the first of these to an illustration of society's complicity in the crimes of a commercial civilization. The second was an ill-conceived description of the hazards of the only competitive industrial world Howells knew: publishing and printing. In it, an inventor created a new process which would throw hundreds of printers and engravers out of work; refusing to listen to the pleas of his fellows, he tried to market his invention until, at last, he was convinced that a device such as his, so right for a just society, could only bring misery in an unjust one. So he died by his own hand, drinking the prussic acid which was a part of his new invention.

8. *A Hazard of New Fortunes*: Realism and Critical Realism

Howells knew that it was his "most vital" book; Henry James thought it "simply prodigious"; contemporary reviewers declared it entitled him to be rated "among men of genius"; by 1903 the reputation of the work was so well established that *Harper's Weekly* could allude to it as the work which had been "taken for granted" as the "meridian" of Howells' career; a young Kansan named William Allen White spent the summer of 1891 reading it enthusiastically to his sweetheart, when he should have been convincing her to become the grandmother of his grandchildren. And the place this novel takes in Howells' development —the gradual widening of his scope before it, the decline into gentle banality after it—suggests that it is the work upon which, as he and his contemporaries believed, his reputation will finally rest. Starting with this hypothesis, that it is the climactic work of the man who was, as we have seen, the leader of the comic and realistic age in American sensibility, it is worth examining as a "realistic" work, as an example of "critical realism," and then, perhaps, as a novel with lasting value.

We have seen that the initial hallmark of literary realism was truthfulness, a truthfulness best achieved by fiction which is close to autobiography and which was verified by the sensory experience of the writer. It was fitting, therefore, that for his best work, Howells should have returned so specifically to the autobiographic mode and employed as central figures those representations of himself and his wife out of whose early adventures he had fashioned a mode of fiction which he believed he could make most specifically his own. Basil and Isabel March, the protagonists of *Their Wedding Journey*, became the central figures whose new fortunes were the theme of the later book, the consciousnesses from whose perspective the bewildering events of New York in the turbulent years that ended the 1880's were seen. The March of *A Hazard of New Fortunes*, like the March of *Their Wedding Journey*, was the Howells of actuality, seen at enough distance and with enough objectivity to become part of the higher truth of fiction, but close enough to the fact to have his basis in the felt and remembered emotions of the world of social reality. The Marches were pictured as entering middle age, at a stage when things went "*sans baisser.*" They were thoroughly decent people who felt ". . . if it had ever come into their way to sacrifice themselves for others, they thought they would have done so," but "never asked why it had not come in their way. They were gentle and kind, even when most elusive; and they taught their children to loathe all manner of social cruelty." One of Mrs. March's objections to going to New York was that she couldn't make her sympathies "go round two million people."

In all this, Howells was describing his own placidity and self-contentment before his awakening, and that of the middle class which he represented. His eyes, as we know, were actually opened by the trial of eight anarchists, most of them German, in Chicago. The shock to March's complacency was more concentrated and personal. The eight martyrs dwindled to the intense dramatic point of one: an old German socialist who became the focus of Howells' feelings and a personalization of the eight remote victims. Lingg, Spies, and Fielden became, in their fictional apotheosis, "Lindau," a character patterned after the romantic German watchmaker who had lovingly and patiently taught young Howells German so they might sit and read Heine together. Like the Haymarket anarchists, Lindau was victimized not for his deeds, but for his opinions; and like them, he met his death as a result of the struggle between capital and labor. This, then, became the novel about Howells' participation in the Haymarket Affair, and the artistic distance at which Howells placed his materials contracted often enough to make the identification certain. March had hired Lindau to do translations for the journal he was editing. The owner of the magazine insisted that March fire the German because of his socialism, and March was forced to risk the sacrifice of everything he had worked for in order to stand by the old man. Fearful for his position, and sick at heart over the grief he must cause his family, March nevertheless decided to stick by him. After he made his decision, he felt "the misery of the man who stakes the security and plenty and peace of home upon some cast, and knows that losing will sweep from him most that most men find sweet and pleasant in life." Things turned out as well for March as they did for Howells, but not before both had had their horizons "indefinitely widened."

No better summary of Howells' feelings at the moment he decided to "risk his reputation and his livelihood" could be written; the emotions of *A Hazard of New Fortunes* had been aroused in him by "the bombs and scaffolds of Chicago"; but these emotions had to be made concrete and given the permanence and the higher reality of fiction, and Howells knew neither the circumstances attending the Haymarket disaster nor the city in whose streets it occurred. But he did know New York, and "opportunely" there was a great streetcar strike during his first year in the city, and it enabled his story to find a way to "issues nobler and larger," and provided him with a denouement and an "impressive catastrophe" when a fatal shooting marked the dispute between traction owners and workers. Actual occurrences, then, were the foundation of his best novel; the autobiographic technique was used to give the work the solid basis in what the author had observed and felt. But the "actuality" was consistently transformed, by selection and arrangement, into the "reality" of fiction. The terminology was Howells' own, and he used it in his preface to the 1909 edition to distinguish between the unassimilated fact of sensory experience, and the assimilated fiction which tries to get as close as possible to the truth of the original fact.

The exception to the generally successful transformation of the palpable was the long first section where Howells described the search of the Marches for a New York apartment. Howells admitted that in detailing their quest so minutely he did not in his "zeal for truth" adequately distinguish between "reality and actuality." There were several reasons for this lapse. The first was that Howells was trying, among other things, to write the first novel of serious consequence about New York, striving to get some of its vast, sprawling, teeming life into fiction. Before narrowing his focus down to the lives of those involved in the fortunes of the magazine, he wanted to let his consciousness rove about the larger scene in the midst of which his drama was to be played. As a device for enabling the reader to explore New York physically, the house-hunt served its purposes adequately, if not admirably. Other, less aesthetic, matters were important in causing this initial section to get out of hand. Perhaps Howells had in mind the words J. Henry Harper had written at a time he greatly feared the publisher's reactions to his growing radicalism; Harper suggested that he write a series of sketches which would get at the truth about the variety of New York life. And undoubtedly, the excuse he made for himself was true—that he had begun his book at the moment of overwhelming grief over the death of his daughter Winifred, and that he had mechanically clung to the reportorial technique as a routine in which he could forget his torment.

The unwieldy size of the initial section, too, served as an index to the extent of Howells' liberation from the dramatic technique to the freedom of the organic. Deeply immersed in Tolstoy, he could not fail to see that *War and Peace* and *Anna Karenina* were great books in every way, and that part of their sweep and inclusiveness was their concern with the involvements and complexities of human fates. Although Howells had the general design of *A Hazard of New Fortunes* well in mind, he found it growing and changing as he wrote, compelling "into its course incidents, interests, and individualities" which had not been part of his original intentions, specializing and amplifying with an inner necessity of its own. The dramatic habit was so strong, however, that he felt he had to tie his plots together, and the means he chose was the new enterprise, the co-operative magazine *Every Other Week;* in the operation of this journal, old Dryfoos was the financier, Fulkerson the manager, and March, Beaton, Alma Leighton, Woodbury, and Lindau the contributors to either its artistic or literary contents. The characters could all be logically related through the magazine; what was not so probable was the coincidence Howells used to relate some of them with an almost stage-like dramatic economy, introducing them to each other and to the audience by a series of coincidences which stretch belief to the breaking point. While the Marches hunted for their apartment, they happened to look at rooms kept by Mrs. Leighton, who happened to have been hostess at a similar establishment in the country, where her daughter Alma happened to be temporarily infatuated with the bright but unscrupulous young artist, Cecil Beaton. Alma happened to be an artist as well, and her sketch for the cover of the new magazine happened to be the one which Fulkerson accepted. Another of Mrs. Leighton's country guests had happened to be Mrs. Horn, whose niece, Margaret Vance, happened to meet Conrad Dryfoos on their charitable excursions to the poor of New York's East Side. The restaurant Fulkerson happened to frequent, happened also to be the one favored by Lindau, and therefore the place where the fateful meeting between March and his old German tutor could take place. When March mused upon these coincidences attendant upon the birth of his magazine, "It seemed to him that there were no crazy fortuities that had not tended to its existence, and as time went on, and the day drew near for the issue of the first number, the sense of this intensified till the whole lost at moments the quality of a waking fact, and came to be rather a fantastic fiction of sleep."

But once these initial illogicalities were assumed, once the reader accepted the fictional premise of an almost dream-like unreality about the fortunate magazine, the dramatic contrivance faded, and the subsequent interminglings were motivated and probable, and illustrated the sense of the social dependence which Howells felt growing upon him. There was not only one, not even two centers of interest in the book; there were actually seven: the story of the Marches, that of Alma Leighton and Cecil Beaton, that of Beaton and Christine Dryfoos, that of Fulkerson and Miss Woodburn, that of Conrad Dryfoos and Margaret Vance, that of the elder Dryfoos; and all of them are bound together by their involvement with *Every Other Week.* Like Basil March, Howells had grown; whereas before he had had difficulty in making his imagination and sympathies extend beyond the fates of a few people in their corner of the world and "go round two million people," he knew he must make the effort, or fail as an artist. The intermingling of the fates of his main characters with their constellations of subordinate characters (ranging from the indigent Frenchman searching amid refuse for his dinner, to Mrs. Horn, the arbiter of one range of New York high society), the almost "fantastic fiction" of their many points of involvement, seemed to illustrate the "complicity" which the Haymarket Affair had proved to him was the truth of modern human relations, a truth which had been seared into his consciousness by the agonies of men whose lives he had before considered remote and foreign, and whose actions he had considered criminal. Basil March felt this complicity in his roamings about New York; at first the sights had awakened in him only an aesthetic interest which made him promise himself to get the sights and sounds of the crowded pavements "down in his sketch book"; then they gradually began to affect his sensibilities more deeply, and he found that he "could not release himself from a sense of complicity" with them, "no matter what whimsical, or alien, or critical attitude he took. A sense of the striving and the suffering deeply possessed him, and this grew more intense as he gained some knowledge of the forces at work —forces of pity, of destruction, of perdition, of salvation." Significant the sequence of forces, to begin with pity and destruction and end with salvation; significant, too, that the deep sense of complicity which March felt was associated with a growing religious sense, for on these roamings, he "wandered about on Sunday not only through the streets, but into this tabernacle and that, as the spirit moved him, and listened to those who dealt with Christianity as a system of economics as well as a religion."

The elaboration of character and complexity of plot enlarged his technique and made it capable of carrying this feeling of complicity and interdependence; but, meanwhile, Howells clung to the original essence of his dramatic theory: the objective portrayal of character in action so that the characters might speak for themselves, indeed, so that the whole work might speak for itself, making whatever moral it would purely through total presentation. Whatever judgments were passed were to be formed by the reader after he watched the drama unfold before his eyes. Part of character in action, of course, was the character's expression of judgment. And since Basil March was the fictional mask of the author, there would be naturally a temptation to view March's judgments as those which the reader should accept. But March is amply disqualified from omniscience by the complexity of his character with its many defects as well as its virtues. And one of these defects made him a prejudiced observer. Was Lindau justified in his avowal of the justice of resorting to violence in answer to violence? On this point March was scarcely fit to judge, since his primary defect was a lack of decision, an unwillingness to take matters in his own hands, an almost fatal willingness to see all sides of every question; and this hesitancy made his verdicts less than oracular. In the two major decisions he had to make, the choices were taken out of his hands by the intervention of what seemed beneficent circumstance. When he was offered the new job with Fulkerson, he had little choice but to accept, since he at the same time lost his old one; when he decided to stand by Lindau and prevent Dryfoos from firing him, Lindau made the decision pointless by resigning. It was with this characterization in mind that the reader was forced to view what seemed to be the moral judgment upon "men like Lindau, who renounce the American means as hopeless, and let their love of justice hurry them into sympathy with violence." And while, as we shall see, the general structure of the novel, and especially its handling of the character of Lindau, seemed to support this conclusion, nevertheless the reader was given the freedom of accepting or rejecting March's overt statement of it, because of its consistency with his characterization.

The similar complexities of the other characters operated to produce the same "dramatic" avoidance of easy moralizing. Where the Gerrish of *Annie Kilburn* was loathsome in his greedy stupidity, the Dryfoos of *A Hazard of New Fortunes* was in many ways an honest and, by his standards, a benevolent man. His antagonism to Lindau, it finally turned out, had not been based upon a despotic opposition to radical opinion, but upon an understandably indignant reaction to Lindau's insults. (One of the reasons for making Dryfoos Pennsylvania Dutch was to enable him to understand the German in which Lindau's remarks were spoken.) The men of whose seemingly heartless discharge Fulkerson had told Lindau and the other dinner guests had been, it finally was revealed, all rehired; and at the end, it was from Dryfoos' house that Lindau's funeral took place, the old and bewildered capitalist's desperate gesture of atonement for the hurt he had caused. And every character is shaded similarly; none can be used to grind the axe of any "moral." What Percy Wetmore said of painting, March and Howells thought in terms of writing. Alma Leighton reported her teacher as not caring "for what he calls the literature" of a piece of painting or sculpture; "he says that will take care of itself if the drawing's good." And as the "literature" or "story" was not the first thing in a painting, so the "moral" was not the primary thing in a story; March reminded his wife of what she had always heard him declare, in connection with his descriptive articles on New York: if he "went to work at those things with an ethical intention explicitly in mind," he would "spoil them."

Despite this dramatic absence of overt preachment, the novel was nevertheless permeated with the morality which had given meaning to Howells' (and Twain's) earlier works. But it had ceased to be the neat and impersonal certainties of the moral social scheme of *The Rise of Silas Lapham*, where a character had been asked to sacrifice himself for altruism. In the humbling uncertainties following Haymarket, Howells retreated to the bedrock of personal morality. When faced with a moral choice, the worthy characters of *A Hazard of New Fortunes* fell back upon the simple golden rule of personal relations; those who were immoral acted out of selfishness and a disregard for others. Those who acted morally acted unselfishly, with an inner necessity prompting them to help and not to hurt. There was no question here of considered philanthropy, or reasoned altruism; there was simply an intuitive and instinctive humanism; the moral characters seemed to say to themselves: I cannot willfully hurt another; and they proceeded out of a deep inner conviction of the rightness of this unreasoned belief. What was it that filled them with this conviction? March answered his wife's question with: "Well it won't do to say, the Holy Spirit indwelling. That would sound like cant at this day. But the old fellows that used to say that had some glimpses of the truth. They knew that it is the still, small voice that the soul heeds, not the deafening blasts of doom."

The character who damned himself utterly by his failure to follow this simple moral principle was Cecil Beaton, who wandered through the pages of the novel egocentric, uncaring, his acknowledged artistic brilliance no compensation for his lack of the essential spark of disinterested love. He was first introduced in the midst of a momentary qualm of conscience about his selfishness towards his father, then successively he spurned Alma Leighton because she could be of no social use to him, plunged Christine Dryfoos into an agony of passion, and considered marrying her for her money. And finally he stumbled into his studio, wishing he could kill himself but, when the pistol missed fire, laughing "with cynical recognition of the fact that he had got his punishment in the right way, and that his case was not to be dignified into tragedy."

His case could not achieve catharsis, but Conrad Dryfoos and old Lindau were saint and near-saint, and they met a tragic end, their blood a remission for the sins of selfishness of the chance world of American laissez-faire economics. Saints, however, are abnormalities, and part of Howells' theory of realism, as we have seen, was to treat of the abnormal and the normal in their proper ratio and relation. In the more densely populated world of normality, men like March and Fulkerson could find happy endings by following the inner voice of human decency, and make *A Hazard of New Fortunes* no exception to Howells' comic view of the world. For even after the agony and the anguish, even after March had seen Lindau battered down by a policeman's club and Conrad fall with a bullet in his heart, March could say that despite these things, rather, *because* of these things: "God did not make us despicable," even though it had become popular to despise ourselves. "Whatever end He meant us for," he told his wife soberly, "He must have some such thrill of joy in our adequacy to fate as a father feels when his son shows himself a man. When I think what we can be if we must, I can't believe the least of us shall finally perish."

In all its elements, then, *A Hazard of New Fortunes* adds up to a representative and climactic work of nineteenth-century American realism. Its view of life was still one which found significance and value in the world of physical appearances. It found its task to be the truthful representation of that world by the selection and arrangement from experience which the author could verify and authenticate, for it was largely his own experience. The illusion of vitality and reality was sustained by the dramatic technique of objective narration, together with the larger and more life-like structure of the many-charactered, organically plotted novel. While no preachment intruded in the work, the whole was infused with the vision of a man who believed that the world in which we live, for all its imperfections, was still one in which a moral scheme could bring peace to those who lived by its laws, and despair to those who did not.

This, despite the social inequities, despite the sombre realization that in the chance world of commercialism "someone always has you by the throat." This realization did not destroy the fundamentally comic faith that invested the book with its mature optimism; instead it formed the basis for its enlargement from a work of "realism" to a work of "critical realism." For the difference between the comic tone of *A Hazard of New Fortunes* and the tone of his earlier works was more than simply a deepening of the serious side of Howells' comedy; it was, as well, a shift in the emphasis of his view of man. In the earlier works, his view had been satiric and individualistic; that is, he was primarily concerned with a gently satiric exposure of those personal insufficiencies which prevented the individual from pursuing a life of good conduct leading to happiness; and the cure was simple: allow reason and common sense to rule in matters of affection; not that reason should usurp emotion, but rather that, in the hierarchy of personality traits, emotions should allow themselves to be guided by reason.

But then, after the Haymarket cataclysm, there was a widening of perspective, a shifting of the focus from reform of the individual in his personality to the social environment in which, perforce, the individual lives and grows; and there was the attempt to show truthfully and honestly the inadequacies of that environment. There was no specific reform proposed for these insufficiencies of social organization; that would have made the work unbearably polemical and would, in Howells' mind, have been an unforgivable intrusion of the ethical upon the aesthetic. Instead, these insufficiencies were revealed with as much honesty and as much aesthetic intensity as the author could manage, so that their revelation would shake the "easy acceptations" of the reader, and make him start thinking about that which he has taken for granted.

The metaphor of the "shifted focus" is not entirely apt. Instead we might talk about that kind of literary impression which centers not only upon the individual but upon the backgrounds as well, upon the institutions of which the individual is a part, which he makes and which, in turn, mold him. For the individual was not forgotten. Far from it; his institutions were revealed through him. Not forgotten, either, was the fundamental belief in the efficacy of reason and common sense. One of the delights of the work, for example, was the characterization of Miss Woodburn, the Southern belle who outwardly appeared almost a caricature of the moonlight-and-magnolia conception of Southern womanhood, but who was full of cheerful and level-headed common sense. "No such South," as her father talked about, "had ever existed to her knowledge, and no such civilization would ever exist, to her belief, anywhere. She took the world as she found it, and made the best of it." But there was no dominance of the theme of anti-sentimentalism. Instead there was an analysis, as truthful as Howells could make it, of a society whose structure would have to be changed so that commonsensical individuals might lead lives of which they could be proud, instead of feeling the retrospective shame of their lives of "pushing and pulling, climbing and crawling, thrusting aside and trampling underfoot" and getting to the end "covered with blood and dirt and sin and shame." It was this shift of emphasis, from reform of the individual to exposure of the inequities of social arrangements, that made *A Hazard of New Fortunes* a work of "critical realism."

True to his beliefs, honest in the realization of the inadequacies of his own experience (March was shown hanging his head in acknowledgment that "his share of the calamity was, by comparison, pitifully small"), Howells tried to show the chance world of the economic jungle in the only phase in which he knew it —the publishing of a magazine which he used as the image in little of the contemporary American scene. It was part of Howells' careful artistry that he made no attempt to relate all, or even most, of the elements of the microcosm to the whole; to have pretended it was a miniature industrial enterprise would have been ridiculous, and it would have given the novel the static, allegorical quality which he wished, at all costs, to avoid. So he went out of his way to emphasize the differences, as well as the similarities, between the production of *Every Other Week* and the usual commercial venture by showing it as a co-operative production in which "labor" would share in the profits. A nice irony was achieved when Fulkerson, the originator of the co-operative venture, maintained its virtues, and the virtues of community ownership of natural gas resources, and then, almost in the same breath, pointed out "a short, dark, foreign-looking man going out of the door. 'They say that fellow's a socialist,'" Fulkerson informed March. "'I think it's a shame they're allowed to come here. If they don't like the way we manage our affairs let 'em stay at home.'" And it was not only for satiric purposes that Howells made the magazine unlike the larger social pattern which it indistinctly symbolized, but for purposes of artistic theory; for by keeping it different, by preventing it from assuming any one-to-one correspondence with the whole complex of laissez-faire industry, he prevented it from slipping into allegory or didacticism and kept its integrity as a segment of life, truthful in its own right, as well as meaningful as an echo of larger issues.

And echo these concerns it did. In its operation was involved capital (Dryfoos), management (Fulkerson), and labor (the contributors and editors ranging from March down to Lindau). As the enterprise developed, the man who owned the means of production exercised his autocratic power over it, and threatened to ruin those who actually produced it; and with this exercise of power and its consequences, March became suddenly aware of his identification with every other worker in the chance world of individualistic commercial civilization. Again Howells avoided too facile an identification between microcosm and macrocosm by ending the small "labor controversy" in which the magazine was involved before the participants in this dispute were sucked into the larger turmoil of the streetcar strike. March's minor role in the whole calamity America was facing had been his education; it enabled him to see the strike in quite different a light from that in which he would have viewed it from his insurance office in Boston. He was able to sense his "complicity" with the strikers; and when he met a policeman on riot-duty, he felt for the first time "like the populace," although, Howells adds with a delicate sensitivity for truthfulness of characterization, "he struggled with himself" and finally "regained his character of philosophical observer." He was, however, even in this character able to see the similarities between his own turmoil, small in its way as it was, and that of the strikers as they stood "quietly about in groups on the corners . . . quiet, decent-looking people," and feel their helplessness in their one-sided willingness to submit their grievances to arbitration, so like his own helplessness in dealing with Dryfoos. And just as March had been educated to sensitivity, so had an immoralist like Beaton remained unchanged in his selfishness. It was through his eyes that Howells first introduced the strike, and to him it was simply a cause of "rage toward the men whose action would now force him to walk five blocks"; and so he told a policeman: "If you'd take out eight or ten of those fellows . . . and set them up against a wall and shoot them, you'd save a good deal of bother."

Through Beaton, the reader saw the capital-labor struggle through the eyes of selfishness, through March, he saw it from the standpoint of the awakening consciousness of a man of good will, and through the reaction of Margaret Vance and Conrad Dryfoos, he was able to perceive how these struggles could affect two unworldly sensitivities who took literally the teachings of their religion. And in an age which had become accustomed to the intellectual short-cuts and emotional avoidances so pleasantly provided for them by the popular stereotypes of the day, *A Hazard of New Fortunes* was the kind of a work which presented the disproportions and the inequities to the reader, shaking his conventional acceptations, forcing him to face not only the facts but the feelings attendant upon those facts. *A Hazard of New Fortunes* was, in short, a work of "critical realism."

By skillfully portraying his world of actuality, Howells created a significant form which represented the general world of American nineteenth-century society. He made his most adroit "use of symbol" to bring these worlds together. He linked the private selfishness of Cecil Beaton to the public selfishness of Dryfoos, making the connection between their two worlds through an intaglio ring. In the first area, Beaton, as part of his unfeeling selfishness, had thoughtlessly trifled with the symbol of marriage: in admiring the ring on Christine Dryfoos' hand, he had changed it from the finger on which she had worn it "to the finger on which he said she ought to wear it," leaving her to glow with the "softened fire" of a young girl after the attentions of a wooer. When Dryfoos tried to protect his daughter by driving Beaton away, Christine stripped off the jewelry which her father had bought her, and he "mechanically picked up the intaglio ring . . . and put it on his little finger." At this point Conrad entered. Furious over his daughter's actions, Dryfoos became even more enraged over Conrad's sympathy with the strikers, those "lazy devils" who had "ruined business." Conrad meekly answered the Gospel of Wealth with the new, yet old, Gospel: "I can't help it. I pity them; my whole heart is with those poor men." With that, Dryfoos struck his son in the face and "the blood began to trickle from a wound that Christine's intaglio ring had made in his temple . . ." and "he looked at him with a kind of grieving wonder, and said 'Father.' " After Conrad's death, old Dryfoos leaned over his son's coffin and saw it—"the wound that he had feared to look for, and that now seemed to redden on his sight. He broke into a low, wavering cry, like a child's in despair, like an animal's in terror, like a soul's in the anguish of remorse."

The ring, which Beaton used to wound Christine, Dryfoos used, quite literally, to wound his son who represented the antithesis to his social immorality, and the reader suddenly saw the two worlds contract into one, the personal deepening into the social, the microcosm broadening into the general.

9. *A Hazard of New Fortunes*: Deeper Meaning

Its kind established, its representativeness described, the question still remains of its value; what is its claim to be called not only a work of "realism," and further, of a realism which is "critical," but also a novel which is "good" and "beautiful," and therefore has a more than transitory interest? The temporarily educational worth of a book which helped its readers not only to understand intellectually, but also to feel emotionally the truth of matters which other writers had been helping them to avoid, is apparent; and Howells, who never for a moment would consent to the divorce between the true and the beautiful, between life and art, would have maintained that this in itself was an aesthetic value. But he had, too, seen and understood the difference between the "actual" in life and the "real" when it was transformed into art; one of the conditions of all art, he had declared, is that it is a "created world" different from, because simpler than, the world of actuality. And *A Hazard of New Fortunes* was, as we have seen, such a created world with the "stricter limits" of art. But it was, as we have seen too, a created world which the normal intelligence could identify and verify as a representation of the actual world of its experience; and its purpose was to enable people to understand themselves and their society better. Now the attack most generally made upon the realistic method of fiction which creates these kinds of worlds with these kinds of purposes, is that it lacks depth and meaning. And this charge must be dealt with seriously; for if a book like *A Hazard of New Fortunes* is simply the story of a number of people in New York City engaged in publishing a magazine, it would not lay serious claim to our continued interest and attention. An analysis will show, however, that it is no more such a restricted story than *Huckleberry Finn* was simply a description of a raft-ride down the Mississippi. *A Hazard of New Fortunes* was a deeply meaningful work of art.

But first: What do we mean by "meaning"? There would be general agreement that most of us mean by "meaning" the way in which something represents something more than itself. The current attention to "symbol" and "myth" in art is a result of the anthropological and psychological findings that the human mind has always known something through something else. The art form has been identified as that symbol, or collection of symbols, which enables the viewer or the reader to apprehend, as one recent philosopher of art has put it, "what was not articulated before." This symbol or group of symbols which performs this service becomes a "significant form": a form which incorporates, in itself, what we think and feel to be essentially truthful about larger areas of experience.

One of the difficulties in the adequate assessment of prose fiction is that its significant forms are different from those of the other arts. It operates by means of what one aesthetician would label "discursive symbolism" as opposed to the "presentational symbolism." By "discursive symbol" is meant that symbol which can be talked about in terms of other symbols (words) with a fair amount of approximation to what the first discursive symbol meant. A "presentational" symbol is that kind of symbol which is incapable of being approximated. Poetry is largely presentational symbolism. Prose fiction, as distinguished from poetry, is largely discursive symbolism—a created world of discursive symbols into which the consciousness of the reader may enter and about which it may roam, interpreting and translating the signs and symbols in a way similar to that in which it interprets and translates the signs and symbols of its own environment. The "meaning" in this kind of created world is the way in which it represents what we think and feel to be essentially true about men in general, about man in essence, and even, perhaps, about God.

Let us, for the present, restrict the discussion to the first two of these three kinds of meaning. The first level of meaning—the representation by the specific fictional instance of truths about men in a particular society—we can call "general meaning," and the second kind of meaning—the representation by the specific fictional instance of man as we feel we would know him wherever he may have lived or will live—we can call "universal meaning." Did the realistic method of prose fiction abandon the attempt to tell us what life means on these two levels?

The answer is that Howells believed that each man is a microcosm. He said in many ways, as F. Scott Fitzgerald asserted later, that if a writer started with an individual, and treated him honestly, he would inevitably broaden into a type, and he believed, conversely, that if one started with a type, he might wind up with a cardboard figure or with nothing. And he believed, too, that if a writer started out with a "meaning" and then sought the character or the situation to embody that meaning, he might end at best with allegory and at worst with sentimentality. The essence of the realistic method was that it started with people and their actions, and the places they acted in, and then believed that if their features were truthfully portrayed and their relations described, then out of these truthful impressions would flow a general significance.

Part of the general meaning which Howells succeeded in capturing in *A Hazard of New Fortunes* was, as we have seen, his portrait in little—the first of its kind in American literature—of the tension between capital and labor which had begun to disturb the national scene. But this was only one of the ways in which the book, by its truth to the complexities of the small and superficial, also managed to summarize the depths. For it represented almost all the ideological tumult which featured the emergence of complex modern America from the simplicities of pre-Civil War agrarian, Jeffersonian democracy. On this level of meaning, the work became an imaginative summary of the bewilderment of millions of Americans at the nightmarish turn their Dream was taking. On this level, the center of interest changed from Basil March as protagonist, to March as observer—watching while old Dryfoos found his values collapsing about his head. The old man had been a sturdy individualist, respected in his community, constructive in his civic life, honest in his accumulation of his moderate "capital" of land and equipment through his "work and saving and steady habits and sense." You know, he told his son, what that "will bring a man to"; and correspondingly, in this view of America, the poor were merely examples of "what laziness and drink and dishonesty, and foolishness will bring a man to." Riches, or, at least, well-being was a product of virtue; poverty a result of vice, and all was as it should be. Since this was so, Dryfoos' deepest convictions, the structure of his moral world, were profoundly shaken by Lindau's "talkin' that paternalism of his." He had "always heard it was the worst kind of a thing for the country," for he had been "brought up to think the best government was the one that governs least." But the discovery of natural gas under his farm and the growth of the industries and urbanization which it fed were irresistible pressures, driving Dryfoos from the land and the environment in which his primitive gospel had had meaning, and into a new world of speculation where his "moral decay began with his perception of the opportunity of making money quickly and abundantly." In this world, his old truths became dangerously false, the extension into social life of the immorality of a Beaton in the personal, and they bring to Dryfoos, as they brought to Beaton, tragedy and disaster. Like Beaton, Dryfoos learned that "to do whatever one likes is finally to do nothing that one likes, even though one continues to do what one will."

The world of selfish individualism fell about Dryfoos as it was falling about America; and the various alternatives to replace it were personalized not only by his son, but by Lindau, by Colonel Woodburn, and by March himself. Woodburn spoke for the Middle Ages, for "the central idea, not of . . . false liberty . . . but of responsibility—responsibility." He told the guests around the capitalist's dinnertable that in a competitive commercial society, where the prosperity of an individual "necessarily lies in the adversity of someone else," it is difficult "to be delicate and chivalrous, or even honest." So Woodburn proposed a return to the system of the early South where, if it had been given time to "eliminate what was evil and develop what was good . . . we should have had a perfect system." This, for Woodburn, would be a world "where the enlightened, the moneyed, the cultivated class shall be responsible to the central authority—emperor, duke, president . . . and it shall be responsible to the working-classes of all kinds for homes and lands and implements. . . . The working class shall be responsible to the leisure class for the support of its dignity in peace, and shall be subject to its command in war." Woodburn, viewing the evils of laissez-faire capitalism from the far but principled right, could see the similarity, yet difference, of a Lindau who saw them from the far left, and wished to shake his hand as "a man of principle and a man of honor—a gentleman, sir." But to Lindau, Woodburn's views represented feudalism, and he answered the old Southerner's vision of the future with one of his own in which the State, the instrument of the citizens who go to make it up, will see that the individual will have work and food, a system where "all the roadts, all the mills and mines and landts shall be the beople's and be ron *by* the beople *for* the beople." But Lindau's Utopia, like Howells' own, had a hint of nightmare in it, a snatch of which was vividly previewed in the dream-like description of Conrad and Lindau falling under the club of a policeman. Conrad "was going to say to the policeman: 'Don't strike him! He's an old soldier! You see he has no hand!' But he could not speak, he could not move his tongue. The policeman stood there; he saw his face; it was not bad, not cruel; it was like the face of a statue, fixed, perdurable—a mere image of irresponsible and involuntary authority." Between the extremes of Lindau and Woodburn stood March, the man of the center, educated out of selfishness into socialness, realizing finally that each was right in theory but wrong in practice, Woodburn's solution an ideal but impossible anachronism, Lindau's tainted with the bloody and violent hint of tyranny, but each containing something of the ideal to which the men of good will must struggle in the pragmatic "pressing toward the social redemption."

From the specific, then, *A Hazard of New Fortunes* stretched out to more general meaning, and became a form significant of the development of those complexities which marked the emergence of modern America at the end of the nineteenth century. This achievement in itself makes a claim upon our continued attention; but there is still a deeper layer of meaning—a layer not only involving Americans at a specific point of history, however climactic this point may be, but involving the truth about man in essence as he sits in "bearded state" far below the flux of transitory social and political manifestations, man as we feel he always has been and always will be. This is the level of the most basic truths we have been able to comprehend about his personality, his aspirations, and his fate. Now these basic truths have been given their varying symbolic representations by those primitive stories usually involving supernatural beings which have come to be named "myths," and one of the major forces in modern fiction has been the reassessment of these stories, rescuing them from the status of either superstitious lie or literal historical truth, awarding them their rightful title of aesthetic truth—of significant forms which express verities not articulated before. In poetry, and in prose fiction which tends towards poetry (romance in its best sense), these myths have been assumed as the pattern of meaning, and symbolic poems and allegorical fictions have been written to illustrate their applicability to the contemporary world. But the realist did not start out with myth and end up with life, but tried to start with life; and if the hypothesis be true that the myth expresses the actual pattern of things, then it must follow that these patterns of living, if caught truthfully through the impressionistic technique, may yield correspondences with those verities symbolized in the "myth."

We note the essential difference between the first and the second mode of fiction. The various "non-realistic" methods start out with one of two judgments about the material with which they deal; either the material (that is, contemporary life) is meaningless, in which case the writer flees from it into mythological "certainties" and creates forms with no regard for the material; or else the material is significant in some predetermined way, in which case the writer applies the particular pattern of symbols, the myth, which he has already decided summarizes the meaning of the material. The realist started from exactly the opposite direction; if a "myth" has any truth or meaning (and there is no reason for doubting that there are false and evil myths as well as good and true ones), it has this truth or meaning by virtue of its symbolic summary of the truth of the actual world of human experience; the actual world, therefore, works out into certain patterns which we can recognize as those patterns which the myth symbolized for past cultures. The actual, in this view, comes first, and the myth later, not the myth first and then the actual. So for the realist, for Howells, the actual would reactivate and demonstrate anew those myths, or parts of myth, which are valid.

There are many clues to the myth that Howells felt his material was reanimating. We remember that he talked about the Haymarket Affair, in the preface to *A Hazard of New Fortunes*, in essentially Christian terminology, speaking of the "remission of sins" which the blood of the anarchists symbolized. And echoes of this symbolism are heard throughout the book itself: Lindau's similarity to Old and New Testament figures; Conrad's sweetness and gentleness which end with his sacrifice. Never obtrusive, these correspondences are seen flittingly through the fabric of reality, reminding the reader of the relation between the real and the eternal. The state of America at this time, personalized in the decay of old Dryfoos, was explicitly described by Colonel Woodburn as a fall from simple innocence to the agonies of sophistication: he showed "how we began as a simple agricultural people" who had been seduced by the "spirit of commercialism" which had "stolen insidiously upon us" and by the "spirit of competition" which had "embroiled us in a perpetual warfare of interests." The phrase "insidiously stolen" and the adjective "infernal" begin to stir dim memories of ancestral voices, and these reverberate and amplify in the personal experience of old Dryfoos whose pleasant, productive, agrarian life had been transformed into a money-making monstrosity by the natural gas which lay beneath his farm, erupting over the natural beauties of the land after "Go-Devils" had been exploded in the well-shafts, calling up the satanic fumes in an eruption of earth and stone and timber and, as Fulkerson humorously put it, assorted "adoptive citizens." Gaining wealth, he lost everything and was driven out of his simple life, his simple morality, his simple joys. " 'I wisht we could go back . . .' " his wife said wistfully. " 'We can't go back!' shouted the old man fiercely. 'There's no farm any more to go back to. The fields is full of gas-wells and oil-wells and hell-holes generally; the house is torn down and the barn's goin'—' " And with his anguished cry, millenniums contract, and we hear the torment of endless generations who have tasted the bitter, necessary fruit of progress.

It would have been tempting to follow this story of America's fall from simplicity with the pattern of the redemption—tempting, but false to the endless varieties of patterns which the actualities seem to take. So Howells continued to use the Hebraic-Christian story not as the mold into which his story would be cast, but as the warp of meaning around which the actual variations wove their complicated changes. Conrad, so full of humble love for his fellows, sacrificing himself for them, lost in grieving wonder at his "Father's" forsaking, came close to a modern representation of Christ. His mother quoted him as insisting gently that "you got to give yourself," and his death symbolized the basic meaning of the need for unselfish love which, as we have seen, permeates the book. But Howells prevented the portrait from slipping into allegory by keeping Conrad human, ineffective, weak; a complex character; there was as much possibility of attributing his actions to the frustrations of impotency as to the satisfactions of altruism. The Christ-pattern was there, deep underneath the natural, reminding us of the oneness of man and his history, giving the character its deepest levels of meaning; but the actuality was there too, reminding us that these myth-patterns are true because they symbolize the actual, and not the reverse.

Even more fleeting is the glimpse of the pattern we catch through the character of Dryfoos. The rigid Calvinism of a Dryfoos was, as Tawney and Weber have shown analytically, but Howells showed aesthetically, equated with laissez-faire capitalism. And for a man like Fulkerson, who, throughout the novel, is treated as the typical American, Dryfoos, Howells told us, was a "fetish," and therefore dimly and a little ironically qualified to serve as part of the Trinity in this indistinct recapitulation of the particular variety of fall and resurrection through which America was passing at the end of the nineteenth century.

And the hope that is eternally contained in this divine comedy of the Christian myth is a hope which was expressed on all levels of meaning of *A Hazard of New Fortunes.* It was a hope that sprang from the essential conviction of the meaningfulness of the seemingly chaotic ugliness through which American life and art were passing. March, walking about New York, saw its architecture as representative of this seeming formlessness which, upon superficial observation, tempted one to abandon faith in the significance of the physical, but then, upon deeper vision, convinced one of the purposefulness of the pragmatist's world:

> Accident and then exigency seemed the forces at work to this extraordinary effect; the play of energies as free and planless as those that force the forest from the soil to the sky; and then the fierce struggle for survival, with the stronger life persisting over the deformity, the mutilation, the destruction, the decay of the weaker. The whole at moments seemed to him lawless, godless; the absence of intelligent, comprehensive purpose in the huge disorder, and the violent struggle to subordinate the result to the greater good, penetrated with its dumb appeal the consciousness of a man who had always been too self-enwrapped to perceive the chaos to which the individual selfishness must always lead.

". . . The chaos to which individual selfishness must always lead." This was the simple vision of *A Hazard of New Fortunes.* In the world of the social Darwinians, individual selfishness would lead to the survival of the fittest and the Gospel of Wealth. But Howells' (and America's) was a different kind of vision. It was a vision which accepted the physical world of appearances with all its complexities and change and becomings and never arrivings and was deeply convinced of the value of that world. It was not the exuberant conviction of the Renaissance man who could cry "The world means intensely, and it means good!" Instead it was the quiet, humble, even a little bewildered assertion of a Basil March: "'*I* don't know what it all means'" but "'I believe it means good.'"

From then on until his death, Howells wrote out his own views on the good society in two Utopian romances, and then, the fund of his experience of social evils exhausted, he returned to tepid reworkings of the themes of his earlier periods. Fiction continued to flow from his pen, but it was old, worn velvet which he went through the weary motions of brushing into freshness, knowing well that his day was past. In *The Day of Their Wedding* (1896) he revisited the Shaker colony of Massachusetts for the love story of a boy and girl of the sect; *The Landlord at Lion's Head* (1897) was a more mature view of the same mixed society of vacationing Bostonians and their country hosts that he had patiently delineated in three of his earlier works, although it gained additional stature by its expert portrait of the "jay" student at Harvard; *The Story of a Play* (1898) lived up to its title, and became the tale of the tribulations of a dramatist in getting his first work produced, and was notable chiefly for the splendidly exaggerated "ham," Lancelot Godolphin; *The Kentons* (1902) was the story of a middle-aged Ohio couple with a marriageable daughter and all the pleasant troubles that seemed to come with a young lady in that state; *Letters Home* (1903) was Howells' attempt at the epistolatory method, a story of courtship and marriage which repeated his earlier favorite theme of the need for common sense in matters of the affections. *The Son of Royal Langbrith* (1904) was the one novel of the late years to deal seriously with social criticism; it was the story of the strange distortions in a family's remembrance of a dead industrialist whose son had been brought up to worship his memory, and whose true character had been that of a greedy and grasping exploiter of those about him. *The Leatherwood God* (1916) became Howells' only historical novel and dealt with an evangelist of early Ohio; *The Vacation of the Kelwyns* (1920) concluded the gentle final years of Howells with a gentle final story of a middle-aged couple vacationing in New England, their relations with the near-by Shakers, and the courting problems of their niece. It is little wonder that readers began to regard Howells as something from another century: he was. Fortunately, he had erected his monument, and the capstone of it had been *A Hazard of New Fortunes*.

CHAPTER V

NATURALISM AND INTROSPECTION

1. The End of the Comedy

When does an "Age" end? The very asking exposes the arbitrariness of all such divisions. We saw that the comic tone —the deep conviction of the value of the world of appearances— was the hallmark of the age of Howells. And this tone did not disappear at once, instead it trailed off like a sigh after the explosion of Haymarket. Twain was still occasionally able to crow to Howells about the immense days when it seemed, with the revolutions in South America, that republics were springing up all over the globe; Howells could agree with Norton that, after all, pleasant people were more numerous than the unpleasant; and he could say in an article bitterly critical of American life that a danger was not that Americans should praise themselves too much, but should "accuse themselves too much."

But these expressions were overwhelmed by increasing weariness and pessimism. By 1895 Twain was sixty, and Howells would become so in two more years, and they knew they were two old men whose day had passed. The death of Winifred in the first months of 1889 left Howells crushed, and the death of Susy Clemens, occurring so tragically while her parents were away on the lecture tour with which her father recouped his shattered fortunes, took the light out of Twain's world. New writers were emerging; for all the continued and unexciting faithfulness of the Garlands, the Boyesens, the Herricks, and the Fullers, there were the younger writers who took Howells as their guide up to a certain point and then, with his blessing, went on into the woods alone: there was Harold Frederic, and Stephen Crane; Theodore Dreiser and Frank Norris, all of whom published promising work in the 1890's. And while Henry James had produced good work, even great work before, his major phase lay just ahead, and his genius symptomatically came to fruition at the moment when that of Howells and Twain was dying.

After *A Hazard of New Fortunes*, Howells had little left to do. While to the outward eye he seemed to be still at the height of his fame and the fullness of his powers, there were signs of his decline. *Harper's* seemed almost eager to shake loose of some of their commitments with him, especially from his continuance of the "Editor's Study" department, about which there had been so much controversy. More important, however, was the growing evidence that he was written out, that he had said all he had to say, and only with effort could force himself to say it over again. From 1890 to 1894 his letters to Norton, along with Twain, the closest and dearest friend of his age, were full of doubts as to his ability to go on in the same line, as to his ability to continue writing fiction; even worse, doubts as to his desire to go on. At the moment of his deepest self-doubts, he was jolted by an episode involving his short-lived editorship of the *Cosmopolitan* from December, 1891, to June, 1892. He had been invited to bring all his prestige and experience to this magazine by John Brisben Walker, who, it would appear, assured him of a free hand in its conduct. Howells immediately set about soliciting material which would, it appears, have made the *Cosmopolitan* the center of the critically realistic, just as he had made the *Atlantic* the stronghold of the realistic; he wrote Garland, for example, asking him if he would do a piece on the growing Farmer's Alliance movement, or anything else on the same lines. It was quite possibly a disagreement about this kind of material that led to the breach between Walker and Howells, about which

Howells was so silent, and which left him without an official editorial connection until 1900, when he relaxed into the Editor's "Easy Chair" department of *Harper's*.

In the meantime, Twain was sinking deeper into the pessimism of his later years. Whereas the early sorrows of his career—the death of his brother on the Mississippi, the death of his first son, both tragedies for which he blamed himself—had been absorbed in the general healthfulness of his optimism, the death of Susy in 1896 was the blow from which he never recovered; for the following four years, his letter paper was still edged with black in gloomy remembrance of his loss. And for the first time Howells and Twain and Aldrich began to talk about reality as if it were a dream: the present a nightmare, the past a pleasant haze of nostalgia. Do you remember, Howells wrote Aldrich, wistfully, the good times they had, the dinners at Ober's where the three of them, together with Ralph Keeler and Bret Harte and James T. Fields, would devour their flattened omelettes and beefsteak with shoe-pegs (champignons), and a blasphemous story from Fields about a can of peaches would be followed by the condescensions of Harte to Twain which must have been so severely galling to the latter. And always there would be the sigh that it all seemed like the vision in a golden haze. What a dream it has been! they would exclaim; or how like two old derelicts they were, Howells and Twain, drifting aimlessly about, their passengers gone, their compass giving no familiar readings.

In this mood Twain was oppressed by his lack of productivity, and his wife would beg him to try to recapture the joy of life which had given the world Huck Finn and the Yankee. But the age whose spirit he was and whose spirit was his, was slipping away until suddenly, everyone seemed to agree at once, it was gone. And in its afterglow, the gloom of personal and financial losses deep upon him, he turned with a cry of rage upon the personal God in whom he had never really believed and the impersonal Fate in which he always had, and wrote the sombre tales of *The Man that Corrupted Hadleyburg* and *The Mysterious Stranger*.

But his pessimism never quite changed to misanthropy; he kept his belief in the goodness possible, though never prevalent, in man in his familial and social relations. We must not be misled by outcries of what seem to be man-hatred in works like *What Is Man?;* for his fiction is more revealing, showing the pervasion of his basic humanistic faith; he pictured the forces which corrupted men, or played with them as if they were meaningless toys, as a fiendish malignance, which he eventually gave the name of Satan. Should he and Howells ever see their children again? without a doubt, he said bitterly, for that would give Malignance another chance to break their hearts.

But his conception of the malice of supra-human Fate caused him to elevate Satan into supreme power in the Universe, and kept something of God among men. In the dark late years of his despair, he lost optimism, but he kept some of his faith in man. This fact has been obscured by the many evidences of the deepening pessimism of his last twenty years, with works like *The Man that Corrupted Hadleyburg* and *The Mysterious Stranger* cited to illustrate the depth of his hatred for his fellow. But when we examine works like these, what do we find?—that men in general do not come out so badly. For on the scale of increasing sympathy, we generally find that the same ordinary, common people he celebrated in *Huckleberry Finn,* like Jack Halliday who led the townspeople of Hadleyburg in their scoffing of the Incorruptibles, ranked high, while the pretentious, self-righteous "pillars of society" were very low. The commoners of Hadleyburg rose to the derision which punctured the pretensions of their respectable bankers and lawyers and civic leaders and ridiculed their own civic hypocrisy with the chorus of "You are not a baaad man." Highest in the scale of sympathies was the old couple who wrestled unsuccessfully with the superhuman temptation placed in their path by the unknown visitor, finally succumbed, and then, with their faith in themselves shattered, were left crushed and dying. And who was lowest of all—lower even than the pompous Incorruptibles? It could not fail to be the "mysterious stranger" himself, a dehumanized figure who came into Hadleyburg, was the victim of a slight which the author did not even bother to record, and then set about coolly to destroy the village's pride with a malevolent practical "joke."

Had Mark Twain wished to change the focus of his readers'

sympathies from the sinful people of Hadleyburg to their tormentor, it would have needed only the slightest of additional touches—the specifying of the man's grievance, the detailing of the injury done him, at least what he looked like, what his name was. Instead Twain kept him nameless and bodiless, an anonymous shadow who slipped into the world of men and slipped out again, and then from afar, with unfeeling malice, manipulated the strings of lustful greed and made the human puppets dance. And what must be remembered is that Mark Twain did not wholly renounce his citizenship in the commonwealth whose motto was: men are a collection of asses, and I'm the biggest ass in the collection. As a matter of fact, he had earlier told something very like the story of *The Man that Corrupted Hadleyburg*, and he had told it on himself; it was a story in *Life on the Mississippi* in which he was the one whose ethics and cupidity came into conflict, with greed the easy victor. There he had related how a dying man in Germany had entrusted him with the secret of a $10,000 cache along the Mississippi, so that the fortune might be given to the poor shoemaker to whom it rightfully belonged. It took very little effort on the part of his companions to persuade him that it would be far more charitable to keep the money themselves, for with the access of sudden fortune, the shoemaker would "shut up shop, maybe take to drinking, maltreat his motherless children. . . ." They soon had talked the poor old man down from $10,000 to a chromo sent as a sentimental remembrance. The point was that Twain immersed himself in the fallibility which he satirized, and in the later, more serious, more bitter description of human corruptibility, he did not completely lose his sense of complicity, his feeling of sympathy. And the second "mysterious stranger"—the title character of the posthumously published work which summarized his later pessimism—was Satan, and there was an undercurrent of terrible anger in the descriptions of the fiend who rules our destinies, how he creates small villages and their populations only to crush them like ants under a board. Helpless, tiny, yet compassionate, the human ants engage our whole sympathies, and our rage is not against man but against Fate.

These are the symptoms of the continuance of some elements of confidence even in Twain's later years. But these elements no longer were segments of the robust and vivifying faith which he shared with the age whose genius he was. Instead they are unintegrated parts of the darkening skepticism and doubt which gathered about his snowy eagle's head, as it was gathering about America's.

Meanwhile, new currents were beginning to flow, one of them carrying the old debris of sentiment and escapism, the other a fresh new surge towards the future. The first counter-current was the revival of historical romance, and it seemed to overwhelm the realistic movement. As early as 1893 one of Howells' fictional publishers had said that "people are getting tired of those commonplace, photographic things. They want something with a little imagination." He could not then foresee that by 1900 people would be buying *Graustarks* and *Prisoner of Zendas* by the millions. By the turn of the century, the fashion of the historical romance had not only captured the general reading public, but had reduced America's centers of culture. When early in 1900, Howells' friend W. H. Bishop invited him to speak at Yale, he warned Howells that he would be in the enemy's country, with regard to opinions about fiction, a country where the only good words were for swashbucklers and their rapiers. Howells answered that he didn't mind being in the enemy's country; he was growing used to it. The thing he complained of, he added, was that it was so poverty-stricken in ideas that a man could not live off of it. In his first essay in *Harper's* "Easy Chair" he despaired of making anyone understand "how wholly" writers of realism had been forgotten, in an age when "the cry . . . is for historical romances, which is answered with volumes in all their hundred thousands." And by 1904, *Collier's* summarized the trend of the times: "The popular novel of today is romantic—romantic in subject and effusively romantic in method. A great deal of adventure, a dash of sentiment, and a strange land for its setting make a fine recipe for a modern novel. All of this is far removed from the minute study of commonplace people which Mr. Howells has made the basis of most of his fiction."

He knew part of the reason for this; the romantic tendency was always present during the supremacy of the "natural," waiting for the time when American sensibility would once again feel the need for probing behind the world of physical appearances; but he felt, too, that there was another, baser reason for the return of interest in the "romanticistic," in the sentimentalism which took the form of the historical romance. He theorized that America's unconscious revulsion from the shameful imperialism of the Spanish-American War made it "more than ever anxious to get away from itself, and welcome the tarradiddles of the historical romancers as a relief from the facts of the odious present." In an attempt to explode these sentimentalisms, Howells wrote one of his best short stories, "Editha," the tale of a girl who embodied all the nonsense about the heroic romanticism of war and whose false sense of values drove her unfortunate lover to enlist. She had visions of him returning heroically home, with some slight wound to testify his courage. Instead, he died miserably in Cuba, and his mother told Editha bluntly that her sentimentalism had killed him. "How perfectly vulgar," said one of Editha's fashionable acquaintances, when she heard of the old lady's accusation, and that helpful phrase enabled Editha to explain everything and to rest in contentment with her sentimentality.

But if the current of historical romance was broad, it was also shallow; running deeper were other currents; younger writers were gratefully accepting the encouragement Howells gave them; to the same allegiance to the truth, to the same unswerving honesty, to careful representation of the normal and the commonplace, they were adding new areas of man's knowledge of himself, going deeper into his social life, spreading wider over his political and economic life, and the unbroken line of serious writers from the 'nineties testifies to the endurance of the basic doctrines of realism. Stephen Crane in *Maggie*, Theodore Dreiser in *Sister Carrie*, Upton Sinclair, Sinclair Lewis in *Main Street*, *Babbitt*, and *Elmer Gantry*, James Farrell in *Studs Lonigan*, all are in a direct line of descent from Howellsian realism and critical realism. The essential similarity, yet important difference in degree, between the generations of realists was symbolized in the tone of a meeting between Howells and Theodore Dreiser in 1900. Dreiser felt that Howells "has been an influence for good in American letters" and had "used his strength and popularity in the direction of what he took to be right"; but there was scorn in Dreiser's eyes as he looked at the man whom he found to be "greater than his writings," and if that was little enough praise, "greater than his reputation." For Howells "had no direct experience" of the "great misery"; Howells had led the sheltered middle-class existence; Howells probably, as Henry James said commiseratingly of him, had known no other woman but his wife. Howells had never, like Dreiser, lived a tortured life of adolescent poverty in a house where love was a stranger; Howells had never, like Crane, slept under a Mexican sky between two bandits or lived with a "madam."

Yet when *Maggie* was refused by publisher after publisher, it was Howells who found him one, and who wrote the essay which launched the young man on his literary career. Crane was frank in his avowal of his discipleship. He was grateful in a way that was hard for him to say, he told Howells, and he always thanked God that he could have the strongest admiration for the work of a man who had been so much to him personally.

Crane believed that he was simply carrying on the work which Howells had begun: the telling of the truth about that which he knew. But there was a difference in degree, if not in kind, between his fiction and that of Howells. The younger novelists were catching and recording the first tremors of cultural change; in this instance, the tremors were of uncertainty, of loss of confidence, a loss of the buoyancy which had made possible the works of Howells, the great works of Twain, the philosophy of William James. The novels of Crane, Norris, Frederic, and Dreiser began to reflect the spread of the feeling that man is no lawgiver, but an absorber; that nature "stands firm," and man must accommodate himself to her, "must record truth, inhuman though it be, and submit to it." This was William James' statement of the "naturalistic" feeling. It also seems to be a summary of the literary position known by the same name.

It is generally agreed that naturalism, the literature of supposedly pessimistic determinism, had its major manifestation in France, especially in the works of Emile Zola. Zola was idolized by Frank Norris, who took him as master and guide, and hence, runs the argument, gave tangible proof of the emergence, in

America, of a new strain of literary technique and attitude in the last decade of the nineteenth century.

What are some of the hallmarks of this supposedly new strain? We must go back to its origins to understand it. Early in his career, Zola cast about for a philosophy to inform his literature and give it meaning, and he thought he found it in Claude Bernard's description of the experimental method of science, and in his interpretations of the theories of Charles Darwin. Here Zola believed he found the rationale for a kind of literature which would report truthfully and objectively, with a passion for scientific accuracy and an overwhelming accumulation of factual detail. Since Darwin had shown that all organisms were shaped by their environment, the way to show what really happens to a person is to portray him in his social and economic surroundings, with as little selection and arrangement of the details of those surroundings as possible. And various corollaries seemed to flow from the neo-Darwinian origins of this literary theory. One of the most striking was the treatment of man as partly animal, especially with regard to his primitive drives of love, hate and hunger. The naturalistic novelist would then go further in the direction of portraying these drives than did his predecessors. A second, and more important corollary, was the assumption of a deep pessimism; for if man develops and changes solely through the buffeting of his environment, if he acts solely through the outer pressures of his heredity and environment, over neither of which he exercises any control, then there is a tendency to see him as a helpless animal without meaning and without hope, reduced to either a pawn of these two forces, or, with pessimism carried one step further (and Twain came near this position in his last years), an insect which some malignant higher force torments with titanic malice.

The first of these distinctions—the extension of truthful representation to wider areas of human experience—would not seem to warrant the division between two kinds of literary sensibility; we have seen that a man like Howells knew that realism must spread out to include these areas of experience. The realistic mode, widening in its interests from those of a Howells, to those of a Robert Herrick, and thence to the interests of a Sinclair

Lewis, remained essentially the same philosophy of art, using the same techniques, but with the extension of the materials upon which these techniques were exercised. What does make a difference is the way in which the newer writers continued to shift the focus of their attention away from the individual towards the natural and social forces which seemed to be enslaving man. But even with their greater emphasis upon natural drives and environmental influence, American writers at the turn of the century did not succumb to complete pessimism. "Naturalism" in the sense of a completely pessimistic determinism never existed save in the mind of its enemies. If it is true that man is simply a helpless creature of external forces, then it follows that man can do nothing about his fate, and therefore it is useless to hope for betterment either of society or of the individual. But the original "naturalist"—the father of them all—Emile Zola, was an ardent reformer, and specifically stated that he wrote his books to show men and their conditions as they are, so that man might take heed of them and make them better. The rigid determinism that supposedly dominated naturalism and differentiated it from other types of literary sensibilities would make it quite impossible for man to affect either his own fate or the fates of others; an individual would be simply the product of external forces over which he has no control; hence there could be no question of a "right" or a "wrong" action, no question of morality, for man could only act as he must. But Zola was a self-proclaimed "experimental moralist"; the putrescent corruption of Nana's body under the ravages of smallpox gave the Rougon-Macquart cycle one of the most moral endings in all literature; the bitter indictment of the unjust social and economic scheme in *Germinal* conveyed the author's moral vision of the just society which would make such miseries impossible.

It is not strange that this should be so. Writing is painful and demands great courage, and it would be difficult to imagine anyone undergoing the strains of creation, the disillusion of watching the transcribed reality fall short of one's vision of perfection, if one believed that it all added up to nothing. Dissatisfaction with his world does one of several things to a writer; if he loses confidence in appearances, he seeks the primitive meanings which he feels are eternally there beneath the flux, or he makes a religion of art; if he remains in his world and seeks salvation in its complexities, he does what Zola did, what Howells did, what in our times a James Farrell does: he writes of things as they are so that people will understand them and try to make them better. This was the answer Danny O'Neill gave to his University of Chicago professor when asked why he wrote of the sordidness of Chicago's South Side.

And the younger American writers at the turn of the century who seem to have been dominated by the pessimistic determinism which has been called "naturalism" turn out to be either writers who wrote for reformation of man, or writers who were groping towards the meanings they felt lay under or above the ordinary world of human social relations.

Dreiser, for example, who at first glance seems so different from what went before (and was hailed by Sinclair Lewis, himself a critical realist of the twentieth century, as the pioneer of new frontiers in American literature); Dreiser's attitude seemed to be summed up in the striking symbol at the beginning of *The Financier,* when young Frank Cowperwood stood before the fish-market's tank and watched the life-and-death struggle between a squid and a lobster, the uneven battle ending, as it must, on the side of the harder armor and sharper claws. For Cowperwood this was the sum of the world's amorality, and it has seemed the sum of Dreiser's world as well. But from the beginning, Dreiser's world of fiction was a moral one.

The fall of Hurstwood in *Sister Carrie* was as moral a tale as the career of Nana. As for the trilogy of which *The Financier* was the first part, it traced the dramatic rise of the immoralist, whose rise brought no more satisfaction than did the "rise" of Silas Lapham; and when the plan of the whole came into view, with the publication of the notes which would have formed the basis of the concluding volume, *The Stoic,* it turned out that Dreiser had designed the series to lead up to—the proof that morality has no place in the Darwinian world of tooth and claw? Hardly; Cowperwood's heirs were to be shown acknowledging that the only peace and satisfaction can come from complicity and feeling with others, and planning the return of their father's fortune to the society from which he had so unscrupulously wrested it.

In Frank Norris, the other presumed "naturalist" of the younger generation of writers, "naturalism" in the sense of pervasive pessimistic determinism is just as hard to find. In *The Octopus,* for example, Presley discovered that the master of the railroad was presumably a victim, helpless in the clutch of the supposedly inexorable laws that govern the affairs of men, just as the earth is in the grasp of natural forces. At least, that is what Shelgrim said, and presumably what Presley believed. But the total meaning of *The Octopus* added up neither to pessimism, nor even to determinism. For according to the scheme of which *The Octopus* was a part, and according to Norris' explicit statement at the end of that work, these vast cosmic forces inevitably worked for the Good. And even social determinism, as well as cosmic pessimism, was ruled out by the structure of *The Octopus,* which did nothing to show the inexorable social necessity of the railroad's actions, and everything to arouse the reader's antipathies against them. The very metaphors applied to the railroad—the title metaphor itself with its connotations of inhuman, faceless death by water—involve the reader in a fierce personal hatred for the machine which was strangling the farmers of the valley; the farmers, victims of the railroad, were warmly personalized; we sympathize with their loves, their loyalties, their griefs; and the only personalization of the cyclopian monster that came tearing through the valley, scattering the carcasses of sheep in its dumb, murderous, iron wake, was the ugly S. Behrman, a man without even a first name, a stereotypical villain if there ever was one, who met a fitting end buried under the flood of wheat pouring into the hold of the India-bound merchantman. This general tenor of criticism of things as they are was reinforced by one of the most moving juxtapositions imaginable: the scenes which alternated between the orphaned child watching her widowed mother starve to death in the bushes, and the dinner party in the sumptuous mansion on the hill just above them. Interspersed with the dying mother's words were snatches of conversation over a decadently elaborate menu, with each course specified; the alternation made an almost unbearably affecting contrast; together with the main dramatic structure of impersonal machine pitted against personal man, it made the work one which stirred the reader with a sense of the injustice and inequality of which he must take heed and change, rather than one which stunned him with a conviction of the overwhelming power of amoral forces over which man has no control, and to which he should deterministically resign himself.

"Naturalism," then, in America, seemed to be no more than a deepening and broadening of the realistic and critically realistic techniques and attitudes extended to larger areas of society. But when one reads the novels of Norris and Crane, and the later works of Harold Frederic, one becomes aware of the beginnings of a difference in kind as well as degree, a difference in treatment as well as a difference in materials. One feels that the surface that Howells revered and portrayed with such loving fidelity was beginning to break up, and through its fissures were welling strange new visions: ogres and demigods, grotesqueries, and distortions of time and space which we associated with the romantics of an earlier time. But these weird landscapes were as real as any pleasant New England countryside described so honestly by Miss Jewett, and the ogres were as genuine, if scarcely as palpable, as the hard-shelled Baptists whom Eggleston showed us. For these were the landscapes and creatures of the human mind, the richly mysterious region where the experience of the individual mind and the experience of the race seem to coalesce; where mythology appears not so much the symbolization of social patterns, as of mental process; where symbols themselves take on new meanings, and become not so much discursive representations of meanings within the story, but presentational things in themselves, the point in palpability where the otherwise unknowable things about the human mind are materialized.

This newer "romanticism" (as Norris termed it) was primarily interested in extending the bounds of literary investigation outward from the normal commonplace of average civilized life in two directions: one was downward, deeper into the inner life of the individual; the other was upward, into the life of the race. And in conducting these explorations, the newer novelists had to abandon the objective techniques of the realists, so well suited to truthful reporting of the average. In place of picaresque looseness, they began to contrive carefully interlaced structures where epical figures worked their way through patterns of symbolism; in place of autobiographical freedom, with its apparent abstention from moralizing, they began to attempt tight contrivances which, in Norris' words, would prove something, would "draw conclusions from a whole congeries of forces, social tendencies, race impulses." As Howells commented, it was the reversal of the realistic mode which in some ways resembled the older scientific method where the documents were collected and then the hypothesis drawn. In the newer fiction, the hypothesis, the insight, was drawn first, and then documents collected in support of the hypothesis: "First the inference, then the fact."

Howells had observed, and to some extent charted, the flow of these new currents towards twentieth-century fiction, one in the direction of the psychological, the other in the direction of the mythical, both of which directions ultimately converged in writers like Faulkner and Steinbeck. As early as 1893 one of his fictional authors had mentioned that the "motive" of his story might be called psychological, and his publisher had replied: "Well, they say that the *roman psychologique* is superseding the realistic novel in France." By 1903, Howells saw that "a whole order of literature" had arisen to which the name "psychological" might be given, as the term "scientific" had been applied to realism. And he saw that the newer impulses were, in many cases, revivals of those tendencies in the literature which dominated the age just before his own—the tendencies best represented by Hawthorne. (He might have added, of Melville, too; but Melville was still deep in the obscurity from which he was only rescued in 1921.) The newer fiction, Howells said, "turning from the superabundance of character" would "burrow far down into a soul or two" and bend its vision inward, as did Hawthorne; or else it would take its clue from "a poet of such epical imagination" as Emile Zola.

Howells himself made some experiments, not very successful ones, with introspection. In several short stories and one short novel in the century's last years he went as far as he could in the unfamiliar grounds of psychological analysis. That this could never be very far was suggested by one of his stories in which Wanhope, a psychologist, proposed to a group, of which the author was a member, that it conduct an investigation into dreams. "That would be rather dreadful, wouldn't it?" Howells asked. "We do dream such scandalous, such compromising things about people." One of these "compromising things" was the subject of *The Shadow of a Dream*, in which a husband's recurrent nightmare was that his best friend, who lived with him, attended his funeral and then married his widow. The husband did die, and the wife did become engaged to the friend, but broke off her impending marriage when she learned the nature of her dead husband's dream.

Although Howells tried to begin to understand this new world with its strangely different kind of reality and was sympathetic to its explorers, although he felt that the fantasy life of the mind should be respected as something "gravely significant," he could not himself develop in this line, for it was, as he confessed to Norton, a new field for his ignorance. The depths of the mind's richness or the heights of the supposed consciousness of the race were not for him, whose ground was the open, sunny meadow of normality and reason. But he could, and did, encourage the younger writers to dive and to climb.

2. Harold Frederic

> "*Mysterious, impersonal, titanic forces . . .*"
> —The Critic

One of these younger men was Harold Frederic, whose fame will rest solely, but securely, on *The Damnation of Theron Ware*, among the four or five best novels written by an American during the nineteenth century. Born twenty years after Howells and Twain, he passed a youth in many ways resembling theirs. His childhood and adolescence were spent in a small New York town and steeped in the freedoms and trials of the lower middle class. Like the elder writers (who were also his idols), he was a printer and journalist, but unlike them, he made journalism his profession, writing only during the hours he could spare from his work first as editor of the Utica *Observer* and the Albany *Evening Journal* and then as London correspondent for the New York *Times.* Apart from *The Damnation,* he produced a series of generally uninspired novels, short stories, reflections, a biography of the future Kaiser, and a Utopia; two of the novels, *Seth's Brother's Wife* and *The Lawton Girl,* are interesting because of the evidence in them of some of the elements which later went into his master work.

Frederic thought of himself as a realist, and declared that he was a Howells man to the end, adding, in this same pronouncement, that he wished to tender "the big man, Mr. Howells," his admiration, gratitude and fealty. With Howells' example before him, he had come to believe that the thing that was worth writing about was "the today . . . the reality" in the "human life about you." He could not restrain himself from writing to his elder, whom he had never met, describing *The Rise of Silas Lapham* as the vision of a master turned upon the most distinctive part of American folk-life for the first time. He visited Howells in Boston in 1888 and carried back from America no other remembrance that could equal the value of that call; and the year before his tragic death, he accepted an invitation to join the Social Science Association because Howells' name was down as one of the members, and with Howells, Frederic wrote, he would "belong to any hose-company or target shoot" that took his fancy.

And yet there were new materials to be explored, not old ground to be gone over again, and so Frederic could not "see all things" as Howells had, nor would Howells have wanted him to do so. Starting with the basic doctrine which Howells preached —a fidelity to the life one knew, an immersion in one's own experience, an unswerving loyalty to the truth and a hatred of the false and sentimental, Frederic found his interest going from the social to the individual, from the inequities in relations between men to the tormenting self-divisions within man, from an analysis of the normal and commonplace to a concern with those hidden recesses of the individual soul where cower lust and fear and primitive ignorance. With the realist's vision of the value of the world of actuality, the world of his own experience, Frederic turned to the materials of his own life in upper New York State.

But he found it, upon honest examination, not the assured society that Howells knew when he had begun to write, but a society in turmoil, doubting the convictions which had sustained it for generations. Frederic saw that his environment was undergoing a spiritual revolution and it became his task to chronicle that change. And with the social certainties exploding about him, he saw that it was the struggle within the individual that would have to be explored. The fall of the social and economic world of a Dryfoos from earlier simplicities had its parallel in the fall of the individual from innocence to disturbing knowledge. And like the corresponding social and economic "advances," the development of scientific knowledge, the sophistication of the individual was attended by possibilities of evil as well as possibilities of good; an advance in knowledge, Frederic saw, could be made at the expense of inner stability; there were primitive emotional balances which could not be disturbed without danger of unsettling the entire personality, without danger of damning the soul.

And with the swinging of his interest from the social to the individual, Frederic, like Crane and Norris, found himself interested in the role played by the primitive passions within man. And like both of these contemporaries, he was eager to go beyond the indirections with which the age of Howells had treated the matter of sexual passion, and analyze it more closely and directly. His life, like that of Crane's, was a personal revolt from the conventions of the preceding era. He had married Grace Williams at her mother's deathbed in 1875; but by 1881 he had placed his wife in an ambiguous position by his close friendship with a young woman, a friendship from which his wife was excluded, just as Alice Ware, in his novel, would be left out of the intimacy between Theron and Celia Madden. And then in 1889, in Belgium, Frederic made the complete break with his wife and began to live with another woman, by whom he had two sons and a daughter. This common-law marriage was, of course, an unmentionable topic and was only alluded to by hint and innuendo at the time of his death in 1899 as the "one grave blemish" on his "brilliant short span." His views on sex were publicly expressed, and their appeal was for more frankness in acknowledging the power of passion; sex, he said, "is the mainspring of human activity." And then he went on to summarize his concepts of sexual ethics, and it was exactly the morality which Howells had illustrated in most of his works: selfishness brings misery, wise unselfishness can bring peace, if not joy. But the forthrightness with which Frederic applied this morality to sexual relations was an index of his loosening of the bonds of nineteenth-century restraint: "What is base about it," he said, "is its indulgence without due regard to the self-respect of one party or the happiness of the other."

But like all other kinds of freedoms, all other kinds of knowledge, Frederic saw, sexual freedom and sexual knowledge had terrible dangers as well as great rewards. He attempted to deal with this theme in the first of his works of serious stature: *Seth's Brother's Wife.* The career of Seth Fairchild, young printer's apprentice and journalist in the upper New York State village of Tecumseh, was closely patterned after Frederic's own experiences in Utica. Although he wrote with a minute fidelity to the rural life: "a sad and sterile enough thing," his main concern was with the moral struggle within Seth, the young innocent, loved innocently by his cousin Annie Fairchild, and lusted after and attracted to his brother's wife, Isabel, full of the sophistication of the city, and bent upon Seth's moral destruction. By an interesting reversal of a century of American literary convention, Annie Fairchild, the girl who was later described as an "angel . . . the sort of woman who enables you to understand all the exalted and sublime things that have been written about her sex," was dark of hair and eyes, while Isabel was a blue-eyed blonde. From the mouth of Isabel came the double-edged truth of the growing impossibility of rural innocence in an age of scientific progress. "The trail of the serpent is over it all," she told Seth. "The nineteenth century is a century of cities; they have given their own twist to the progress of the Age. . . . Perhaps there may have been a time when man could live in what the poet calls daily communion with Nature and not starve his mind and dwarf his soul, but it isn't this century." Seth tried to say, ". . . it isn't all as bad as you paint it"; but he was irresistibly drawn to her sophistication, and away from the innocence of Annie.

But this was just one kind of sophistication; the growing knowledge of the sexual passion. Frederic could agree with the age of Howells that the application of reason to passion could save; and *Seth's Brother's Wife* has a happy ending. When he came to investigate the growing complexities of other realms of the human mind, however, Frederic wrote not a comedy, but a tragedy: the story of the fall of a man, rather than his salvation, through illumination and knowledge: *The Damnation of Theron Ware*. Theron Ware was a Methodist minister whose innocence was in terms of all kinds of knowledge, scientific, historical, ethical, as well as sexual. Frederic made every effort to identify Theron with American innocence; he was described as having "features moulded into that regularity of strength which used to characterize the American Senatorial type in those far-away days . . . before the War." He had an "innocent candor and guileless mind." When his fellow ministers were assembled, it was said of them, too, that "the effect of these faces as a whole was toward goodness, candor, and imperturbable self-complacency rather than learning or mental astuteness." And Frederic pointed out that the effect was pleasantest "on the countenance of the older men. The impress of zeal and moral worth seemed to diminish by regular gradations as one passed to younger faces."

Representative of this simpler, happier, more ignorant time, Theron Ware came to his new ministry in Octavia. The bigotry of the narrow, hypocritical fundamentalists of his congregation prepared him for his revolt against orthodoxy, for the discovery of the depths of his own ignorance. "Strangely enough, after he had weathered the first shock, this discovery did not dismay Theron Ware. The very completeness of the conviction . . . saturated his mind with a feeling as if the fact had been known to him all along. And there came, too, after a little, an almost pleasurable sense of the importance of the revelation. He had been merely drifting in fatuous and conceited blindness. Now all at once his eyes were open: he knew what he had to do. Ignorance was a thing to be remedied, and he would forthwith bend all his energies to cultivating the mind." He met the beautiful Celia Madden who at once opened his eyes to the stringencies of monogamy and the narrowness of Puritanism, the modernist Catholic priest, Father Forbes, who introduced him to religious skepticism, and Dr. Ledsmar, who showed him the road to scientific rationalism. His simple moral defenses breached, Theron was taken by storm. The really extraordinary objectivity of the author—the story was told strictly from the minister's point of view—involved the reader completely with the protagonist, so that he was unaware that the education of Theron Ware was anything but good; he was shown "expanding, growing in all directions," and only gradually was it realized that what seemed improvement was, instead, moral degeneration. When the book was finished, the innocence of Theron Ware was finished too; his eyes could not soften and glow "with the complete and simple assurance of God's goodness."

A Hazard of New Fortunes was, in part, a story of the social fall of America; *The Damnation of Theron Ware* reached out to become a representation of the psychic fall of Americans. Like Americans in general, Theron Ware rose from ignorance to knowledge, and yet the rise was, at the same time, a disaster, a tragedy, and a beneficent and necessary one. Not for anything would we have had Theron Ware cling to his childish, outmoded simplicities. Knowing, feeling that he cannot go on as the attractive simpleton he was and maintain either his dignity or our respect, we cheer his steps towards emancipation, light, truth, only to discover that he, and we, have been ascending the rise to a precipice, that we have been cheering him on to his fall.

Now the techniques employed by Frederic were the techniques of a Howells. There was the same rooting in the actuality which he had seen and heard himself, the same reworking of the autobiographical, the same adherence to the dramatic technique of narration. Frederic had never been a minister, but he did exhaustive research on Methodism. Theron Ware was much like Seth Fairchild, who was obviously the fictional mask for Frederic himself. Father Forbes was patterned after a real priest, a Modernist, whom Frederic had become friendly with in Utica; and Celia Madden was similarly drawn from life. Frederic admitted his discipleship, and in the one critical piece he wrote, referred to Howells' short stories as a standard of excellence, and contemporary critics referred to his treatment, "in much the same spirit," of upper New York State life as Howells had shown in his treatment of New England scenes. This was, then, a work which one can call "realism"—a loving attention to the appearance of things as they are, and the attempt to honestly capture their truth by selection and arrangement. But something seemed to happen when the truth of appearances was a psychological rather than a social truth. The characters Frederic portrayed seemed to become subtly different from a Dryfoos or a Lapham or a Lindau. Just as in the title the theme of the mythical fall advanced from the dim recesses of allusion to the foreground of complete overtness, so in the characterization, significant traits began to emerge and dominate the other aspects of character, transforming the people of Theron Ware's world into archetypes: Father Forbes as religious liberation from fundamentalism, Celia Madden as the embodiment of the pagan gospel of beauty, Dr. Ledsmar as the apostle of pure science. And those wonderful inventions, the Soulsbys, went one step further in the change from the realistic complexity of the characters of the realists to the abstract, symbolic quality of the characters of the world of the mind which the post-realists began to investigate. The Soulsbys were two ex-vaudevillians and snake-oil salesmen who had turned their talents to the production of revivalist "debt-raisings." They were the mountebanks who nursed Theron Ware back to health after he had been broken by his "education" in the terrible complexities of knowledge. And their very names seem to recall, ironically, a world of romance where a Red Crosse Knight could restore himself at the house of Holiness, after his encounter with Despair. A critic at the time saw this change in the technique of fiction occurring, and pointed out that the characters who had most to do with Theron's development—Celia Madden, Father Forbes, Dr. Ledsmar, and the Soulsbys—"while they are perfectly life-like at the time of reading, by some curious mental process present themselves when we come to look back upon the book as a whole . . . , in the light of mysterious, impersonal Titanic forces."

3. Frank Norris

"The dimensions of tortured Titans . . ."

The technique of Frederic, then, seemed to be changing from a technique which used symbols to reinforce meanings already within the scope of the narrative to a "symbolism" whose reference went far beyond the confines of the art work. And in turning his attention to the "inspects" rather than the "aspects," he found himself involved more and more with the primitive passions of ignorant hate, and greed, and lust. What Frederic did tentatively, almost unconsciously, Frank Norris did with boldness. At the time Norris was attending the University of California (1891-1894), Howells already was in the decline of his powers, although at the height of his influence; and while Norris respected the dean of American realism, he thought his method ineffective, and the range of his materials limited. When he read the work of Zola, he believed he had found the way in which literature could tell more about life and its meanings: not in trying to portray average people leading normal and uneventful lives, but in depicting the abnormal and the cataclysmic, the clash of primitive instincts at moments of tremendous and terrible passion.

With his sensitivity and generosity, Howells encouraged Norris' development along these lines, so different from his own, and found it a "rare pleasure" to tell the world of the richness of Norris' promise, finding him steeped in the older realists, and especially in Zola, but transcending them, and himself, in a "rich strain of poetry" and mysticism. And he chose exactly the right words to describe the nature of Norris' return to a poetic mode of fiction, words which named the manifestation with precision and exactness, and foretold the continuation of Norris' methods in writers like Steinbeck and Faulkner. Norris, Howells said, tried to place the forces of modern American life in an "epical relation," trying to see the relation between man and nature, between human drives and natural forces; and in order to demonstrate these relations, Norris slipped the leash of his imagination, permitting it to rove the wilderness of racial memories and ancestral stirrings. His plots, based upon reality, upon a careful observation and documentation, yet transcended the transitory real and became quite conscious allegories of all human activity, and pressed on to the frontiers of symbolic representation of the unknowable. As befitted the personages of an epic, his characters, without being pure autochthons, yet had "something rankly earthy and elemental" in them, giving them the dimensions of "tortured Titans." *McTeague* was a "personal epic," an odyssey of the soul among the low levels of lust and greed, while *The Octopus* was the *Iliad* to McTeague's *Odyssey*, the epic of a nation, as *McTeague* was the epic of an individual, showing, as mythology has always shown, the correspondence between human and natural cycles of birth, growth, and death. This was Howells speaking about a trend which he knew full well led away from that which he had established as the fictional method of his age; and he used words which had not been heard in American criticism since Emerson, used them to encourage the continued building of America's towers of fiction.

In writing his two books which together constitute his important contribution to the development of American sensibility, Norris exploited the fictional possibilities of greed, lust, hatred, and murder. Both *McTeague* and *The Octopus* were violent books. McTeague, the huge, slow-witted itinerant dentist with his purely animal drives—food to fill his belly, beer to dull his senses—was ruined by his wife's civilized but far more destructive vice of greed, and he could only, in the end, turn his strength upon her, crushing her fingernails between his strong teeth and finally beating her to death with his fists. This was strong stuff; and in *The Octopus,* Norris tested his theories of the importance of the primitive instincts and their correspondence to natural forces in a vastly larger laboratory—the great Central Valley of California. *The Octopus* was the story of that valley and of the railroad whose tentacles stretched out to crush the farmers who struggled against it; but more than that, it was a story of man and his beneficent enslavement to the god of fertility and growth. Based upon actual incidents in the bitter war between the ranchers of the San Joaquin and the Southern Pacific, the book was crammed with violence from the opening chapter when a locomotive roared through the flock of sheep and flung their mangled innocence to either side of its iron charge. A vengeful ranch hand galloping into a folk festival and sending shot after shot at the feet of his coolly watching enemy, a stolen locomotive careening along the tracks with a fugitive at the throttle, a gunfight in which nine ranchers were killed as they opposed the repossession of their lands—these were some of the incidents which illustrated Norris' interest in the more uncommon aspects of life as the stuff of fiction.

And in choosing these themes of the inner epic of the mind and the outer epic of man and nature, Norris seemed to have turned to an indirect manner of narration, trying to contrive his incidents to reflect back and forth between each other so that their intensified light would radiate outward to illuminate all of man's relationships, and perhaps, even the relation of man to the earth, and God; in a word, he turned to symbolism. In *McTeague,* the theme of man's imprisonment by greed was symbolized by gold objects in every conceivable form. The dentist's dream was fulfilled when his wife gave him a huge gilded tooth to use as the signpost of profession (Norris even considered calling the book *The Golden Tooth*). He kept the object in their bedroom, where it squatted and dumbly watched the disintegration of his marriage. His wife, Trina, eventually changed her small fortune into gold coins, and would strip herself, and wallow nakedly in a bed of gold. The subplot concerned a maniac's dream of a lost golden treasure. And the final scene was so naively symbolic as to become ridiculous: McTeague, having murdered his wife, escaped into Death Valley with Trina's gold on one side of his saddle, a canary in its cage on the other. He killed a pursuer, but in the struggle found himself handcuffed to the corpse, beside his useless gold, waiting for death with the "half-dead canary chittering feebly in its little gilt prison."

The symbolism in *The Octopus* was often on this obvious level: the locomotive killing the sheep, for example, or the flood of wheat smothering S. Behrman as he fell into the hold of a cargo ship. But the technique was also used to enlarge the story into a hymn to the power of sex. The fertile valley, warm with the promise of boundless fecundity, was really the major protagonist, and the seeding of its fields was described as a cosmic marriage. This titanic mating of earth and man was symbolized by the two human pairings. Vanamee, the sheepherder and mystic, discovered that out of the tragic rape of his beloved came Angèle, the embodiment of eternal physical and spiritual love. Annixter, the young rancher, died in violence, but left his wife, Hilma, the earth-mother; Annixter had first realized his love for Hilma at the very moment that the soil of the valley stirred gigantically with the first sprouting of the green wheat. Norris thus transformed *The Octopus* from a timely and reportorial comment, such as Howells or Garland might have written, into an illustration of the timeless cycle of birth, growth, death, and rebirth.

4. Henry James

Art amid the "howling desert"

While these newer notes were being sounded, while younger writers were deepening and extending realism into symbolism and mythology, exploring the mind and its darknesses, the body and its passions, a writer of Howells' own generation reached the fullness of his maturity and produced his greatest work. While Howells and Twain wearily settled into their winter of despair, Henry James, who had never shared their optimism, had his Indian summer, and in three years published his greatest tragedy, *The Wings of the Dove* (1902), his largest comedy, *The Golden Bowl* (1904), and his most artful and finished tragicomedy, *The Ambassadors* (1903). It was symptomatic of the shift in intellectual climate, in the impalpable atmosphere of sensibility upon which artists either thrive or die, that James, the great writer with a view of life essentially tragic, and with the corresponding passionate belief that the forms and structures of art were the refuge for the developed consciousness, should have written his masterpieces while Howells and Twain felt themselves drifting like old derelicts. It is at the end of the age which Howells had made his own, therefore, that a discussion of his friend Henry James should take its place. And an observation of the important similarities, as well as the deep-rooted differences between the minds and temperaments and art of the two, throws much light upon the men themselves, their age, and upon subsequent history of American sensibility.

The connections between the two writers seemed at first to link them together as the nucleus of a school of American realism, and, indeed, they were so regarded by their contemporaries. They met early and were friends late, and Howells could "scarcely exaggerate the intensity" of their literary association, which began in 1866 and only ended with James' death. They walked and talked together much in these early years in Cambridge; Howells, as assistant editor of the *Atlantic*, helped to give James his start, and from then on was godfather to the younger man's career. In one of their early talks, two or three hours long, Howells, only half in jest, declared that they "settled the true principles of literary art." In an essay on James, and with the subject of the essay as his chief evidence, Howells made his famous declaration that fiction in America had developed into a finer art than that practiced by Dickens and Thackeray. A year after this pronouncement, James wrote Howells that articles "about you and me are as thick as blackberries. . . ." It was a measure of Howells' breadth that he was as unceasingly and uncompromisingly appreciative of the genius of James as he was of the genius of Twain. And Howells' admiration never flagged; when James felt himself despised, his demand reduced to zero, his sales, "tell it not in Samoa," not ten copies, Howells wrote him that he was the first man of letters of his day, that it was upon him, James, and not upon Howells himself, or any other, that "the aspiring eyes" of all writers were bent. For his part, James returned at least a portion of the admiration so genuinely felt and so generously given. Although he felt Howells' lack of the "really *grasping* imagination," although he felt that there was a "whole quarter of the heaven" upon which his back was turned, he nonetheless ranked him first among the other American realists of his times.

The similarities between the two men were similarities of technique, of attitude, of morality, and of world-view, but first and above all of technique. Like Howells, James went to contemporary, perceived life for his subjects; all his stories began with a "germ" dropped into his consciousness from contemporary actuality. This actuality was what he demanded of all his "données" —"actuality," he told himself at one time, "must be my line at present. I may work it with infinite profit." He felt too, along with Howells, that the dramatic method of narration was the finest, and he not only made objectivity one of his requirements, but went even further and insisted, with increasing severity, that his plots be constructed in tight, dramatic fashion. Like Howells, he felt that fiction must be in some fashion a "representation of life," and that the novel must fulfill its function, as he wrote Daudet, "*comme révélation de la vie et du drôle de mélange que nous sommes.*" As little as Howells, did James have to do with violence and primitive passions. While there are many more allusions to relations between the sexes in the novels of James, he felt that "functional Love" must be "counterplotted by roundabout arts—as by tracing it through indirectness and tortuosities." Like Howells, even more than Howells, James knew the difference between "actuality" and actuality removed into art, knew that while art must be related to life, it must be life transformed and changed so that the art form would give the truthful *impression* of actuality. James' short story "The Real Thing" admirably conveyed this truth: the "actually" genteel old couple could not give the impression of reality that the artist desired; so he was forced to turn to the professional models whose gentility was not actual, but who could simulate the tone which the artist was trying to capture. On the way in which this "higher reality" of art differed from the limited actuality, James was again in thorough accord with Howells, whose point had always been that the higher realism of impressionism could stretch out to encompass all of man's experience. James used the words "Case" and "Situation" to distinguish between unassimilated actuality and realism. A "Case," he said, is always "a thing rather void of connections with . . . life at large," is a "barren little instance," a "little limited monstrosity." A "Situation," on the other hand, would have those connections with life at large, would be a "reflection . . . to one's sense of life in general."

As in technique, James agreed with Howells on many aspects of their attitude towards their contemporary world, towards values, even, strangely enough, towards the relative merit of American and European sensibility. The last area of agreement is too often overlooked in face of the almost blinding intensity of the very real differences between the two men on the score of intellectual patriotism. The differences were fundamental; but nevertheless Howells could scarcely have gone further than James in presenting, through his fiction, the superiority of at least some of the values of the New World to those of the Old. For with amazing consistency, James, when confronting Americans with Europeans, portrayed the Americans, in their moral innocence, living under "the high natural light of chance and space and prosperity," as heroes, and the Europeans, in their artful and amoral and sombre decadence, as villains. In "The Last of the Valerii," he described the evil influence of the European traditional past stretching out to curse; in "A Passionate Pilgrim," he suggested that immersal in the spirit of the past brings sadness and tragedy, madness and death. His heroes and heroines were almost invariably Americans who confronted European decadence and either triumphed over it or were overwhelmed by it: Isabel Archer, in *The Portrait of a Lady*, betrayed by the sensitive, sinister expatriates, Gilbert Osmond and Madame Merle; Daisy Miller victimized by the continental attitude towards the *jeune fille;* Christopher Newman, in *The American*, frustrated by the evil of French aristocratic selfishness, triumphing over it, only to have the dead hand of its traditions reach out to snatch his happiness from him; the Puritan New England family in *The Europeans* whose openness and light drive the mercenary Baroness back to the darkness of Europe; the peaceful innocence of the dying American heiress, in *The Wings of the Dove*, spreading its pinions over the Old World evil of Kate Croy and Merton Densher; the healthful good sense of Adam and Maggie Verver rescuing their marriages from the sophisticated and illicit passion of her European mate—in almost every instance the meanings of James' stories reinforced Howells' request "not to think harshly of Americans."

James, too, accepted as his own the simple ethic which motivated Howells' writing; that to give to others is to live, to keep to oneself is spiritually to die. In his first formulations of the idea that later became *The Wings of the Dove*, James felt that the theme of his work would lie in making Milly Theale's "happiness," her "life," her "snatched experience . . . BE, *in fact*, some rapturous act . . . of generosity, of passionate beneficence, of pure sacrifice. . . ." John Marcher, the protagonist of his masterful story "The Beast in the Jungle," found that the Beast for whose spring he had been waiting in terror all his life was the Beast of Nothingness, of a selfish refusal to enter into a sympathetic relation with another. And as in Howells' work, so too in James' was this ethic tested against basically pragmatic premises—pragmatic in their rejection of absolutes, in an abstention from moralizing, in the acceptance of that which "worked" as right, in the rejection of any *a priori* standards of good or evil. When his brother William gave this philosophy its permanent form, Henry blessed him "for a relevant and assimilable . . . philosophy," and considered "Pragmatic invulnerability constituted."

But whereas William James (and Howells) found the test of all ideas to lie in experience and in action, Henry James considered it to reside in the growth of sensitivity of an individual's consciousness; and herein lay the first significant difference between Howells and William James and the dominant American attitude they represented on the one hand, and Henry James on the other. For Howells and William James an idea had to be tested in an active social relationship, with the outcome to be measured in terms of the peace or happiness of those involved in the relationship. But for Henry James the test did not lie in action or in *doing*, but in contemplation, or *being*, in an increase of the total awareness, in a heightening of sensitivity. The meaning of all his novels, the figure in the carpet of his artistic intention, was that consciousness is life, and that the business of the artist was to carry "the field of consciousness further and further, making it lose itself in the ineffable . . .; that," he said, "is all my revelation or my secret."

And it was not just any consciousness in which James was interested, but in the finest and most highly organized sensitivities. Whereas Howells, like Emerson and Whitman before him, and Frost and Sinclair Lewis and John Steinbeck after him, was animated by a love of the common, the familiar, the low, these kinds of consciousnesses scarcely existed for James at all; in a sense, he refused to grant them even the small dignity of life: "Of those who don't react . . . ," he wrote, ". . . it may very well be asked on their behalf whether they are distinguishable as 'living' either before or after [death]." Dull people he thought of as "slugs and jellyfish," not waste, but rather as "the amusement, the attestation of wealth and variety" in nature. To his aristocracy of sensitivity, he was willing to admit newcomers: a bookbinder like Hyacinth Robinson, a wash-tub manufacturer (after his retirement) like Christopher Newman. But even a Hyacinth Robinson, so typically described as standing before life as before a pastry-shop window, seeing the delicacies spread before him, yet condemned by accident of birth to be forever on the other side of the window, even Hyacinth Robinson became a convert to the doctrine of aristocracy of taste. This aristocracy, James saw, was being overwhelmed by what he considered the blatant forces of "vulgarity" and "democracy," two terms which he generally equated, and then linked with the flood of publicity which he thought the worst feature of his age. He would speak of the "hard western ugliness, newspaperism, vulgarity, and democracy," and of the "note of 'familiarity,' the sinking of *manners*, in so many ways, which the democratization of the world brings with it." In *The Bostonians* he pictured Miss Birdseye, the "confused, entangled, inconsequent, discursive old woman," extending a "delicate, dirty, democratic little hand" to her visitor. While Howells and William James saw nothing good in the vivid contributions to what they considered a national culture of the immigrants from eastern Europe, Henry James, viewing New York's East Side, "gasped" and "stared at this all-unconscious impudence of the agency of future ravage" upon the niceties of the English language, viewing the ravagers as "the dragon" of an "alien presence climbing higher and higher, climbing itself into the very light of publicity."

For the dull and the common James had small sympathy then, and with them he had increasingly little desire to communicate. His kingdom of dullness included some promising people—on one occasion, his brother William, for example. When William complained of the tortuous convolutions of Henry's later style (he had said of it on an earlier occasion that "19 out of 20 worthy readers grow intolerant" and cry "'Say it *out*, for God's sake . . .'"), Henry replied with rare ill nature that he would be "greatly . . . humiliated" if William would like one of his books and "thereby lump it" in his affections "with things, of the current age" for which he had expressed his admiration. Whereas Howells detested obscurity, while William James tried to "say a thing in one sentence as straight and explicit as it can be made," while Henry Blake Fuller and Hamlin Garland had independently underlined Herbert Spencer's doctrine of "the economy of attention," Henry James felt more and more that literature could be, should be a "game of skill" played by such "supersubtle fry" as the aesthetes in "The Figure in the Carpet." "Patches of ambiguity and the abysses of shadow . . . ," he wrote Paul Bourget, "really are the clothing—or much of it—of the *effects* that constitute the material of our trade." He finally evolved so complex a style that, when two of the chapters of the eleventh book of *The Ambassadors* were reversed in all but one of the editions, making nonsense of his time scheme, a subsequent half-century of readers missed the error, so nearly was the unintended confusion like the calculated subtlety of the rest of the work.

These departures from the prevailing temper could be summed up under the one major and all-embracing difference—against the comic view of life, the view which animated the age of realism, James set a view which was dominantly tragic. Whereas Howells and Twain through most of their careers envisioned life as completion and fulfillment with human well-being the reward for a life of reason and human misery the result of superstition and passion, James saw the world of appearances as essentially one of frustration and renunciation, a dry and parched waste, a "howling desert." At best, the sensitive consciousness could impose its patterns upon the meaningless chaos of the world of material things, at worst it could suffer in dignity. While Howells and Twain and the writers around them believed deeply in the value of their environment, James believed only in the power of personal perception, and often appeared close to a total withdrawal from the world of the flesh into a world of mental substance in which the personality could strike its hopeless blow for dignity by renunciation and rejection. While Howells believed that reason and common sense taught the lesson of "the economy of pain," the doctrine that the course of action should be chosen under which most persons would suffer least, James felt that the "note of suffering" was necessary to the enlargement of sensitivity, and he would sacrifice the well-being of others to this increase in sensitivity. One of James' stories which directly involved the question of "the note of suffering" against the "economy of pain" was "Georgina's Reasons." It concerned a husband who was secretly wed to a selfish woman from whom he separated and who then bigamously remarried. The husband wished to remarry also, but, in order to do so, would have had to legally dissolve his first marriage, an action which would have exposed the dishonor and crime of his first wife. Confronted by this impasse, "the only endurable denouement" that James could see was to have the husband renounce his own happiness and the happiness of his future wife. In *The Spoils of Poynton*, the drama of Fleda Vetch's inner consciousness ended with her renunciation of love: "That's about the gist of it," James told himself in thinking out the story. "If I want *beauty* for her—beauty of action and poetry of effect, I can only, I think, find it just there; find it in making her heroic. To *be* heroic, to achieve beauty and poetry, she must conceal from him what she feels."

Howells was constitutionally unable to agree with this tragic view of human experience. When as editor of the *Atlantic* he read and accepted *The American*, he objected to its unhappy ending, not as an editor, but as a private reader who honestly could not see why two sensible and intelligent human beings like Christopher Newman and Claire de Cintré, after triumphing over the obstacles in the path of their union, should keep themselves forever apart. For Howells, the world was the proper scene for potential comedy, the comedy of the victory of reason over the darkness embodied by old Madame de Bellegarde. But for James, "the interest of the subject was . . . its exemplification of one of those insuperable difficulties which present themselves in people's lives and from which the only issue is by forfeiture—by losing something. . . . We are each," he continued in this revealing disagreement with Howells, "the product of circumstances and there are tall stone walls which fatally divide us." And then he concluded: "I suspect it is the tragedies in life that arrest my attention more than the other things and say more to my imagination."

James then, like Hawthorne and Melville, and unlike Emerson and Whitman, Twain and Howells, found his artistic strength not in acceptance of his world and his age, but in rejection. And for James, therefore, salvation could never lie in the hopelessly confused world of physical and social appearances, but only in the individual mind. And in so rejecting his environment and substituting for its material values the values of the personal consciousness, he more and more was driven, as Poe had been driven, to erect a temple of art as the only sanctuary for the spirit of the artist, the only significant structure for the sensitive. "Oh art, art," he cried, "without thee, for me, the world would be, indeed, a howling desert." When Hyacinth Robinson, the impoverished young "hero" of *The Princess Casamassima*, was given the means to travel, he learned from his new experiences that the things worth fighting for were "the splendid accumulations of the happier few"—"the monuments and treasures of art, the great palaces and properties, the conquests of learning and taste. . . ." These, for Hyacinth, and for James as well, were the "fabric of civilization as we know it, based, if you will, upon all the despotisms, the cruelties, the exclusions, the monopolies and rapacities of the past, but thanks to which, all the same, the world is less impracticable and life more tolerable." It was Art, Art, "the anodyne, the escape, the boundlessly beneficent resort" which was "all discrimination and selection" while life was "all inclusion and confusion." James' assertion of "the fatal futility of Fact" was a complete revolution from a dominant American tradition which had begun with Emerson's worship of the natural fact as symbol of the spiritual.

From this rejection of fact to the religion of art was only a step, and James took it. He turned his back upon the whole range of possibilities of finding value in the process of his contemporary life, and asserted the supremacy of form and structure of the fine arts.

But the miracle of it was that James, turning his eyes more and more on art, appeared to many readers to say more and more about life; not the social life, not the broad swath of human relationships about which Twain and Howells had so much to tell, but about the secret inner life of the mind. He appeared to have proven, for a succeeding generation of poets and poetic novelists, that one way to get nearer to the truth of human consciousness (and unconsciousness) was by an art form so carefully contrived, so demanding of attention, that the reader is forced into complete participation, into a world of the author's art, compelled to live in it, react in it with the same intensity as in the world of the finest perceptions.

The work in which James felt he reached his greatest perfection of technique was, by a pleasant coincidence, a work for which Howells had unwittingly provided the "germ" and in which a figure with some echoes of Howells' own personality was the "hero" and central recording consciousness. *The Ambassadors,* as is well known, began with an incident reported to James by Jonathan Sturges. One day in Paris, Sturges told him, Howells had suddenly advised him to "live all you can," that he, Howells, was too old and for him it was too late, but that Sturges was young and should "live!" James recorded the anecdote in his notebook on October 31, 1895, and at that time sketched the first summary of the novel that was finally to emerge after the turn of the century. He would make his hero, he thought, the editor of a magazine—not a novelist, for that would be "too like W.D.H."—and he would give him "a little supersensual hour in the vicarious freedom of another."

How much richer, deeper, and infinitely more complex than this bare statement is the meaning of the finished novel only its careful reading can reveal. On the surface the story appears to be little more than the author's summary: A middle-aged American comes to Paris, an emissary from a wealthy New England matron, to rescue her son from Old World evil and decadence. The emissary becomes convinced that the Old World has done the boy good, and uses his persuasion not to make him go, but to make him stay. More "ambassadors" are sent to rescue both man and youth; the latter, it is hinted, will go back; while the man, too, will return, he has "lived" and has been forever changed. But it may be at least suggested that the novel said as much as James could say about the area of consciousness as it extends deeper and deeper into the ineffable. The novel said it largely through the complexities and ambiguities which were a result of James' strict adherence to dramatic form and to the point of view of his main character. Without the intervention of the author to tell us what we should believe, the reader is thrown back upon his own skill, his own resources of imagination and perception. And he finds that there are always at least two ways of reading the various signs in the world which James has made. What, for example, is "best" for Chad Newsome?—to return to Woollett and his mother or to stay in Paris with Madame de Vionnet? We know that James regarded publicity as the blatant beast which democracy had loosed on the world, and it is a job as advertising manager for an unspeakably vulgar product which is balanced against Chad's continued life of refinement in Paris; so it would seem that to go back to America and Mrs. Newsome is wrong, to stay in Paris is right. Yet the case for Woollett and America is given serious consideration. The Puritan view is sustained by a consistent analogy to the biblical themes of temptation and fall. Little Bilham, the "little artist man," has abandoned activity for aesthetic contemplation and serenity, and half-humorously calls the latter an evidence of "the trial of the serpent." Waymarsh, sturdy and simple as a prophet from the Old Testament, glooms out "to demand justice," to "save" Strether in spite of himself. "Yet," James wrote ambiguously, "it was somehow just this communication that showed him [Strether] to himself as more than ever lost." (Strangely enough, James originally meant to call this representative of American simplicity "Waymark," the man who marks the way for the pilgrim to follow; by changing the final letter he suggested not a path but a bog.) And finally Strether tries to make an arrangement between Mamie Pocock, who brings with her "the breath of fresh Western air," and Little Bilham, for he feels he must "put on record somehow" that his "fidelity—fundamentally unchanged after all—" is to the Puritan, American gods. "I feel," he tells Bilham, "as if my hands were inbrued with the blood of monstrous alien altars—of another faith altogether."

Not knowing which is fundamentally right—Woollett or Paris—one can never be sure of the morality of the characters and their actions. For Bilham, Madame de Vionnet is "virtuous"; for Mamie Pocock's sister-in-law, Sarah, (again the Old Testament reference in the name) she is "hideous." The ambiguity is reflected in her very dress; when Strether thinks her innocent she is dressed in black (although a black that is "light and transparent"); when he knows her guilty, she is in pure white, with just a touch of sable in the scarf at her bosom.

This moral ambiguity must be viewed in light of the narrative method and fictional structure—a structure which is, in itself, paradoxical. For the theme of the work may be regarded as "freedom," and yet the story is told under the ultimate in narrative restrictions, under the imposition of a form which allows the author a minimum of liberty and imposes upon him a maximum of limitations. James constructed *The Ambassadors* in rigid act and scene divisions; each group of three books constitutes one act of a four-act "play," with the climax of each act occurring regularly at the end of every third book. The method of narration is almost entirely scenic, the characters entering and leaving with the rules of the stage governing their actions. Very little is told that is not either a reflection of Strether or a statement of one of the characters. To bear out the analogy to the stage, the metaphors are consistently those of the theatre: it is the "performance of Europe" which the Pococks are said to be watching; Strether is the "hero," but he leaves the stage to the "heroine"—Madame de Vionnet. Attendance at a play is used as the setting for the introduction of Strether's mission: it is a drama in four acts during which a bad woman dressed in yellow makes a weak young man do terrible things. Strether's first view of *his* young man is at another play—this time at the Comédie Française.

To what purpose? Is it simply a *tour de force*, a feat of intellectual acrobatics which James was performing? It impresses the reader as more than that. One senses that in the form itself lies a clue to the meaning of the work, that the dramatic method is in itself part of what James is so painfully trying to understand. He shackles himself to portray freedom; to tell the story of an escape from dullness to the liberty of imagination and sensitivity, the artist confines himself to the prison of one man's perceptions and to the stringent requirements of the stage. "Freedom" within bonds; "liberty" within confinement; these seem some of the clues to the figure in the carpet. With this hypothesis furnished by the paradox of the form, we can turn to the center of the book, to its "germ" located at its structural heart; it is spoken in Gloriana's garden, just after Strether has met the "bad" woman and tells Little Bilham that the important thing in life is to "live." But then he does not equate "life" or "living" with "freedom," but with the "*illusion* of freedom," and it is therefore with "illusion," with "imitation," with "acting," in short, it is with *Art* that *The Ambassadors* seems to be concerned—with the achievement of a sense of freedom by man who is actually bound hand and foot. Strether uses another metaphor: "The affair of life," he tells Little Bilham, is "at best a tin mould, either fluted or embossed, with ornamental excrescences, or else smooth and dreadfully plain, into which a helpless jelly, one's consciousness is poured." He then follows this with the statement about the need for an "illusion of freedom," and then ends with the warning: "Therefore, don't be, like me, without the memory of that illusion."

It is art, then, that *The Ambassadors* is about—art and the way in which men and women, by reacting artfully, can have their "illusion of freedom" and live, and by not reacting artfully, remain dead. The pilgrimage of the man from Woollett was into an aesthetic world—beginning with the play in London, and continuing into Paris where the very "air had a taste of something mixed with art." It was in the garden of the great artist, the garden of Gloriana, that Strether began to understand that "he shouldn't reach the truth of anything until he got rid" of "his odious ascetic suspicion of any form of beauty." At the climax of the work, when Strether received his supreme test of the knowledge of the essentially primitive sexual depths of Madame de Vionnet's motives, the French countryside in which the recognition took place reminded him at once of both a painting he had wanted to buy (and then didn't) and "essentially more than anything else a scene and a stage." The flavor, the taste of the helpless jelly of consciousness lay in its art; without art, without manners, relations, selections, discriminations, without gentlemanly lies like those told by Little Bilham and Maria Gostrey and Madame de Vionnet, the jelly is flat, the consciousness does not exist. Life, worldly success, activity, accomplishment, without art is death; renunciation, failure, with art, is life.

Strether is willing to admit the terribly precarious hold upon reality which this view provided. When the Pococks came to Paris, bringing the viewpoint of Woollett and America with them, Strether asks himself if it is possible that he has begun to live in "a false world" and if his irritation with the Pococks might not be "but the alarm of the vain thing menaced by the touch of the real." And he comes near to despair when he finds that Chad has not been made over by Madame de Vionnet after all, but remains Chad, an unimaginative brute. But he maintains his own "artistry" to the end by being "right," by renunciation, by not, out of the whole affair, getting anything for himself, and proving to himself that it "made more for reality" to be "silly" with Maria Gostrey, and Little Bilham, with Madame de Vionnet and little Jeanne, than to be "sane with Sarah and Jim."

Life through art, in a world in which we are otherwise dead; the little comedy of consciousness triumphant simply through "being" amid the great tragedy of the wasteful world; that is what *The Ambassadors* seemed to be about. That is why the phrase "there we are," or its variations, is sounded throughout the book. It is a phrase full of resigned acknowledgment of limitations and constrictions. Its verb is the simple verb of "being." But true "being," full existence as a sensitive consciousness, was the highest state James could imagine. And while, in Gloriana's garden at the beginning of his pilgrimage of perception, Strether could only think "so there they are," at the end he is able to say as the last words of the novel: "then there we are." He had reached the celestial city of "being," but even that city was "there" in a corner of the world of frustration. That is why, too, at the end, Maria Gostrey "sighed it at last all comically, all tragically away"; "comically" because Strether had been a success and had enjoyed his illusion of freedom; tragically because the illusion is, after all, an illusion, and played out on the stage of life, played in the man-made garden of art tragically located in the chaotic jungle or the parched and "howling desert" of actuality.

It can be seen here—the abyss between James and Howells, despite their many agreements; it can be seen here the way in which the world view of a writer intermingles with his art, with his selection from and forming of the materials he finds within him and about him. James' tragic view of life led him into an increased involvement with the dramatic method because it produced form removed from the wastefulness of the living process with its loose ends, its apparent lack of meaning. Howells wanted a small part of the dramatic technique because it would lead him closer to life, because it would give the illusion of greater verisimilitude, would appear to mimic the process of living where the sensory data are supplied, but the conclusions and judgments are left to the faculties of the perceiver. But Howells used the dramatic method as part of a looser form in which he tried to give a sense of the dynamic, never arriving, always becoming relationships of the pragmatist's world. For James, on the other hand, this air of improvisation, this feeling of the unfinished was anathema. Seeking, as he was, to create art forms in which "the great stew-pot or crucible of the imagination" has intervened between the perceiver and the wasteful world of living to perform "a chemical transmutation to the aesthetic," he could only despair at the autobiographic mode, the picaresque structure. His eye was on Art; Howells' was on Life.

EPILOGUE

We have come to the end of our story, always aware of the danger of using words like "end" or "beginning" to describe the infinite complexities of the history of human sensibility. But within the area bounded on one side by the Civil War and the other by the closing decade of the nineteenth century, we have traced the development of one man's sensibility and have shown how that representative man helped to shape the creative expression of the age which saw the emergence of modern America. This characteristic expression was "realistic": it found meaning and value to reside in the world of physical appearances, in the world of democratic, middle-class, empirical American life. It was "comic": it believed that the application of human reason and common sense could result in a happy ending, and it applied its satiric analysis to the world which it loved so that it would become even better. It started, this characteristic expression, with an attack upon the lie in society and in literature, continued and strengthened into the conviction that the function of art was to enable man to know himself and others better, told Americans the truth about the world of their normal physical and social arrangements, and provided the ground upon which future writers could build when they would turn to the telling of truth about the individual and his passions as well.

It remains to remind ourselves how the age of Howells and its techniques of literature have stretched forward to mingle with contemporary consciousness, to become a part of ourselves. But first, it must be acknowledged that a large area of modern intellectual attitude in America stems not from Howells (and eventually from Emerson), but from Henry James (and ultimately from Hawthorne). James' view of the world as "a howling desert" has become Eliot's view of it as a Waste Land. And many of the most sensitive poets and poetic novelists of the years after 1918 have taken this great contemporary poet of secular despair as their model and guide, and have been shoring up fragments of art against the ruins of the modern world. But at the same time, the attitudes of the age of Howells have persisted to produce a major mode of modern American literature.

Although Howells' age was not an age of poetry, nor is our own, the spirit of Howells produced a poet in Robert Frost whose work is charged with the same basic belief in the meaningfulness of modern American life. Howells' "romance of the commonplace" became Frost's "synecdoche," for Frost sees all the facts of the physical world as significant in their own terms, and as representative of something larger and higher. He has known that by catching the most humble actualities of the field and the farm and the woods and the most humble emotional responses to them, he could create poetry. And as Howells did, so does Frost attack the dark immorality of unreasoned devotion to primitive impulse or sentimental premise. The old New Englander lurching through the poem "Mending Wall" like an old stone-age savage, a rock in either fist, mouthing incantations like "good fences make good neighbors," is asked "Why?" Why do good fences make good neighbors? Why indeed must such unverified superstitions, refuted by both nature and reason, make walls between people? And with the asking of the question, Frost carried over into the twentieth century the anti-sentimentalism of Howells and Twain. An awareness of this truth leads us to a proper reading of Frost's poem "The Egg and the Machine," a poem that has been mistaken as a Thoreau-like rejection of science and technology. With the clue supplied by the avowed sympathies of Frost with Howells, we can hypothesize that such a sentimental withdrawal from the realities of modern life would be out of place. And so a close reading of the poem proves. For the verse is not written in the first person; it is not Frost who is the subject, but a "he," and the tone the poet takes towards this "he" is a satiric and disparaging one. "He" is described as giving the rail "a hateful kick"; not a "kick full of hate," we notice, but a "hateful kick," the hatefulness becoming an attribute of the kicker as well as a description of his emotions towards the thing kicked. We are dealing with a child-like man who lashes out against an inanimate, insensate thing which has hurt him, like a peevish and unreasoning baby. And "he" then is described as digging up some turtle eggs, and preparing to splatter the bits of living stuff against the engine, the machine. "He" is willing to destroy life to satisfy his primitive rage against modern technology. This, then, is no romantic poem, but a satiric one, a satire against a futile and foolish, sentimental attack on modernity.

But it is not upon poetry, but upon fiction that the age of Howells would have most influence. What it gave to twentieth-century America was a faith in its own materials as the subject for short story and novel. Regionalism in fiction, so lovingly fostered by Howells, flowered in Twain, and continues to flourish. The local realism of writers like Erskine Caldwell or James T. Farrell is close to the philosophy of art enunciated by Howells. And while there is a radical difference between the world views of William Faulkner and Howells, Faulkner's concern with his own provincialism, his careful observation of his own people in their own setting are attitudes for whose acceptance Howells had fought. Novelists in our age have taken this for granted—that a writer could confront his own environment with courage and honesty; but it was Howells who helped to make it possible.

More directly, the extension of Howells' techniques into more overt symbolism, and the extension of his materials to include wider areas of social life and deeper areas of human consciousness, have produced writers like Dos Passos and Thomas Wolfe and John Steinbeck, all of whom start with the fundamental proposition that life is significant, that human beings deserve attention and sympathy. And the techniques Howells developed to capture an impression of truthfulness have been used, with but little change, in the works of Robert Herrick, Sinclair Lewis, and one of the most competent novelists practicing his craft today: James Gould Cozzens.

In the works of Cozzens (and in those of a lesser, but commendable talent like J. P. Marquand), there is the continuation of the basic attitudes and techniques of the age of realism which were, as we have seen, those of the British eighteenth century as well. Not that Cozzens could not, and did not, write in the symbolic mode so characteristic of modernity. In *Castaway*, for example, he created a horror-filled, Kafka-esque fiction about a soulless modern man turned loose in a huge department store, crammed with every conceivable comfort for the body. Imprisoned in materialistic abundance, the man tries to call out, but is only answered, in the terrible fastness, by "faint halloos in kind." Through this nightmare, Cozzens examined the plight of the individual lost in a modern world of things. But then, at this point in his development (with *The Last Adam* standing between his early and his later method), he turned to an examination of relationships, of togetherness, of human social awareness, and he obviously decided he would be committing an act of artistic pride to continue to look at life as an allegory. And so he returned to the older realistic tradition, and unpretentiously decided to write about the life he knew as clearly and unobscurely as possible, and began writing novels about society, and about men with social intelligences as central figures. In *Men and Brethren*, *The Just and the Unjust*, and *Guard of Honor*, the mature social scientist becomes the hero: a priest, a lawyer, and a judge turned Army administrator; and in his choice of materials for these works, and in the methods by which he treats those materials, Cozzens demonstrates the continued vitality of the major tradition of the Anglo-American novel stretching from Fielding and Defoe through Howells and Twain.

Like these earlier writers, Cozzens is concerned with the rejection of sentimentality, the rejection of false myth. In *Guard of Honor*, this sentimentalism concerns the race problem, and here, like the Howells of *An Imperative Duty*, he explores and exposes the reverse kind of lying about life which would make the Negro something more rather than something less than he is. The same kind of wrong-headed insistence upon a principle with no sanction in fact which could tempt Howells' heroine to a meaningless self-sacrifice leads Cozzens' Lieutenant Edsell to risk the disruption of an Army air base. Cozzens demonstrates that the first step towards a knowledge of our world is the ridding ourselves of false preconceptions. Then he shows how mature men must go on, through observation, through painfully won experience, through analysis and evaluation with our rational faculties of the world of sensory perception, to understand the complexities of the world of moral relativity. In this world there are no ethical absolutes, but only relationships. Truth means "consistent with something else"; ideas are qualified by the company they keep; sexual morality is to not hurt or humiliate a friend; general morality means the governing of the passions by civilized mature intelligence and reason. The kind of world Cozzens sees through his fiction is therefore a meaningful world, infinitely complex in its relationship, constantly shifting and changing in its values, but nevertheless the kind of world which can be kept functioning by the application of reason to its problems, and can be disrupted by acts of lawless violence. A Benny Carricker, the hot-shot pilot of *Guard of Honor*, could, in the world of Hemingway or Faulkner, punch a Negro pilot in the nose and cause scarcely a stir; in the world of Cozzens, a punch in the nose can threaten the unravelling of society. In this world, the mature social scientist can continue to perceive clearly and act reasonably, convinced that in the vexations and perplexities of the change and the flux, there is a meaning which holds it all together. And he, and we, can be convinced that the lights of mankind are "no more than stars among the innumerable stars," but stars nevertheless, and worthy of our attention. Cozzens, it is clear, is working in the direct tradition coming through Howells.

These are the lines of continuity in materials and techniques of fiction coming from the age we have examined. As important as the influence of Howells' fiction and his criticism, however, was the effect of his literary appreciations with their breadth and range and tolerance. Hating and proscribing only the cheap, the false, and the meretricious, the literature which tells the currently popular lies about life, he welcomed and encouraged all forms of literary truth and sincerity. The roll call of those talents to whom he introduced the American public, or for whom he helped to win an audience, is impressive: Henry James as well as Mark Twain, De Forest, Eggleston, Jewett, Murfree, Cable, Harte, Frederic, Garland, Norris, Crane, Dostoievsky as well as

Tolstoy, Turgenev, Ibsen and Shaw, Verga, Galdós, and Palacio Valdés.

Despite these contributions, and despite the efforts of a small group of scholars and historians to give him his due, Howells has been for two generations a prophet with little honor. Those writers who might have been expected to acknowledge some indebtedness have been put off by the conventional attitude which held him to be bourgeois and sissy. The attack on Howells as a prude first came from an aesthetic fugitive from his age, a man whose spiritual home was in the 1840's and '50's with Edgar Allan Poe, despising middle-class American democracy with all its beliefs in reason, science, and progress. Ambrose Bierce it was, the bitter Bierce, who noted the transfer of Howells' editorial activities from *Harper's* to the *Cosmopolitan*, and seized the occasion to excoriate him and all that Bierce felt he represented. "He can tell nothing that he has not seen or heard," Bierce said, "and in his progress through the rectangular streets and between the trim hedges of Philistia, with lettered old maids of his acquaintance curtseying from the door-ways, he has seen and heard nothing worth telling." Howells, he went on, had "shifted his smug personality and his factory of little wooden men and women on wheels to the *Cosmopolitan*, and his following of fibrous virgins . . . and oleaginous clergymen has probably gone with him. . . ." Then Gertrude Atherton blamed Howells for making American literature "the most timid, the most anaemic . . . the most bourgeois, that any country has ever known." That was in 1904, and four years later her temper was even worse as she accused him of blighting American letters with his "hopelessly narrow, finicky" standards. And from then on, successive condemnation of Howells invariably implied his prudish reticence. John Macy found him overrefined; Alexander Harvey branded him the leader of the "sissy school"; Mencken expressed his revulsion at the sight of lady critics fawning over Howells and no more questioning his novels "than they would their own virginity"; Sinclair Lewis, in his Nobel Prize speech labelled Howells the darling of the vicar and the old maid. And the cumulative effect of all of this was to obscure the direct line of development from Howells, through the realists and critical realists of the twentieth century, for whom Lewis was the primary spokesman.

Another, and perhaps more important reason for the contemporary disapproval of the late nineteenth century has been the loss of confidence of many of our best writers and thinkers in the values which nourished Howells and Twain. Writers for whom the modern world has become a Waste Land, turned towards the image of Melville, sitting on a wind-swept dune, telling Hawthorne that his search for meaning had been fruitless, that he had made up his mind to be annihilated. These writers of the twenties took T. S. Eliot's poem as their text, and wrote poetic and prosaic illustrations of its truth. The world they saw about them was an empty and a meaningless one, and the job of the writer, their job, was to identify that lack of meaning and make it bearable. Scott Fitzgerald's *The Great Gatsby* was one expression of this view of the writer's role in a world without meaning. Its protagonist was a hero manqué, one whose visions of greatness could have had a realizable object in another day but which, in modern America, could only be projected upon racketeering and upon the unrewarding love of a girl who embodies the American dream of success and wealth. And like the creatures in *The Waste Land*, the narrator of *The Great Gatsby* was a man whose loss of purpose was symbolized by his sexual impotency: Nick could not take Jordan into his arms until Gatsby, the demigod of the American dream, had achieved his Daisy. For his account of modern spiritual barrenness, Hemingway, too, used the symbol of sexual sterility. Jake, in *The Sun Also Rises*, had been rendered impotent by a war wound, and had become a representation of the emptiness of the modern world through which the lost generation moved, they liked to think, like tragic hollow men. Only when they are involved in the primitive irrational ritual of a fiesta do these people live, and when the fiesta is over, they lapse into the somnabulism of their empty lives. In this kind of world, the only meaning, the only morality is "not to be a bitch–it's what we have instead of God." Another narrative on this same theme was the first major work of the novelist whose influence has almost matched that of Hemingway: William Faulkner's *Soldier's Pay*. Here the symbol of the modern world was a soldier so deeply wounded as to be imbecile as well as emasculate; and the other protagonists of the novel had to assert their faith in some kind of purpose by compelling a tawdry Southern flapper, the direct ancestor of Temple Drake, to carry out her part of the code of life in a senseless world by marrying her helpless, dying fiancé. And then, at the very end of the twenties, Faulkner gave us his vision of modern life as a tale told by an idiot, signifying nothing: Benjy Compson, the thirty-three-year-old, feeble-minded castrato of *The Sound and the Fury*, driven through the streets of Jefferson, Mississippi, by a bullying Negro, a broken flower in his fist.

With the sensibility dominant that could give its age this kind of symbol, it is little wonder that Howells and what he stood for—the significance of normal, commonplace American life—could get little hearing. But perhaps there are indications that this era is passing. Faulkner recently told a class of college women that they should strive to complete the unfinished work of God even in so humble and ordinary a place as their own middle-class kitchens; while it is scarcely to be expected that he will practice this preaching, this most recent of his public statements is indicative of a trend away from the view of an empty and meaningless world which dominated his early works and those of Hemingway. After the imbecile soldier, after the idiot with the broken flower, Faulkner has finally worked his way back into some kind of acceptance of the world as a place with a pattern, a place where there is a small reservoir of truth, not much perhaps, but enough to keep the world going, a truth which can be overheard by a young boy like Chick Mallison and an old lady like Miss Habersham in *Intruder in the Dust*. Hemingway's evolution towards acceptance is even more clear. He began with the meaningless world of *The Sun Also Rises* and "A Clean Well-Lighted Place"; in this world the only prayer could be a bitter invocation to nothingness: "Our nada who art in nada, nada be thy name." Hemingway's fiction then became a progressive description of the struggles of his heroes to make a code by which man can live. This code is first one of negation: "not to be a bitch," then a code of love between man and woman in *A Farewell to Arms*, then an expansion to all mankind, for he discovered for whom the bells toll, and his hero, Jordan, could die convinced that "the world is a fine place and worth fighting for." And finally, in *The Old Man and the Sea*, Anselmo, the Hemingway hero grown old, feels his kinship not only with man (the young fisherman) and beast (the fish), but with the stars which are his brothers. And in this world of significant relations, Hemingway can recreate in simple terms the myth of tragedy due to man's own responsibility, the myth of the beneficent and necessary fall which has often been man's final, deepest acceptance of the moral meaning and value of his world.

This shift in sensibility, so well charted by the general development of these two spokesmen for one aspect of the 'twenties, is best illustrated in the works of the most significant talent to arise in the generation that came just after the one which called itself "lost." Robert Penn Warren has analyzed the painful cleavage between reason and emotion, science and faith, head and heart which was the cause of the alienation of his predecessors. Warren has described the conflict as one between allegiance to "the world" (science, reason, moral relativity) and "the idea" (faith, the absolute, that which satisfies man emotionally). His Southern heroes, Adam Stanton in *All the King's Men*, Jerry Beaumont in *World Enough and Time*, reject "the world" for "the idea" and bring misery to themselves and those around them. In doing so they become representative not only of modern Southern man, but of the modern artist as well. For Warren's Southern characters are tormented by the vision of a world which apparently is as meaningless as the dissociated spasmodic jerk of an old man's eye-muscle as he dozes against the cracking wall of a desert shack: the world of The Great Twitch. Jerry Beaumont and Adam Stanton must impose their patterns of chivalric "idea" upon this world, and Jack Burden must abandon himself to a lost and empty and impotent existence. But both Jack Burden in *All the King's Men* and Jerry Beaumont in *World Enough and Time* finally realize that the world of The Great Twitch is not the real world, that the real world has pattern and meaning, however obscure the pattern, however fluid and changing the meaning. They discover that the man, the artist, cannot reject his world, but must strive to fuse it with the idea.

Warren, like all artists of the first rank, represents for us the state of our sensibility; and perhaps he illustrates its contemporary movement away from rejection to an acceptance, critical and wary as it might be, but an acceptance nevertheless of the natural surface of things, of social man and his complexities and his responsibilities. We see indications of this shift demonstrated in the recent works of many of the major novelists. There is a significance in things, says the Colonel Ross of Cozzens' *Guard of Honor;* there is a small amount of truth, enough to make the world go, declares the Gavin Stevens of Faulkner's *Intruder in the Dust;* there is reason for the old man's tragedy, and hence a basis for human dignity and responsibility, says the Hemingway of *The Old Man and the Sea;* man can choose between good and evil and has the power and the responsibility to make the right choice, the characters of Steinbeck's *East of Eden* agree; and Jack Burden, in Warren's *All the King's Men,* goes to live in his father's house, and, after having lived in it, accepts it and is ready to go out of it and into "the convulsions of the world and the responsibilities of time."

And as these, some of our most sensitive authors, begin to accept their world, perhaps more of our writers will be prepared to live in their fathers' house. If this be true, we may be entering a cultural climate in which it may be possible to read with sympathy those writers of an age of acquiescence, who derived from that acceptance a hope and a sense of proportion.

Their hope was based upon a reverence for living and all its manifestations, upon a faith that the world of social man is a world in which decent men can believe in the possibility of making decent lives for themselves, and can be helped to make that decency and to enjoy it by their arts. It was a critical, often a bitter hope; but it was vibrant with the conviction that the world we live in is worth the artist's attention, that there is meaning in the flux and change, that in the very change and process which seems to make a mockery of absolutes there are values that are worth living by.

And above all a sense of proportion. Theirs was no religion of art for the few, theirs was a religion of life with art for the many. They had the conviction that the fine arts can only preserve their supreme position as the highest emotional resource of man if they, at the same time, take their lowest position as the most dependent and contingent of human activities. Linked with the other, and more basic "arts"—the art of human relationships, the arts of family and group and social living, the art of living with one's God, the fine arts enable us to recognize value, sense significance, feel joy. Howells felt that a simple act of goodness is the highest artistic action that can be taken, for it is a part of conduct which is the "beautifullest" thing of all. Feeling this, he set art below humanity; but, having set it there, he spoke up for the right of the artist to serve human needs in whatever way his talents took him. In his own honest, sensible, consistent work, he kept alive and growing a major American tradition of an intuitive reverence for the homely and the native, showed us how this intuition could be part of an age of science, and prepared the grounds for much that we find in subsequent American literature.

NOTES

Key

ABT, William Dean Howells, *A Boy's Town* (New York, 1890)
HL, Manuscript collection of the Houghton Library, Harvard University
Hunt, Manuscript collection of the Huntington Library, San Marino, California
JF, F. O. Matthiessen, *The James Family* (New York, 1947)
"EEC," "The Editor's Easy Chair," *Harper's*
"ES," "The Editor's Study," *Harper's*
LFA, William Dean Howells, *Literary Friends and Acquaintances* (New York, 1900)
LHJ, *The Letters of Henry James*, ed. Percy Lubbock (New York, 1920), 2 vols.
L in L, *Life in Letters of William Dean Howells*, ed. Mildred Howells (New York, 1928), 2 vols.
MLP, William Dean Howells, *My Literary Passions* (New York, 1895)
NHJ, *The Notebooks of Henry James*, ed. F. O. Matthiessen and Kenneth B. Murdock (New York, 1947)
USC, Manuscript collection of the University of Southern California
YOMY, William Dean Howells, *Years of My Youth* (New York, 1916)

PROLOGUE

Page

13 "not a very good draughtsman . . ." Introduction to *Recollections of Life in Ohio*, William Cooper Howells (Cincinnati, 1895), v.

14 "In school . . ." *MLP*, 8.
For the books available to Howells, see *MLP*, 4-5.
"at the ends . . ." *MLP*, 62.

15 "public a place . . ." *YOMY*, 142.
everyone had enough . . . *ABT*, 78.
"Simon Girty . . ." *YOMY*, 55.
"almost unrivalled fitness . . ." *Ibid.*, 21.
"Saturdays spread over . . ." *Ibid.*, 22.
"god of poetry . . ." *ABT*, 81.
"nothing else . . ." *LFA*, 36.

16 "honor and worship . . ." *YOMY*, 182.
Howells would occasionally chafe . . . See his letter to C. E. Norton of December 28, 1874, regarding the responsibilities which made it impossible for him to take up an historical work on Venice, *Hunt.*
agreed to read and edit . . . *L in L*, I, 105.
"as thick as blackberries . . ." See his letter to Howells, March 28, [1883], *HL.*

17 "virile . . ." "EEC," *Harper's* CXIII, 473 (August, 1906).
the definitive picture . . . This is the essence of James' tribute to Howells in "Letter to Mr. Howells," *North American Review* CXCV, 561 (April, 1912).

18 taught him the way . . . See his letter to Howells, no date, but possibly 1877 or 1878, where he tells Howells how much he owed to his training, *HL.*
"fibrous virgins . . ." "Dispatch from San Francisco, May 22," *Literary Digest,* IV, 110 (May, 1892).

19 "really *grasping* . . ." *LHJ*, I, 30.
the big man . . . See letter from Harold Frederic to Hamlin Garland, May 12, 1897, *USC.*
dead wood . . . See Sinclair Lewis, "Speech on Acceptance of the Nobel Prize," New York *Times*, December 13, 1930, 12.

20 De Forest could argue . . . *European Acquaintance* (New York, 1858), 120.

Page

"flung the Stars and Stripes . . ." Mark Twain, *Innocents Abroad* (New York, 1906), I, 98.

"no one knows . . ." Letter to Miss Victoria M. Howells, January 18, 1862, *L in L*, I, 47.

"vulgar, vulgar . . ." Letter to his mother, October 13, 1869, *LHJ*, I, 22.

"not to think . . ." Letter to Miss Victoria M. Howells, April 26, 1862, *L in L*, I, 58.

21 "the approximate vision . . ." Ortega y Gasset, *Revolt of the Masses* (London, 1932), 142.

"We are eight . . ." Letter from Robert Frost to Hamlin Garland, February 4, 1921, *USC*.

CHAPTER I—BACKGROUND

23 Friedrich Schlegel's introduction of the term "romantic . . ." See F. O. Lovejoy, "On the Meaning of 'Romantic' in Early German Romanticism, Part I," *Modern Language Notes*, XXXI, 385 (1916).

"search for an unseen world . . ." C. M. Bowra, *The Romantic Imagination* (Cambridge, Mass., 1949), 9-10.

1. Strains of Idealism

25 "No author, without a trial . . ." Nathaniel Hawthorne, Preface to *The Marble Faun* (Boston, 1897), 15.

"come nearer . . ." *L in L*, I, 31.

Howells' preference for *The Blithedale Romance* . . . *LFA*, 55.

"the conception of intellectual . . ." William James, *The Varieties of Religious Experience* (New York, 1928) 162. This is James' definition of morbid-mindedness.

"my way is still . . ." Letter to Henry Blake Fuller, January 17, 1904, *L in L*, II, 181.

"the supreme contemporary example . . ." William James, *op. cit.*, 84.

"the meal in the firkin . . ." Ralph Waldo Emerson, "The American Scholar," in *Works* (Boston, 1903), I, 111.

"a presence of force . . ." *LFA*, 61. Howells quoted Emerson: "I ask not for the great, the remote, the romantic . . ." in *Criticism and Fiction* (New York, 1891), 79.

27 "after many years . . ." *ABT*, 11.

"their life." *Ibid.*

"in every thought . . ." *Ibid.*, 14.

"wholly outside . . ." *LFA*, 45.

2. The Classical Tradition

Page

27 "most of the goods things . . ." "EEC," *Harper's*, CXXV, 151 (June, 1912).
Howells did not ride on the elephant . . . *ABT*, 107.
28 "If the eighteenth century . . ." "EEC," *Harper's*, CVIII, 641 (March, 1904).
"Instead of . . . sleeping . . ." *LFA*, 146.
29 "poor, honest herd . . ." "ES," *Harper's*, LXXIII, 154-155 (June, 1886).
"Kindness and gentleness . . ." *MLP*, 15.
"later . . ." *Ibid.*, 26.
"not a master . . ." *Ibid.*, 27.
"When fair Aurora . . ." *YOMY*, 76.
"first three loves . . ." *MLP*, 26-27.
"the reading of Don Quixote . . ." *Ibid.*, 21.
30 "gross in its facts . . ." *Ibid.*, 107.
"free and simple . . ." *Ibid.*, 21.
"went to heights . . ." *Ibid.*, 58.
"instinctive liking . . ." *Ibid.*, 60.
31 "it was no more possible . . ." *Ibid.*, 71.
"grotesqueness . . ." *Ibid.*, 72.
"admired other authors . . ." *Ibid.*, 71.
"farthest reach . . ." *Ibid.*, 101.
"Its chief virtue . . ." *LFA*, 118.
went throught them all . . . *MLP*, 34.
"how false and how mistaken . . ." *Criticism and Fiction*, 22.
32 "Byron is the essence . . ." "Alfieri," *Atlantic*, XXXV, 538 (May, 1875).
"not make out that Wordsworth . . ." *MLP*, 81.
" 'the moving accident' . . ." *Italian Journeys* (1867), 1; and indirectly in "Henry James, Jr.," *Century*, XXV, 28 (November, 1882).

3. The Brahmin Culture

34 "the common sense of the invisible . . ." J. R. Lowell, "The Function of the Poet," in *The Function of the Poet and other Essays* (Boston, 1920), 13.
"Great poetry," *Ibid.*, 74.
"glad and proud . . ." Letter to J. J. Piatt, March 4, 1859, *L in L*, I, 23,
35 "to make sure of its presence . . ." *YOMY*, 181.
"the wisest and finest . . ." *LFA*, 24.
"the largest part . . ." Letter to James Russell Lowell, June 22, 1879, in *L in L*, I, 270.
"keep on cultivating . . ." Quoted in *L in L*, I, 88.
"particularly delighted . . ." Letter to James Russell Lowell, August 21, 1864, *L in L*, I, 84.

Page

"the apostolic succession . . ." *LFA*, 37.

"Boston State-House . . ." Quoted by S. I. Hayakawa, ed. *O. W. Holmes: Representative Selections* (New York, 1939), ix.

36 "oriental side . . ." Oliver Wendell Holmes, *Works* (Boston, 1891), XI, 307.

"If for the Fall . . ." *Ibid.*, III, 182.

"He liked horizons . . ." *LFA*, 177.

"an 'imaginary' story . . ." Oliver Wendell Holmes, "The Professor's Story, Part I," *Atlantic* V, 89 (January, 1860).

4. Sentimentalism in America

37 "an abode of enchantment . . ." Sylvester Judd, *Richard Edney* (Boston, 1850), 10-11.

"had read of so many . . ." quoted in Herbert Ross Brown, *The Sentimental Novel in America* (Durham, N. C., 1940), 364.

"to become a clerk . . ." *Ibid.*, 365.

"It is a dark thread . . ." *Ibid.*, 368.

"nascent fictionists . . ." William Dean Howells, *The Vacation of the Kelwyns* (New York, 1920), 56.

39 "Because I write . . ." "The Memorial of A. B. or Matilda Muffin," *Atlantic*, V, 190 (February, 1860).

40 "A promise is a promise . . ." "My Last Love," *Atlantic*, V, 145 (February, 1860).

"How they have loved . . ." [Marian James], "Some Account of a Visionary," *Atlantic*, V, 207 (February, 1860).

"Now we all need . . ." *Atlantic*, XVII, 380 (March, 1866).

"a female rake . . ." Charles Reade, "*Griffith Gaunt*," *Atlantic*, XVII, 596 (May, 1866).

41 "a fashion so remote . . ." *MLP*, 152.

The synopsis is paraphrased from a letter to "Dear Foster," May 13, 1863, *USC*.

42 "tinged . . . with . . . passionate . . ." [William Dean Howells], "Scintillations from the Prose Works of Heinrich Heine," *Atlantic*, XXXII, 238 (August, 1873).

"sweat the Heine . . ." Quoted in letter to William Cooper Howells, August 25, 1864, *L in L*, I, 88.

"The German poetry . . ." See his letter to Don Lloyd Wyman, September 5, 1865, *USC*.

"misfortune . . ." Letter to James T. Fields, September 29, 1861, *Hunt.*

he had almost entirely changed . . . See letter to T. W. Higginson, November 20, 1866, *USC*.

CHAPTER II–THE ATTACK ON THE SENTIMENTAL

1. Beginning the Attack: Higginson

Page

44 His advice . . . Thomas Wentworth Higginson, "A Letter to a Young Contributor," *Atlantic*, IX, 401-411 (April, 1862).

"young girl who seeks . . ." [Thomas Wentworth Higginson], "*Esperance*, by Meta Lander," *Atlantic*, XVII, 525 (April, 1866).

"in keeping close . . ." Thomas Wentworth Higginson, *Atlantic Essays* (Boston, 1871), 31.

2. Howells' Defense of Romance

46 "fidelity, not merely . . ." Nathaniel Hawthorne, Preface to *The House of the Seven Gables* (Boston, 1897), 13.

47 "absolving it from any cumbrous . . ." [James Russell Lowell], "*Sir Rohan's Ghost*, by Harriet Prescott," *Atlantic*, V, 254 (February, 1860).

" 'It's not, properly speaking . . .' " William Dean Howells, *The World of Chance* (New York, 1893), 58.

"a novelist in the sense . . ." [William Dean Howells], "*Yesterdays with Authors*, by James T. Fields," *Atlantic*, XXIX, 498 (April, 1872).

"The book is a romance . . ." [William Dean Howells], "*Joseph Noirel's Revenge*, by Victor Cherbuliez," *Atlantic*, XXXI, 105 (January, 1873).

48 "Certain premises . . ." [William Dean Howells], "*Prudence Palfrey*, by Thomas Bailey Aldrich," *Atlantic*, XXXIV, 228 (August, 1874).

"like the poem . . ." [William Dean Howells], "*Detmold*: A Romance by W. H. Bishop," *Atlantic* XLIV, 265 (August, 1879).

"Talking of talks . . ." Letter to Edmund Clarence Stedman, December 5, 1866, *L in L*, I, 116.

49 "for certain rich poetical . . ." William Dean Howells, "Henry James, Jr.," *Century*, XXV, 26 (November, 1882).

3. The Rejection of Europe: Howells and De Forest

"America is beginning . . . to judge . . ." *Nation*, III, 189 (September, 1866).

50 Howells was a professional . . . The worth of his estate was given in *Publishers' Weekly*, CXCVIII, 1706 (November 27, 1920).

53 "pleasant flavor of individuality," *Nation*, III, 189 (September, 1866).

"Most tourists," *North American Review*, CIII, 612 (October, 1866).

54 "one critic for 40,000,000 . . ." Letter to Henry James, June 26, 1869, *L in L*, I, 144.

"The author of *Italian Journeys* . . ." *Nation*, XII, 44 (January, 1871).

4. The Rejection of the Old World: Twain

Page

57 "an amount of pure human nature . . ." [William Dean Howells], "*The Innocents Abroad*, by Samuel S. Clements [*sic*]," Atlantic, XXIV, 766 (December, 1869).

"immensely . . ." Letter to S. L. Clemens, December 3, 1880, *L in L*, I, 290.

"all good . . ." Letter to S. L. Clemens, October 17, 1889, *Ibid.*, 427.

5. The Attack on the Sentimental in Literature: Howells

59 he hoped no one else . . . Letter to James T. Fields, October 22, 1866, *Hunt.*

60 through somebody else's . . . See letter to Ralph Keeler, September, 1871, *USC.*

"is apt, if anything . . ." [William Dean Howells], "*Prudence Palfrey* by Thomas Bailey Aldrich," *Atlantic*, XXXIV, 227 (August, 1874).

"giving not so much . . ." William Dean Howells, "Mr. Aldrich's Fiction," *Atlantic*, XLVI, 695 (November, 1880).

61 "it is hard . . ." William Dean Howells, "The New Historical Romances," *North American Review*, CLXXI, 942-943 (December, 1900).

"Do I, then . . ." *Ibid.*, 945.

"that which it is loath . . ." William Dean Howells, *Literature and Life* (New York, 1902), 122.

"we have no name . . ." *Ibid.*

62 "in which all the disagreeable . . ." "ES," *Harper's*, LXXIII, 478 (August, 1886).

"or what that reader . . ." "ES," *Harper's* LXXV, 318 (July, 1887).

"horrid tumult of the swashbuckler . . ." "The New Historical Romances," *North American Review*, CLXXI, 936 (December, 1900).

"facts of the life of toil . . ." "ES," *Harper's*, LXXXIII, 965 (November, 1891).

"lust of gold . . ." "The New Historical Romances," *North American Review*, CLXXI, 936 (December, 1900).

6. The Attack on the Sentimental in Literature: Eggleston, Harte, Twain

69 "a real human being . . ." Quoted by J. B. Harrison, *Bret Harte: Representative Selections* (New York, 1941), xiii.

7. The Attack on the Sentimental: Twain and Warner's *The Gilded Age*

73 to be "authentic . . ." *Mark Twain to Mrs. Fairbanks*, ed. Dixon Wecter (San Marino, Calif., 1949), 19.

8. THE ATTACK ON THE "FUNGUS CROP OF SENTIMENT" ABOUT THE SOUTH

Page

77 "Every loyal American . . ." William Dean Howells, *A Fearful Responsibility* (Boston, 1881), 3.

79 our first American novel . . . praised its honesty . . . [William Dean Howells], *Miss Ravenel's Conversion from Secession to Loyalty*, by J. W. De Forrest [*sic*], *Atlantic*, XX, 120 ff. (July, 1867).

an American realist worthy . . ." "ES," *Harper's*, LXXV, 639, (September, 1887).

82 "What would you say . . ." Quoted by E. L. Tinker, "Cable and the Creoles," *American Literature*, V, 322 (January, 1934).

CHAPTER III–TOWARDS A PHILOSOPHY OF LITERARY REALISM

1. THE REASON FOR REALISM

88 "He can . . . write solely . . ." *LHJ*, I, 30.

89 "dominating the intellectual . . ." Ralph Gabriel, *The Course of American Democratic Thought* (New York, 1940), 147.

90 the life one has lived . . . See his letter to Don Lloyd Wyman, February 6, 1867, *Hunt.*

with the naked eye . . . See his letter to Ralph Keeler, September, 1871, *USC.*

"came," and seemed "to have come . . ." Letter to T. S. Perry, January 28, 1886, *L in L*, I, 378.

short, lively sketches . . . See his letter to Mrs. James T. Fields, undated, *Hunt.*

"there is hardly any law . . ." [William Dean Howells], "Thomas Purnell's *Literature and Its Professors*," *Atlantic*, XX, 255 (August, 1867).

"faithful spirit . . ." [William Dean Howells], "*The Story of Kennett*, by Bayard Taylor," *Atlantic*, XVII, 777 (June, 1866).

"felicity in expressing . . ." [William Dean Howells], "*Norwood*, by Henry Ward Beecher," *Atlantic*, XXI, 761 (June, 1868).

"honest enough to let himself . . ." [William Dean Howells], "*Innocents Abroad*, by Samuel S. Clements [*sic*]," *Atlantic*, XXIV, 765 (December, 1869).

"what . . . life is . . ." [William Dean Howells], "*The Story of a Bad Boy*, by Thomas Bailey Aldrich," *Atlantic*, XXV, 124 (January, 1870).

"the form of fiction . . ." Quoted in *L in L*, I, 162.

"most distinctly . . ." *Ibid.*

"Fleshly eyes . . ." *LHJ*, I, 30.

2. The Scientist as the New Hero

Page

91 "with the most heart . . ." *Atlantic*, XIX, 637 (May, 1867).
"the inquiry was inquiry . . ." *LFA*, 153.
92 "Goethean face and figure . . ." *LFA*, 269.
94 "those who entirely reject . . ." Sidney Lanier, *The English Novel and Essays on Literature* (Baltimore, 1945), 62.

3. Taine in America

95 "write a three-number . . ." George Cary Eggleston, *The First of the Hoosiers* (Philadelphia, 1903), 297.
96 "reign of democracy . . ." Hippolyte Taine, *History of English Literature* (Philadelphia, 1908), IV, 66 ff.
97 "admirably brilliant . . ." [William Dean Howells], "*History of English Literature*, by H. Taine," *Atlantic*, XXIX, 241 (February, 1872).
98 "making what changes . . ." *LFA*, 138-139.
99 "For the present . . ." [A. G. Sedgwick], "*Middlemarch*, by George Eliot," *Atlantic*, XXXI, 492 (April, 1873).
"It is hard . . ." [William Dean Howells], "*Liza*, by Ivan Turgenieff," *Atlantic*, XXXI, 239 (February, 1873).
"the most precious contribution . . ." [William Dean Howells], "*Threading My Way*, by Robert Dale Owen, *Atlantic*, XXXIII, 232 (February, 1874).
100 "impose a mechanical morality . . ." G. P. Lathrop, "Growth of the Novel," *Atlantic*, XXXIII, 695 (June, 1874).
"teaches us not . . ." *Criticism and Fiction*, 112.
"powerful sketches . . ." "ES," *Harper's*, LXXIV, 483 (March, 1887).
101 "we must ask ourselves . . ." *Ibid.*, 826 (April, 1887).
"contributes his share . . ." *Ibid.*, 641 (September, 1887).
102 "novelty and interest . . ." "EEC," *Harper's*, CVII, 806 (October. 1903).

4. The Autobiographical Method: Howells

"Is it true? . . ." "ES," *Harper's*, LXXIV, 825 (April, 1887).
106 "Mrs. Farrell . . ." *L in L*, I, 205.
"temptations to the fictionist . . ." *Ibid.*, 209.
"outdid themselves . . ." *LFA*, 186.
107 "simulacrum . . ." *L in L*, I, 174.
either a Padre Libera . . . The different identifications are made by James L. Woodress, Jr., in "Howells's Ventian Priest," *Modern Language Notes*, LXVI, 266-267 (April, 1951), and Mildred Howells, in *L in L*, I, 192.

Page

"strong motive . . ." Letter to John Hay, December, 18, 1875, *L in L*, I, 215.

His wife's sister . . . *L in L*, I, 74-75.

108 "brutal exaltation . . ." Letter to Victoria M. Howells, January 18, 1862, *L in L*, I, 47.

that part of himself . . . *L in L*, II, 301.

Mark Twain . . . insisted . . . See his letter to Howells, July 24, 1882, *HL*.

"softening cynic . . ." *LFA*, 105.

journeyed to Crawfordville . . . *L in L*, I, 297.

109 The situation for *Fennel and Rue* . . . *L in L*, I, 375-376.

The genesis of *The Lady of the Aroostook* . . . *L in L*, I, 265.

the account of Sylvester Baxter . . . *L in L*, II, 17.

description of Quebec . . . *L in L*, II, 13.

110 "You have had . . ." Henry James, "Letter to Mr. Howells," *North American Review* CXCV, 560 (April, 1912).

5. The Autobiographical Method: De Forest, Harte, Eggleston, Garland, Twain

113 People like Edward Dowden . . . Mark Twain, "In Defense of Harriet Shelley," in *How to Tell a Story* (New York, 1906), 49.

Lafayette Hawkins . . . See his letter to Howells, May 10 [1874?], *HL*.

Colonel Sellers . . . The identification is made by Dixon Wecter, *Sam Clemens of Hannibal* (Boston, 1952), 161. In a letter to Howells, May 7 [1875?], Twain says that he drew Sellers from life, from one of his relatives, but not his brother.

114 Tom Blankenship and his parent . . . See Wecter, *op. cit.*, 149-150.

115 "burlesque of a farce . . ." Quoted by Dixon Wecter, *op. cit.*, 188. Wecter also quotes a letter in which Twain declared that all his books were autobiographical, *op. cit.*, 65.

"Uncle Sam" Smarr . . . Dixon Wecter, *op. cit.*, 107-108.

6. Local Color

116 "we have the whole . . ." [William Dean Howells], "James's *Hawthorne*," *Atlantic*, XLV, 284 (February, 1880).

117 "know his environment from himself . . ." "EEC," *Harper's*, CXXIV, 636 (April, 1912).

118 more sense of "locality" . . . See his letter to Charles Warren Stoddard, January 3, 1873, *Hunt*.

"sell monstrously . . ." See his letter to Howells, March 17, 1879, *HL*.

nineteen-twentieths . . . See his letter to Howells, December 6, 1886, *HL*.

"bits of local color . . ." Letter to Howells, March 19, 1872, *HL*.

Page

119 downright hatred . . . See, for example, Twain's letter to Howells of June [?], [1879], *HL*.

"felicity in expressing . . ." *Atlantic*, XXI, 761 (June, 1868).

told Cable of the pleasure . . . *L in L*, I, 302.

"There is no greatness . . ." "ES," *Harper's*, LXXV, 641 (September, 1887).

"didn't make North Georgia . . ." *L in L*, II, 281.

very tint and form . . . [William Dean Howells] "*Deephaven*, by Sarah O. Jewett," *Atlantic*, XXXIX, 759 (June, 1897).

120 "work upon English literature . . ." Notebook of Hamlin Garland, *USC*.

121 expressed the sad spirit . . . "ES," *Harper's*, LXXXIII, 638 (September, 1891).

romantic and badly motivated . . . See Howells' letter to Garland, November 6, 1892, *USC*.

"The flush of wild adventure . . ." "EEC," *Harper's*, CXXXIII, 629 (September, 1916).

"perfectly true to life . . ." Letter to Hamlin Garland, July 22, 1917, *L in L*, II, 373.

122 most grateful . . . See a letter from Alice French to Howells, January 4, 1888, *HL*.

"How would Mr. Howells . . ." See letter from Henry Harland to Howells, August 3, 1887, *HL*.

sadly detached modern . . . See letter from Henry Blake Fuller to Howells, June 3, 1895, *HL*.

7. Techniques for Truth

"hard and dry . . ." "EEC," *Harper's*, CXII, 959 (May, 1906).

123 "tell itself . . ." [William Dean Howells], "*Edelweiss*, by Berthold Auerbach," *Atlantic*, XXIII, 762 (June, 1869).

"He seems the most . . ." [William Dean Howells], "*Liza*, by Ivan Turgenieff," *Atlantic*, XXXI, 239 (February, 1873).

"The novelist's business . . ." [William Dean Howells], "*The Circuit Rider*, by Edward Eggleston," *Atlantic*, XXXIII, 745 (June, 1874).

124 "plucks her people apart . . ." [William Dean Howells], "*The Legend of Jubal and Other Poems*, by George Eliot," *Atlantic*, XXXIV, 103 (July, 1874).

8. Dramatic Method and Organic Form

126 "You wretch . . ." Letter to Ralph Keeler, September, 1871, *USC*.

"the good old sort, like De foe's [*sic*] . . ." William Dean Howells, "Mark Twain," *Century*, XXIV, 782-783 (September, 1882).

127 "I don't know that you are bound . . ." Brice Maxwell in *The Story of a Play* (New York, 1898), 90.

Page

"a finished story . . ." William Dean Howells, "Henry James, Jr.," *Century,* XXV, 29 (November, 1882).

128 "has surprised the prime secret . . ." "EEC," *Harper's,* CXXXII, 636 (March, 1916).

131 "the more art resembles . . ." "EEC," *Harper's,* CIX, 967 (November, 1904).

132 "work of art . . ." *Ibid.*

9. "Symbolism" and "Use of Symbol"

134 "mystic symbol . . ." Nathaniel Hawthorne, *The Scarlet Letter* (New York, 1883), 50.

135 "my books are water . . ." Quoted in De Lancey Ferguson, *Mark Twain: Man and Legend* (New York, 1943), 196.

"the true standards of the arts . . ." Edmund Burke, "On the Sublime and Beautiful," in *Burke's Writings and Speeches* (Boston, 1901), 128-129. Quoted in *Criticism and Fiction,* 7.

10. Impressionism and Realism

137 "a few distinct touches . . ." [William Dean Howells], "*Tales,* by Björnsterne Björnson," *Atlantic,* XXV, 505 (April, 1870).

pre-Raphaelitism of Hans Christian Andersen . . . [William Dean Howells], "*Only a Fiddler,* by Hans Christian Andersen," *Atlantic,* XXVI, 632 (November, 1870).

138 "preoccupation with the common things . . ." A. Schade van Westrum, "Mr. Howells on Love and Literature," *The Lamp,* XXVIII, 27 (February, 1904).

"Supposing there were . . ." William Henry Bishop, "Authors at Home," *The Critic,* IX, 260 (November, 1886).

139 "the true artist will shun . . ." William Dean Howells, *Their Wedding Journey* (Boston, 1872), 86.

"it is well to remember . . ." [William Dean Howells], "*Prudence Palfrey,* by Thomas Bailey Aldrich," *Atlantic,* XXXIV, 228 (August, 1874).

"every writer of fiction . . ." William Dean Howells, Introduction to *The Actor Manager* by Leonard Merrick (London, 1918), vi.

"in a moment . . ." William Dean Howells, Introduction to Leo Tolstoy's *Master and Man* (New York, 1895), vi-vii.

11. "Morality" in Realism

141 "social purity . . ." *YOMY,* 42.

"cleanly respectabilities . . ." *Ibid.,* 142.

"very Victorian . . ." *Ibid.,* 146.

142 "love-makingest . . ." Letter to John Hay, March 18, 1882, *L in L,* I, 311.

Page

"It is a confounded pretty foot . . ." Quoted in Brown, *The Sentimental Novel in America*, 366.

Oliver Wendell Holmes questioned the propriety . . . Review of E. H. Clarke's *Sex in Education*, *Atlantic*, XXXII, 737 (December, 1873).

it would be well . . . See H. M. Alden's letter to Howells, March 10, 1888, *HL*.

143 "with slender legs, and tribute to woman . . ." Quoted in De Lancey Ferguson, *Mark Twain: Man and Legend* (New York, 1943), 105 and 129.

"lustfully hypersensitive . . ." Bernard DeVoto, *Mark Twain at Work* (Cambridge, Mass., 1942), 15.

"were not dreamed of . . ." Quoted in DeVoto, *ibid.*, 16.

"with the question of sex . . ." *NHJ*, 247.

144 "make something of it . . ." *NHJ*, 77.

"were a Frenchman . . ." *NHJ*, 55.

"for a French public . . ." *NHJ*, 170.

145 "intensely a moralist . . ." William Dean Howells, "Emile Zola," *North American Review*, CLXXV, 592 (November, 1902).

"One of the best written books . . ." A. Schade van Westrum, "Mr. Howells on Love and Literature," *The Lamp*, XXVIII, 31 (February, 1904); also a similar statement in letter to S. L. Clemens, August 9, 1885, *L in L*, I, 371.

"wonderfully well done . . ." Letter to Robert Herrick, September 7, 1906, *L in L*, II, 230.

recognize man's . . . See his letter to Hamlin Garland, July 15, 1914, *USC*.

"through which the pioneer . . ." William Dean Howells, "The Novels of Robert Herrick," *North American Review*, CLXXXIX, 815 (June, 1909).

"why . . . look at it . . ." "EEC," *Harper's*, CXXXV, 434-435 (August, 1917).

146 "so provoking . . ." *Harper's*, XLVII, 460 (August, 1873).

"could not help feeling . . ." *Eclectic Magazine*, XVIII, 122 (July, 1873).

"Miss Vervain's seizing . . ." *North American Review*, CXX, 212 (January, 1875).

"has had the good fortune . . ." *Nation*, XX, 12 (January, 1875).

"error of taste . . ." *Scribner's Monthly*, XVIII, 151 (May, 1879).

"The whole thing . . ." Letter from Grace D. Pattan, New York *Tribune*, December 4, 1882, 10.

147 "pitiless reality . . ." New York *Tribune*, December 18, 1886.

"Man gains a knowledge . . ." *Century*, XXV, 464 (January, 1883).

Page

"We are ready to admit . . ." *Literary World*, XVIII, 5 (January, 1887).

" 'every half-bred rogue . . .' " *L in L*, I, 307.

150 Dixon Wecter reports . . . *Sam Clemens of Hannibal*, 77-78.

151 has been pointed out . . . George Arms in his Introduction to *The Rise of Silas Lapham* (New York, 1949), xiii.

152 "superficial treatment . . ." A. Schade van Westrum, "Mr. Howells on Love and Literature," *The Lamp*, XXVIII, 30-31 (February, 1904).

"ludicrous immorality . . ." William Dean Howells, "The New Historical Romances," *North American Review*, CLXXI, 941 (December, 1900).

12. Pragmatism and Realism

Mabie's attack was in *The Andover Review*, IV, 417-429 (November, 1885).

153 "a new name . . ." This was the subtitle of William James' *Pragmatism.*

"sense of what life . . ." William James' *Pragmatism* (New York, 1907), 4.

"abstraction . . ." *Ibid.*, 51.

154 our beliefs adjust . . . *Collected Papers of Charles Sanders Peirce* (Cambridge, Mass., 1931-35), I, ¶ 321.

"looking away from . . ." James, *Pragmatism*, 54-55.

"noise of facts . . ." *Ibid.*, 40.

"We shall never . . ." *Their Wedding Journey* (Boston, 1872), 110.

"truth independent . . ." James, *Pragmatism*, 64-65.

155 "the same thing . . ." "ES," *Harper's*, LXXV, 156 (June, 1887).

"the salvation of the world . . ." James, *Pragmatism*, 285.

13. Rejection of Moralizing

156 "ruthlessness . . ." [William Dean Howells], "*Norwood*, by Henry Ward Beecher," *Atlantic*, XXI, 761 (June, 1868).

"His moral would have been good . . ." William Dean Howells, "*Griffith Gaunt*, by Charles Reade," *Atlantic*, XVIII, 767 (December, 1866).

"tendencious . . ." William Dean Howells, Introduction to *Dona Perfecta* by B. Perez Galdós (New York, 1896), viii.

157 "hortatory . . ." "ES," *Harper's*, LXXVI, 642 (March, 1888).

14. *The Gilded Age*, *Huckleberry Finn* and *The Rise of Silas Lapham*

"morality penetrates all things . . ." "ES," *Harper's*, LXXIII, 962 (November, 1886).

163 "Our gross appetities . . ." *Harper's*, LXXIV, 824 ff. (April, 1887).

CHAPTER IV–CRITICAL REALISM

1. Industrialism and Corruption

Page

171 "found sympathy and assistance . . ." Allan Nevins, *The Emergence of Modern America* 1865-1878 (New York, 1927), 382.

172 "It had to come . . ." Allan Nevins, *John D. Rockefeller* (New York, 1940), I, 622.

2. Sentimentalists Preferred Blondes

174 "The Troubles of Labor," *Frank Leslie's Illustrated Newspaper*, LXIX, 101 (September, 1889).

3. Howells' Early Attitudes Towards Society

"Many of us who will vote . . ." [William Dean Howells], "Politics," *Atlantic*, XXX, 638 (November, 1872).

177 "Our social and political system . . ." [William Dean Howells], "*Four Years Among Spanish Americans*, by F. Hassaurek," *Atlantic*, XXI, 254 (February, 1868).

"new observer . . ." [William Dean Howells], "A New Observer," *Atlantic*, XLV, 848 (June, 1880).

178 "the more smiling . . ." "ES," *Harper's*, LXXIII, 641 (September, 1886).

"all the pain . . ." William Dean Howells, "Mrs. Johnson," in *Suburban Sketches* (1871), 26.

179 "referred to our national . . ." James Realf, Jr., "Men of Letters," *The Californian*, III, 309 (February, 1893).

4. The Haymarket Affair

180 "The Bill of Rights in most states . . ." Edward Everett Hale, *How They Lived at Hampton* (Boston, 1886), 356.

"Everyone would be glad . . ." *Nation*, XLII, 377 (May 6, 1886).

"In American labor history . . ." Henry David, *The History of the Haymarket Affair* (New York, 1936), 3.

"Socialists, to the number of 600 . . ." *Nation*, XLII, 394 (May 6, 1886).

181 "an illuminating demonstration . . ." Tarbell, *The Nationalizing of Business* (New York, 1936), 162.

"Chicago Police would have been . . ." *Ibid.*, 163.

"the blatant cattle . . ." *Ibid.*

182 "the ruffians . . ." *Letters of James Russell Lowell* (New York, 1894), II, 394.

"call attention to some . . ." Michael Foran, *The Other Side (A Social Study Based on Fact)*, (Washington, 1886), viii.

"chimerical ideas . . ." *Ibid.*

Page

"wrathful fervor . . ." Percy MacKaye, *Epoch, The Life of Steele MacKaye* (New York, 1947), II, 96.

"seductive glamour . . ." *Ibid.*, 127.

183 "roared and rose . . ." *Ibid.*, 149-150.

"through reading their trial . . ." Letter to T. S. Perry, April 14, 1888, *L in L*, I, 413.

"civically murdered . . ." Letter to Hamlin Garland, January 15, 1888, *L in L*, I, 407.

184 "hideous . . . damnable . . . abominable . . ." Letter to Francis F. Browne, November 11, 1887, *L in L*, I, 402.

"thinking and feeling much . . ." Letter to Garland, *L in L*, I, 407.

"a dynamiter . . ." Letter to T. S. Perry, *L in L*, I, 413.

185 "accumulation . . ." Laurence Gronlund, *The Cooperative Commonwealth* (Boston, 1896), 66 ff.

5. The Invalidation of *Criticism and Fiction*

"the prophet of 'critical realism . . .'" Vernon Louis Parrington, *Main Currents in American Thought* (New York, 1927), III, 241.

"at least one short novel . . ." Howells, writing in J. Henry Harper, *House of Harper* (New York, 1912), 321.

186 "ill-advised Study-presence . . ." "ES," *Harper's*, LXXXIV, 642 (March, 1892).

187 "It used to be one . . ." *Criticism and Fiction* (New York, 1891), 127-128.

6. The Theory of Critical Realism

190 "the conventional acceptations . . ." William Dean Howells, "Henrik Ibsen," *North American Review*, CLXXXIII, 3 (July, 1906).

191 "know one another better . . ." "ES," *Harper's*, LXXV, 639 (September, 1887).

"appeals to no sentimental . . ." "ES," *Harper's*, LXXVIII, 159 (December, 1888).

192 "to set a few people . . ." Letter to E. E. Hale, August 30, 1888, *L in L*, I, 416.

He found Harold Frederic's work . . . See his letter to Sylvester Baxter, July 11, 1890, *Hunt*.

"full of the . . . life . . ." "ES," *Harper's*, LXXXIII, 639 (September, 1891).

"any conscientious and enlightened . . ." Letter to Howard Pyle, October 30, 1893, *L in L*, II, 40.

"to hit the fancy . . ." William Dean Howells, "The New Historical Romances," *North American Review*, CLXXI, 943 (December, 1900).

"truth about ourselves . . ." "EEC," *Harper's*, CXII, 959 (May, 1906).

Page

193 "something to think about . . ." William Dean Howells, "The Novels of Robert Herrick," *North American Review,* CLXXXIX, 812 (June, 1909).

"People began to see . . ." "EEC," *Harper's,* CXXIX, 310 (July, 1914).

"Literature which was once . . ." "Mr. Howells's Speech," *North American Review,* CCXII, 8 ff. (July, 1920).

195 "the workingmen *as* workingmen . . ." Letter to John Hay, January 7, 1884, *L in L,* I, 357-358.

"in the wage-takers . . ." William Dean Howells, "Are We a Plutocracy?" *North American Review,* CLVIII, 187 (January, 1894).

"in their fatal existence . . ." "EEC," *Harper's,* CX, 806 (April, 1905).

"In one thing the labor side . . ." Letter to W. C. Howells, July 24, 1892, *L in L,* II, 26.

"three or four years . . ." Letter to T. S. Perry, December 26, 1911, *L in L,* II, 310.

196 "theoretical socialists . . ." Letter to W. C. Howells, February 2, 1890, *L in L,* II, 1.

"something like science . . ." "EEC," *Harper's,* CXXIX, 312 (July, 1914).

197 "almost a better world . . ." "ES," *Harper's,* LXXV, 478 (August, 1887).

"sincerity and reality . . ." Letter to Miss Aurelia H. Howells, September 5, 1897, *L in L,* II, 79.

"We may not think the republic . . ." William Dean Howells, "The Modern American Mood," *Harper's,* XCV, 201 (July, 1897).

"misery is of such ancient . . ." "EEC," *Harper's,* CVI, 327-328 (January, 1903).

198 "by building themselves shanties . . ." *LFA,* 58.

"for a hopeless reversion . . ." William Dean Howells, "Lyof N. Tolstoi," *North American Review,* CLXXXVIII, 857 (December, 1908).

7. *Annie Kilburn*

"someday . . . do justice . . ." Letter to Mrs. Achille Fréchette, November 18, 1887, *L in L,* I, 404.

8. *A Hazard of New Fortunes*

201 "most vital . . ." William Dean Howells, *A Hazard of New Fortunes* (New York, 1952), xxii.

"simply prodigious . . ." *LHJ,* I, 164.

"among men of genius . . ." *The Spectator,* March 8, 1890.

"taken for granted . . ." *Harper's Weekly,* November 7, 1903.

204 Harper's suggestion was relayed to Howells by Alden in a letter, September 14, 1888, *HL.*

Page

216 "significant form," Susanne Langer has been the most influential recent critic to use this term, following Clive Bell and Roger Fry; "presentational symbol" and "discursive symbol" are distinguished by her in *Philosophy in a New Key* (Cambridge, Mass., 1942), 97 ff.

CHAPTER V–NATURALISM AND INTROSPECTION

1. The End of the Comedy

225 Twain crowed about the immense days . . . In a letter to Howells, November 22, 1889, *HL.*

"accuse ourselves too much . . ." William Dean Howells, "The Modern American Mood," *Harper's*, XCV, 200 (July, 1897).

226 eager to shake loose . . . Letters to Howells from Henry Alden, Editor of *Harper's*, especially those of September 1 and September 22, 1891, suggest the willingness of the magazine to drop or change "The Editor's Study," *HL.*

227 Do you remember . . . The party at Ober's is described in a letter from Howells to Aldrich, May 7, 1902, *HL.*

What a dream . . . . The feeling about reality being a dream is contained in letters from Howells to C. E. Norton, December 1, 1890, March 20, 1892, October 16, 1892, and March 11, 1894; and from Twain to Howells, September 24, 1896, *HL.*

228 Malignance another chance . . . The statement about giving malignance another chance to break their hearts is paraphrased from a letter from Twain to Howells, September 24, 1896, *HL.*

230 "people are getting tired . . ." William Dean Howells, *The World of Chance* (New York, 1893), 58.

enemy's camp . . . The exchange between Bishop and Howells on Howells' engagement to speak at Yale is in three letters, December 30, 1899, February 7, 1900, and February 9, 1900, *HL.*

"how wholly . . ." "EEC," *Harper's* CII, 156 (December, 1900).

"The popular novel of today . . ." *Collier's*, XXXIII, 19 (August 13, 1904).

the romantic tendency . . . William Dean Howells, "The New Historical Romances," *North American Review*, CLXXI (December, 1900), 935.

231 "has been an influence . . ." "The Real Howells," *Ainslee's* (March, 1900), 137-142.

232 Howells had known no other woman . . . *NHJ*, 313.

He was grateful in a way . . . See his letter to Howells, August 15 [no year], *HL.*

"stands firm . . ." William James, *Pragmatism*, 16.

Page

238 "draw conclusions from . . ." Frank Norris, *The Responsibilities of the Novelist* (New York, 1903), 22.

"a whole order . . ." "EEC," *Harper's*, CVII, 149 (June, 1903).

"turning from the superabundance . . ." William Dean Howells, "A Possible Difference in English and American Fiction," *North American Review*, CLXXIII, 135 (July, 1901).

239 "gravely significant . . ." William Dean Howells, *The Shadow of a Dream* (New York, 1890), 59.

he could not himself develop . . . His letter to Norton about psychology being a new and unknown field is of March 11, 1906, *HL*.

2. Harold Frederic

240 Frederic thought of himself . . . Frederic's declarations of allegiance to Howells are in a letter to Hamlin Garland, pasted in a copy of *Rose of Dutchers's Coolly*, May 12, 1897, *USC*, and in three letters from Frederic to Howells, May 5, 1885, December 11, 1890, and June 16, 1898, *HL*.

241 "one grave blemish . . ." *The Bookbuyer*, XVII, 602 (January, 1899).

"is the mainspring . . ." Quoted in Paul Haines, "Harold Frederic," 138 (Unpublished doctoral thesis, New York University).

244 Frederic's careful documentation of his work is attested by Louise Imogen Guiney. "Harold Frederic: A Half-Length Sketch from Life," *The Bookbuyer*, XVII, 601 (January, 1899). The autobiographical basis of his works is proven in Haines, *op. cit.*

245 "while they are perfectly life-like . . ." *The Critic*, XXVIII, 310 (May 2, 1896).

3. Frank Norris

246 "rare pleasure . . ." William Dean Howells, "Frank Norris," *North American Review*, CLXXV, 769 ff. (December, 1902).

4. Henry James

250 "scarcely exaggerate . . ." Quoted in *LHJ*, I, 10.

"settled the true principles . . ." Letter to E. C. Stedman, December 5, 1866, *L in L*, I, 116.

In an essay . . . William Dean Howells, "Henry James, Jr.," *Century*, XXV, 28 (November, 1882).

A year after this pronouncement . . . See letter to Howells, March 28 [1883], *HL*.

"tell it not in Samoa . . ." Letter to Robert Louis Stevenson, August 5, 1893, *LHJ*, I, 207.

"the aspiring eyes . . ." Letter to Henry James, Jr., December 13, 1894, *L in L*, II, 55.

"really *grasping* imagination . . ." *LHJ*, I, 30.

Page

"a whole quarter of the heaven . . ." Letter to Howells, May 17, 1890, *LHJ*, I, 165.

251 "actuality must be my line . . ." *NHJ*, 52.

"*comme révélation de la vie* . . ." Letter to Daudet, June 19, 1884, *LHJ*, I, 108.

"functional Love . . ." Letter to H. G. Wells, March 3, 1911, *LHJ*, II, 182.

"a thing rather void . . ." Letter to Mrs. Alfred Sutro, June 25, 1913, *LHJ*, II, 320-321.

252 "the high natural light . . ." *LHJ*, I, 31.

253 "snatched experience . . ." *NHJ*, 172.

"for a relevant and assimilable . . ." Letter to William James, October 31, 1909, *LHJ*, II, 142.

"Pragmatic invulnerability . . ." *Ibid.*

"the field of consciousness . . ." "Is There a Life After Death?" *In After Days* by William Dean Howells, Henry James and others (New York, 1910), 223.

"is all my revelation . . ." *Ibid.*, 229.

254 "Of those who don't react . . ." *Ibid.*, 201.

"slugs and jellyfish . . ." *Ibid.*, 203.

"hard western ugliness . . ." *NHJ*, 102.

"note of 'familiarity,' . . ." *NHJ*, 82.

"stared at this all-unconscious . . ." Henry James, *The American Scene* (London, 1907), 138.

255 "'Say it out . . .'" *The Letters of William James* (Boston, 1920), II, 278.

"with things of the current . . ." Letter to William James, November 23, 1905, *LHJ*, II, 43.

"say a thing . . ." *The Letters of William James*, II, 277.

"game of skill . . ." *NHJ*, 224.

"Patches of ambiguity . . ." Letter to Paul Bourget, August 19, 1898, *LHJ*, I, 289.

two of the chapters of *The Ambassadors*. See Robert E. Young, "An Error in *The Ambassadors*," *American Literature*, XXII, 245-253 (November, 1950).

256 "note of suffering . . ." Henry James, *Partial Portraits* (London, 1918), 13.

"the only endurable . . ." *NHJ*, 6.

"If I want beauty for her . . ." *NHJ*, 217.

"the interest of the subject . . ." Letter to Howells, March 30, 1877; published for first time in *JF*, 500.

257 "Oh art, art . . ." *NHJ*, 68.

"the anodyne, the escape . . ." *NHJ*, 145.

"all discrimination and selection . . ." *NHJ*, 138.

Page

258 "Live all you can . . ." *NHJ*, 226.
"a little supersensual . . ." *NHJ*, 228.

259 "Waymark" and "Waymarsh . . ." *NHJ*, 376.

263 "the great stewpot," *LHJ*, II, 182.

EPILOGUE

269 "consistent with something else . . ." James Gould Cozzens, *Guard of Honor* (New York, 1949), 146.
"among the innumerable stars . . ." *Ibid.*, 631.

270 "He can tell nothing . . ." Ambrose Bierce, "Prattle," in *The San Francisco Examiner*, May 22, 1892, p. 6.
"the most timid . . ." Gertrude Atherton, "Why Is American Literature Bourgeois?" *North American Review*, CLXXVIII, 772 (May, 1904).
"hopelessly narrow . . ." Gertrude Atherton, quoted in *Current Literature*, XLIV, 159 (February, 1908).
overrefined . . . John Albert Macy, *The Spirit of American Literature* (New York, 1913), 278-295.
"sissy school . . ." Alexander Harvey, *William Dean Howells* (New York, 1917), 180.
"than they would their own virginity . . ." H. L. Mencken, *Prejudices: First Series* (New York, 1919), 53.

275 He set art below humanity . . . See letter to C. E. Norton, August 11, 1895, *HL*.

INDEX